F O U N D I N

MW01037403

"The San Francisco 49ers won five Super Bo
early history. Dave Newhouse went digging for it and found it. A must-read for every
49ers fan and every pro football fan."
   —**Scott Ostler,** sports columnist, *San Francisco Chronicle*

"Football, San Francisco, and the era in which both grew up, written by the only man
who could have done it. One hell of a good read!"
   —**Jerry Izenberg,** author of *Rozelle: A Biography*

"*Founding 49ers* is a delightful journey back to a time when the National Football
League was more about players and games than corporate sponsors and television
ratings. The original 49er Faithful, who sat on bench seats at Kezar Stadium,
epitomized the franchise that never quite reached the gold standard that came with
winning a championship. Dave Newhouse captures that Niner era perfectly."
   —**Jim Street,** 49ers beat writer during the 1970s

"Dave Newhouse's newest book is must reading for anyone interested in the iconic
49ers franchise, with unforgettable portraits of Frankie Albert, Hugh McElhenny,
Y. A. Tittle, John Brodie, and R. C. Owens and the Alley Oop pass. Newhouse's book
enriches the already rich list of football literature."
   —**Lowell Cohn,** sports columnist, Santa Rosa (CA) *Press Democrat*, and
      author of *Rough Magic: Bill Walsh's Return to Stanford Football*

"Dave Newhouse has performed a valuable public service, not just for 49er fans
but for anyone who watches the NFL and wonders how the league became so
monstrously popular. Future NFL scholars will consult these pages for insights and
anecdotes. But this isn't a dreary history book. It's a helluva ride and a rich read."
   —**Mark Purdy,** sports columnist, *San Jose Mercury News*

"This book provides us insight as to where it all began—the names, the personalities,
and the legends who are every bit as prominent as the fascinating history of this great
organization."
   —**Steve Mariucci,** NFL analyst and former 49ers and Detroit Lions
      head coach

"*Founding 49ers* might as well have been acted out on a different planet; this was life
in the NFL before the corporations took over. The seats at Kezar were wooden planks,
nothing fancy, no luxury boxes. If you want to walk in the cleat marks of 49ers
founders and their brethren, read this book."
   —**Barry Gifford,** novelist, playwright, 49er fan

"A brilliantly written book filled with great 49er history and wonderful personal insights
from the men who built this franchise . . . the inside depths of the ups and downs."
   —**Susan Owens,** widow of 49er legend R. C. "Alley Oop" Owens

To Michelle—

Founding 49ers

A 49er fan
extraordinaire.

Dave Newhouse
8-18-15

Founding 49ers

The

Dark Days

before the

Dynasty

Dave Newhouse

Black Squirrel Books™
Kent, Ohio

© 2015 by The Kent State University Press, Kent, Ohio 44242
All rights reserved
Library of Congress Catalog Card Number 2014048974
ISBN 978-1-60635-254-0
Manufactured in the United States of America

BLACK SQUIRREL BOOKS™ 🐿™
Frisky, industrious squirrels are a familiar sight on the Kent State University campus and
the inspiration for Black Squirrel Books™, a trade imprint of The Kent State University
Press. www.KentStateUniversityPress.com

Library of Congress Cataloging-in-Publication Data

Newhouse, Dave, 1938–
  Founding 49ers : the dark days before the dynasty / Dave Newhouse.
     pages cm
  Includes bibliographical references and index.
  ISBN 978-1-60635-254-0 (pbk. : alk. paper) ∞ 1. San Francisco 49ers (Football team)—
History. I. Title.
  GV956.S3N44 2015
  796.332'640979461—dc23
                                    2014048974
19 18 17 16 15   5 4 3 2 1

To Lou Spadia, the last founding member of the 49ers, and the foundation of this book.

Contents

Foreword

San Francisco has been my home since 1941, though I hardly qualify as a native. I was born in Cincinnati, Ohio. My dad, Thomas Burton, went to medical school at age 36, when he was the father of three boys. After graduating, he wanted to go west. It was a coin flip between Santa Barbara and San Francisco, and San Francisco won. He started at Franklin Hospital and did his internship and residency there. Then he became a family doctor, the kind in those days who went from house to house.

The 49ers started in 1946, but they didn't change the town any more than the baseball Giants did when they moved from New York in 1958. I mean, everyone was excited about the 49ers, because it gave us a real professional football team. But what really changed the town was World War II—the war changed everything! Having the 49ers here gave you something to do on Sunday.

When I attended Lincoln High School, I could get into 49er games for free by becoming an usher. When I was in college, at San Francisco State, we'd get into games by slipping an usher a buck.

One 49er I liked was Hugh McElhenny. He'd run sideways, and he was smart. A short screen pass to McElhenny, and off he went. But the 49er I liked best was Riley Matheson, a linebacker in 1948 whose nickname was "Rattlesnake." He was really good; even Bill Walsh remembered the Rattlesnake.

You had to like quarterback Frankie Albert, with the way he ran the bootleg and quick-kicked. His backup in the 1940s was Bev Wallace, who allegedly could hit a handkerchief from 60 feet. Then the 49ers picked up Y. A. Tittle in 1951. I don't know how Albert took that, because the All-America Football Conference took guys who were local draws. Albert went to Stanford, while Tittle went to Louisiana State University. But Albert dinked passes, whereas Tittle could throw deep.

I saw Joe Perry run 58 yards for a touchdown the first time he carried the ball (in 1948). Later in life, he lived downstairs from my ex-wife and daughter. But the only 49ers I recognized in public back then were Albert and Norm Standlee, another Stanford guy who played fullback and linebacker. You'd see guard Dick Bassi at a bar, the Florentine Garden, if someone pointed him out.

The first big-name guy I recall the 49ers drafting was tackle Leo Nomellini in 1950, the team's first season in the National Football League. I still remember that Paul Salata, who played end in 1949 and '50, wore No. 55. That was when ends' numbers were in the 50s, tackles' numbers in the 40s, guards in the 30s, centers in the 20s, quarterbacks in the 60s, fullbacks in the 70s, and halfbacks in the 80s and 90s.

The dumbest trade in all of professional sports involved the 49ers: Tittle for lineman Lou Cordileone of the New York Giants in 1961. Cordileone lasted one year with the 49ers. You'd see that jackass doing the Twist at the Condor Bar. And all Tittle did for the Giants was win three straight (conference) championships.

When the 49ers were new to San Francisco, and I was a kid in the Sunset District, the town was Irish Catholic. The parishes defined where you were from. The Sunset District had Holy Names, St. Anne's, and, later, St. Gabriel's. The Richmond District had Star of the Sea, St. Monica's, and then St. Thomas. Living on one block, you'd have Murphy, Sullivan, O'Connor, and on and on and on . . . all Irish Catholic.

The Sunset District was just vacant lots and sand dunes when the 49ers started in 1946. After the war, construction rebuilt that entire area. All three Burton sons—Phillip, Bobby, and myself—did well in sports, especially basketball. I was the youngest. We played at Jefferson Playground at 17th and Kirkham. Then our family moved to Sloat and West Portal. I asked my daughter, "Why aren't kids going to the playgrounds anymore?" Nobody got shot at the playground when I played basketball with guys who were older and better, like war veterans. We'd play from dawn to dusk. At San Francisco State, I scored 20 points against Bill Russell and the University of San Francisco. I'm six foot four. I was a good player, not very good. I was smart.

Then I went into the army and spent two years in Austria and Germany. My mom sent me the Sporting Green, the sports section from the *San Francisco Chronicle*. I remember reading about McElhenny getting hurt (in 1954) and missing the rest of the season. When I got back home in 1955, a 49er ticket was $8. I was used to $3.50. Plus the 49ers weren't too good then, not like in the AAFC, where they were always No. 2 to the Cleveland Browns. Then those two leagues merged, and the 49ers kind of faded in the NFL. They didn't make the smartest moves. They drafted John Brodie when they could have had Jim Brown. Cleveland took Brown. Brodie had a terrific career with the 49ers, but Brown only became the game's greatest running back.

Back then, I'd bet on football and a horse now and then. The 49ers were playing Cleveland in an exhibition, and the oddsmakers laid six on the Browns to win. I was with a basketball buddy, Mike O'Neill, who liked to gamble. The Lucky Club at Stanyan and Haight, next to Ray's Smoke Shop, was a bookie joint. We had to get down, and we were chasing the bet, $100 each on the Browns. I said, "Mike, 100?" And Mike said, "It's only money." So the 49ers won, and then we read how the Browns' coach, Paul Brown, said he didn't worry about winning exhibition games. Talk about mistakes you make in your life.

I wound up drinking one night with quarterback Bobby Layne. I remember Red Hickey and the Shotgun offense. I remember the "Red Dog" linebacker blitz. I saw Slingin' Sammy Baugh and Buddy Young at Kezar Stadium. I also saw Ollie Matson at Kezar, when he was in college at USF.

You'd jump on a streetcar to get to Kezar. Candlestick Park was a pain in the ass to get to. There was none of this corporate stuff at Kezar. You pissed in a trough and sat on a bench, but I was there to watch a football game. You'd go to the Kezar Club, a shot and beer place, and get drunk. It was part of life. I stopped going to games, by and large, when the 49ers left Kezar (in 1970). By that time, what had changed San Francisco even more than World War II were the beatniks and hippies. Then, finally, the 49ers had some success in the early 1970s.

But I didn't look at the 49ers making us into a major-league city. I mean, there were Chicago, Boston, New York, Philadelphia. . . . Those were major-league cities. San Francisco has its charm, like Jeanette MacDonald singing "San Francisco" in a movie. San Francisco has Nob Hill, the Barbary Coast, the Tenderloin. We're a good, nice city.

Eddie DeBartolo, the 49er owner who turned the team into a dynasty by hiring Walsh, is like a guy I grew up with in North Beach. I was there when the 49ers played in Pittsburgh in 1981. The Niners were up at halftime, and this is just when the franchise was finally turning the corner. So I said to Eddie, "What would you have given before the game to be where you are at halftime?" I mean, these were the Pittsburgh Steelers! Someone else said, "There's still two more quarters." The 49ers went on to win the game (17–14), but I'm the kind of guy who would say something like that. Then I sat in Eddie's booth later that year watching "The Catch," when the 49ers finally beat Dallas and went to their first Super Bowl. Brodie was in the booth with tears in his eyes. He was an emotional guy.

I've served San Francisco and California as a state senator and congressman. Then I left Congress because of alcohol and drug addiction. I'm clean now—no whiskey, no drugs, no nothing. I've always tried to speak the truth, even if it's often laden with epithets. How do people react to my swearing? I don't know, and I don't care. As my mother and father would say, "Profanity is a sign of a limited vocabulary." It's hard to hide the real me; people see it.

I'm in my early 80s, but I still have a law practice in San Francisco. I'm also chairman of the State Democratic Party. I lost my jump shot a long time ago, but I still play racquetball twice a week. The biggest thing in my life right now is a foundation I run that helps foster kids. I've always rooted for the underdog, like the 49ers over their first 35 years. I remember taking my daughter to a Virginia Slims tennis tournament. I told her the player I was rooting for, and she asked, "Why?" I said, "Because she's the underdog."

I also pull for the underdog. The *California Journal* said this about me after I was termed out of the state senate in 2004: "Gone will be the Senate's most vehement partisan voice for social services for the poor, the Senate's angriest voice against tax breaks for businesses and the wealthy, its loudest voice for the protection of workers, its fiercest pro-labor advocate, and its disciplinarian." I guess my underdog philosophy came from my parents, because we lived a life of beans, hot dogs, and macaroni and cheese.

I've remained a 49er fan, though I'm not as big a fan as my daughters and grandchildren. I was a big Alex Smith fan when he played for the 49ers. He's a nice kid. But if I ever played for the 49ers with Jim Harbaugh as their coach, I'd never believe a word he told me. I'd rather play for his brother, Baltimore Ravens coach John Harbaugh.

The 49ers have left San Francisco—a total screwup. You know what it would have cost me for season tickets in Santa Clara? One hundred and twenty grand for the right to buy $350 tickets. Their leaving is saving me money. It's business, so I get it. The NBA's Golden State Warriors are coming back to my side of the Bay, from Oakland. It's business again, so I get it.

But I don't think the 49ers leaving San Francisco will be the end of the city. I just assumed that the 49ers would always be here.

John Burton
Chairman, California Democratic Party

Acknowledgments

The author wishes to thank all those who contributed in telling the story of the San Francisco 49ers' first 30 years.

Bringing the story to life again, of course, was Lou Spadia. But the project couldn't have gotten off the ground without the presence of Ken Flower and Louise "Lulu" Spadia-Beckham.

The following 49ers, who played between 1946 and 1976, were interviewed for this book: Ken Casanega, Jesse Freitas, Pete Wismann, Sam Cathcart, Paul Salata, Gordy Soltau, Bob St. Clair, John Brodie, Charlie Krueger, Dan Colchico, Len Rohde, Frank Nunley, Preston Riley, Cedrick Hardman, and Delvin Williams.

Others graciously offered their time in providing a historical perspective that authenticated those earlier 49ers. Future 49er head coach George Seifert and Pro Football Hall of Fame quarterback Dan Fouts relived having watched the team play as San Francisco teenagers. Joe Vetrano Jr. shared memories of his father, Joe "The Toe" Vetrano, the franchise's original placekicker. Josephine Ann "Midge" Morabito Tassi shed light on her father, Tony Morabito, who founded the 49ers in the mid-1940s, and then guided them into the NFL in 1950.

Mario Basso, Lou Spadia's friend of 75 years, spoke of their growing up in San Francisco during the Depression. Spadia's children—Lou Jr., Doss, Kate, and Louise—discussed their upbringing in a loving home. Sportswriter-caricaturist Dave Beronio covered the 49ers from their inception in 1946; possibly the last journalist left from that beginning. Bob Fouts, Dan's father, was a 49er broadcaster in the 1950s and 1960s. Lon Simmons was the radio voice of the 49ers from the late 1950s, with one interruption, through the 1980s. Former DeBartolo-era 49ers' president Carmen Policy offered perspective on his predecessor, Lou Spadia, and Carolyn Hoskins spoke about her late husband, 49ers' defensive lineman Bob Hoskins.

A number of the book's interviewees were in their late 80s and early 90s when quoted between 2012 and 2014, while former Pittsburgh Steelers executive Ed Kiely was 95 when contacted in 2013. But their minds were lucid and their insights invaluable.

The author is grateful to John Christian of the Hayward Area Historical Society, home of the *Oakland Tribune* (pre–computer technology) library, which contains yearly newspaper clippings of the 49ers' history from 1996 dating back to their embryonic roots during World War II.

Nick Peters provided additional material, Michael Dobson and Chad Newhouse assisted the author technically, and Ted Schroeder and Andy Jokelson diligently proofread the manuscript during its development.

The author appreciates everyone who made this book a reality, including Frank Atkinson, who pointed the way to a publisher; Kevin Donahue, who located original 49er quarterback Jesse Freitas; Donn Bernstein, who knew the whereabouts of AAFC-NFL 49er halfback Sam Cathcart; and San Francisco 49ers' archivist Jerry Walker, who provided important photographs and enthusiastic support.

Special gratitude goes to Joyce Harrison, acquiring editor of The Kent State University Press, who believed in this project from the start; to Jonathan Knight and Scott Ostler, who read a rough draft of the manuscript and recommended it for publishing; to Erin Holman, whose precise editing of the final manuscript was invaluable and who kept the author on deadline; and to managing editor Mary Young, Will Underwood, Susan Cash, and others at the Kent State press who facilitated the process.

The author is grateful to his son, Casey Newhouse; his lovely wife, Michelle; and their two wonderful children, Callan and Campbell, who have brought our families closer together, even with a distracted writer.

And thanks, as always, to Patsy Newhouse for her loving support and endless patience while her husband typed away the hours, days, weeks, months, and years on this labor of love.

Introduction

High on a San Francisco hill that climbs halfway to the fog lived a native son who was the last man standing from the launching of the Bay Area's oldest and most successful big-league sports franchise—the pro football 49ers.

Lou Spadia was indirectly responsible for the birth of the team in 1946. His initial jobs included equipment assistant, ticket seller, and office clerk—often grunt work. But with capable hands, a single-minded purposefulness, a quick mind, and unbounded loyalty, this son of struggling Italian immigrants ascended through the team's organizational chart to become its general manager and, finally, its president and part owner.

Lou Spadia, an American success story.

Loyalty and purpose can only carry a man so far for so long, sometimes. Despite 30 years of fierce commitment to the franchise, then owned by the Morabito family, Spadia (SPAY-dee-yuh) wasn't rewarded with a single league championship. After the DeBartolo family purchased the 49ers in 1977, new general manager Joe Thomas cruelly demoted Spadia from president to a lowly position in community relations, reminding him daily of his humble 49er beginnings.

Spadia left the 49ers, humiliated, in 1979. The franchise then won multiple Super Bowls without him. Approaching retirement age, he reenergized himself by cofounding the Bay Area Sports Hall of Fame, a successful nonprofit that raises millions of dollars for local youth activities. His goal was to help poor kids, like himself, achieve a better life. Before stepping away from it, he was inducted into the same hall he created.

His life's work done, Spadia filled his days by swimming laps and entertaining family and friends in his Nob Hill condominium directly across

1

from the majestic Grace Cathedral, while listening to cable cars clanging their way up and down California Street. Then, upon entering his 90s, life changed. Illness, idleness, living alone, and lifelong depression turned Spadia into a recluse. He could see the end coming, and he not only accepted it, he welcomed it.

As an *Oakland Tribune* sportswriter and columnist, I had written about Spadia's separate careers over four decades. Then by accident, or perhaps fate, our lives intersected once again in September 2012. While attending the memorial service of 49ers' great R. C. "Alley Oop" Owens, I learned from Ken Flower, Spadia's buddy and ally, about his friend's declining health. "He's frail, and he uses a cane, but his mind is clear," noted Flower. "Why don't you go see him?"

Thus I visited Spadia at his Gramercy Towers residence. We sat by the indoor/outdoor pool (the roof was closed that day) and had a pleasant talk. He spoke of having to give up swimming, and before that jogging, two exercises he depended upon, for he liked being physically fit. Sadness was in his voice, and in his eyes, as he spoke of those two forfeitures.

After 45 minutes, he grew fatigued. "I need to lie down," he said. He held my arm as we walked back to the elevator. That's when the thought hit me: Why hadn't Spadia, who knew the 49ers' history better than anyone still living, written his memoir? I put that question to him. He answered that he had begun a memoir years ago with *San Francisco Chronicle* sports editor and good friend Art Rosenbaum, who then passed away during the project.

Spadia squeezed my arm.

"Why don't you do it?" he said excitedly.

"Oh, no, Lou. I didn't come here with that in mind," I said, caught off-guard. "I'm retired. I just wanted to pay you a visit."

"We get along," he persisted. "So why don't you do it?"

We reached the elevator, we were about to separate, and he awaited some form of reply. And I hadn't yet come to grips with the question. My mind was spinning. Quickly considering his advanced age and weak physical condition, I sought a specific number that made some sense.

"Lou, you don't know what you're asking," I said, finally. "A book like this would take, at least, 10 interviews."

Without missing a beat, he grinned impishly. "I've got a few months left," he said.

Then up the elevator he went, and back home to Oakland I went. I called Flower to inform him about my conversation with Spadia, thinking that would be the end of it. A few days later, Spadia's daughter, Louise Spadia-Beckham, phoned from her Paso Robles, California, home. We hadn't ever met, but I discovered she could be persistent in the sweetest way.

"Our family has been after Dad for a long time to do his memoirs, and you're the perfect person to do them with," the daughter known as Lulu said eagerly. "He adores you."

Adores me? Now hold on a minute, Lulu. It's true that during my half-century as a journalist, Spadia ranked at the summit of sports executives who returned my calls regardless of what I had written, good or bad, about them or their team. Nonetheless, "adoration" hardly describes the often-strained relationship between a front-office sports figure and a sports scribe.

That explanation didn't stop the tenacious Lulu, who wouldn't take no for an answer. She said that she would drive up to facilitate the first interview. Surrendering meekly, I returned to Gramercy Towers a week later after first researching the 49er franchise's roots in the 1940s.

Perhaps I was the right person to undertake this project. I am a Bay Area native, and I saw my first 49ers game in 1948 against the Chicago Rockets. I watched two Pro Football Hall of Famers that day—Joe "The Jet" Perry of the 49ers and Elroy "Crazylegs" Hirsch of the Rockets, though I couldn't have foreseen their greatness; I was only 10. This was at a time when the 49ers and Rockets played in the fledgling, yet doomed, All-America Football Conference, viewed as a "B" version of the more established National Football League.

The final curtain dropped on the AAFC the next year, when I saw the 49ers play the Baltimore Colts—not of Johnny Unitas, but of Y. A. Tittle. Those earlier Colts were among four AAFC teams accepted by the NFL in 1950, along with the 49ers, the Cleveland Browns, and football's New York Yankees. The Colts folded after the 1950 season, and the 49ers then drafted Tittle off their roster. The Yankees became the Dallas Texans in 1952, a one-year failed experiment, before they evolved into the Baltimore (now Indianapolis) Colts in 1953.

That 1949 Niners-Colts game left an indelible impression on me. Tittle had marched the Colts to the San Francisco goal line, where bodies collided and a Niner was helped to the sideline. Sitting behind that end zone, I saw 49er defensive end Hal Shoener point at a Baltimore player. On the next play, a Colt was carried off the field. This was my first sense of the violent, redemptive nature of football.

In the 1950s, the 49ers trained at Menlo Junior College, a fifteen-minute bike ride from my Menlo Park home. On a photo day, the team's photographer recruited me to throw a pass to star end Gordy Soltau at a designated spot. I was naturally nervous, but Soltau caught my wobbly toss. My one NFL completion—Soltau instantly became my favorite 49er.

The early '50s coincided with the infancy of television. If his parents were fortunate enough to own a TV set, and if the 49ers were playing in the Eastern or Central time zone, a Bay Area boy could watch a Sunday morning football game in his pajamas. Life just couldn't get any better. On one of those Sundays, in 1952, 49er rookie Hugh McElhenny received a punt at the six-yard line and wove his way through all 11 Chicago Bears, it seemed, to score as I watched, agog, on the living-room floor. That remarkable run marked the coronation of McElhenny as "The King."

Such memories haven't faded 60-plus years later. But in reflecting upon the 49ers' history—spanning their decades of disappointment to their "Team of the '80s" dynasty—I'm still amazed that the franchise didn't win a single league championship, either in the AAFC or NFL, between 1946 and 1981. A 35-year shutout, yet, amazingly, there are eight 49ers in the Pro Football Hall of Fame who retired before the DeBartolo family acquired the team in 1977. Even more amazing, the DeBartolo era, despite amassing Super Bowls, hasn't produced superior talent at certain positions.

Those unsuccessful 49ers of yore placed an entire backfield in the Hall of Fame: The "Million Dollar Backfield" of quarterback Tittle, halfbacks McElhenny and John Henry Johnson, and fullback Perry. No other NFL team can make that same full-house backfield distinction. Those playoff-deprived 49ers also put two superb tackles, Leo "The Lion" Nomellini and Bob "The Geek" St. Clair, in the Canton, Ohio, hall, joined there by rugged linebacker Dave Wilcox and ageless cornerback Jimmy Johnson.

And here's another nugget for trivia nuts: The 49ers also fielded pro football's only "All Initial Backfield" of Y. A. Tittle, R. C. Owens, J. D. Smith and C. R. Roberts. Smith became a thousand-yard rusher and Owens a one-of-a-kind wide receiver.

So why didn't the Morabito-owned 49ers win more with such obvious talent? They didn't have enough *quality* players on their rosters—quantity doesn't beat quality—unlike the much later, well-stocked 49ers who benefited from Bill Walsh's genius and Eddie DeBartolo's largess. That same Super Bowl formula continued more recently under the York-DeBartolo ownership and coach Jim Harbaugh's strong stewardship. But those ancient 49ers, victimized by wasted draft picks and unsatisfactory coaching, remain locked into a what-happened, what-if, where-did-we-go-wrong mentality.

"It was disappointing," recalled St. Clair, who played for the 49ers from 1953 to 1964. "We needed players."

"It was depth," added center-linebacker Pete Wismann, who joined the Niners in 1949 in one league and finished with them in 1954 in another. "Other teams had more established players—bigger and better men."

Today's generation of 49er Faithful—the team's undying fan base—would be stunned, nevertheless, to learn that some of the greatest 49ers toiled on losing teams, let alone recognizing their names. And those same greatest 49ers never played in an NFL championship game.

Don't just take my word for it: When *Sports Illustrated*'s esteemed pro football writer, Paul "Dr. Z" Zimmerman, selected his All-Century Team in 1999, he named Bill Walsh, Joe Montana, Jerry Rice, and Deion Sanders from the DeBartolo era, and—surprise!—Hugh McElhenny, Jimmy Johnson, Dave Wilcox, Tommy Davis, and Henry Schmidt from the Morabito era.

Zimmerman, who picked McElhenny as a "third-down back," said: "The King could turn a short pass into a crazy-legged, broken field-adventure." As for cornerback Johnson, he wrote, "Jimmy Johnson and Deion Sanders will be remembered as pure downfield cover guys, so feared that they often went entire games without being tested deep."

Of Wilcox, Zimmerman said: "No outside linebacker manhandled tight ends the way Dave Wilcox did; he was impossible for a tight end to hook [block]." Tommy Davis was a 49er placekicker-punter from 1959 to 1969; despite this double duty, he averaged a club-record 44.7 yards on 511 punts. Schmidt was a 49er for only two seasons, 1959–60, but Zimmerman called him pro football's greatest "wedge-buster" on kickoff coverage.

By Zimmerman's count, that's five to four, Morabito era over DeBartolo era, in terms of all-time greatness. So there you have it. One small step behind McElhenny in importance as a 49er running back, though not in speed, is Perry, still the franchise's definitive fullback. Johnny Strzykalski, (Stry-KALL-ski), J. D. Smith, Delvin Williams, Wilbur Jackson, Roger Craig, Garrison Hearst, Charlie Garner, and Ricky Watters were all quality 49er backs, like the current mighty-mite, Frank Gore, just not in the same regal, racehorse class as The King and The Jet.

The 49ers haven't produced a better offensive tackle than St. Clair or a finer defensive tackle than Nomellini. Fred Dean and Charles Haley were superb pass rushers, but Cedrick Hardman created as much fear in the 1970s. He just lacks their cache of Super Bowl rings. The 49ers' finest set of defensive ends? Hardman and Tommy Hart. And the 49ers' best defensive line in hunting down quarterbacks? The "Gold Rush" foursome of Hardman, Hart, Cleveland Elam, and Jimmy Webb.

No 49er offensive line protected its quarterback better than Len Rohde, Randy Beisler, Forrest Blue, Woody Peoples, and Cas Banaszek shielded John Brodie, who was sacked an NFL-record eight times in 1970. That line lacked only a catchy nickname: "The Impenetrables"?

More recent Faithful are convinced Brent Jones is the team's greatest tight end. But in the 1970s, Ted Kwalick was the 49ers' most athletic tight end ever, catching passes that looked uncatchable. Vernon Davis, though, may surpass both men as the franchise's definitive tight end. Wilcox is, without question, the franchise's greatest outside linebacker. However, current inside man Patrick Willis should retire as the 49ers' best overall linebacker.

As for the Niners' greatest center, two archaic snappers, Bill "Tiger" Johnson and Bruce Bosley, share that all-time distinction. Many 49er followers are convinced that defensive back Ronnie Lott is the franchise's hardest hitter. But back when face masks amounted to a single bar or none at all, 49er linebacker Hardy Brown broke countless noses with his feared "shoulder block." And John Henry Johnson, also in the 1950s, rearranged facial structures permanently with his lethal forearm shots. The latter is, arguably, the meanest man the NFL has produced since setting up shop in 1920.

While some Faithful can't name another 49er quarterback besides Joe Montana or Steve Young, Brodie spent 17 seasons in San Francisco, producing three consecutive division titles with passing numbers that surpass even those of some Canton inductees. His years of service represent the 49ers' record for longevity. His competitiveness remains, too, as he has regained some of his speech and his mobility following a severe stroke in 2000.

But if not for the team's first quarterback, the magical and mercurial Frankie Albert, would there even be a 49ers franchise today? While it's true those 49ers of old don't have championship rings to squeeze over broken knuckles, a bunch of them still could out-play more recent 49er heroes who have Super Bowl rings on multiple fingers.

"Oh, sure, automatic," said St. Clair. "McElhenny and Perry? C'mon. Compare them to today's players? Look, Mac, Joe, and all the players back then had off-season jobs. Some even had in-season jobs. If the players of my era conditioned themselves like today's players, where football is all we worried about? C'mon."

St. Clair is the one San Franciscan in the Canton hall who played high school, college, and professional football in his hometown. And the playing surface at Kezar Stadium, the 49ers' first home, also is named Bob St. Clair Field. How many NFLers can boast of such distinction?

Even though those old 49ers weren't consistent winners, they certainly were interesting. A professional boxer and a professional wrestler played on the same 49er defensive line. An assistant coach and an offensive lineman were mayors. And that offensive lineman ate his steak raw, straight off the bone. One 49er head coach nearly was blind. A 49er running back was the NFL's first known gay player. A 49er defensive tackle's hobby was bird-watching; this same lineman also won the first injury suit ever against the NFL. A 49er wide receiver quit football to become an actor and a painter. And let's not forget the 49er placekicker who mentored actor Jack Nicholson as a boy and whom Nicholson remembered in an Oscar acceptance speech.

Adding to the 49ers' uniqueness, they remain the only NFL team owned by two widows who were sisters-in-law: Josephine and Jane Morabito.

Though the pre-DeBartolo 49ers didn't win one NFL title, they did win playoff games in the 1970s with players colorfully named Goober, Fudge-hammer, Lone Wolf, and Fontana Wagonwheel. Those 49ers might have gone all the way if not for those darn Dallas Cowboys.

Carmen Policy served as the 49ers' legal counsel and then team president under his boyhood friend, Eddie DeBartolo, during the team's glory years in the 1980s and 1990s. Policy was asked how much he knew about 49ers' history before the DeBartolo family took control. "Not much," he admitted. "I remember some games on TV. [Dick] Nolan was the coach. He's the only [49ers] coach I could recall. I remember the quarterback [long pause] John Brodie. I knew that they played Dallas in the playoffs, they were close games, and Dallas won. Growing up in Ohio [Youngstown], and our connection to Cleveland [and the NFL's Browns], I'd hear the names Leo Nomellini and Frankie Albert. But the truth of the matter is that, prior to 1977 when the DeBartolos bought the team, most people in Ohio thought of San Francisco as being halfway around the world. Their football team was not one to inspire Easteners to become fans."

This book will serve as a history lesson for Policy and younger 49er fans who believe that the franchise began with Bill Walsh and can't believe that life existed before him. This book is a fond remembrance of, and a fitting tribute to, those forgotten 49ers and Lou Spadia, whose memoir will be completed by his players, his close friends, and his loving family.

For he did have only a few months left.

1 Pre-1946

Football in the Fog

As America nervously welcomed the 1940s by entering a world war and, simultaneously, exiting a national Depression, San Francisco continued to exude charm, panache, and a stoic resilience. But the game of football "The City That Knows How" knew best was political.

With its foggy climate, rolling hills, cable cars, picturesque bridges, sprawling waterfront, five-star restaurants, and diverse nightlife, San Francisco then, as now, was an international tourist attraction. And it was saved by its sturdy political backbone, which rebuilt a crumbled and charred city ravaged by the 1906 earthquake and fire.

As the 1940s approached, San Francisco had everything a major city required, except for a big-league sports presence. San Francisco was stopped short every time it sought a National Football League franchise. The eastern establishment regarded the western United States as Death Valley in terms of lucrative athletic turf, overlooking San Francisco's successful, though spotted, sports background.

A San Franciscan became the first heavyweight boxing champion under the Marquess of Queensberry rules (with gloves on), when "Gentleman" Jim Corbett KO'd the great John L. ("I can lick any man in the house") Sullivan in 1892. Another San Francisco pugilist, Abe Attell, won the world featherweight championship in 1903. He held that title for nine distinguished years, then sullied his fistic exploits by serving as bag man for gambler Arnold Rothstein, who orchestrated the Black Sox Scandal, which led to the Chicago White Sox throwing the 1919 World Series.

In the 1930s, San Francisco native Angelo "Hank" Luisetti changed basketball forever with the running one-hander, the forerunner of the jump shot. He scored fifty points in a single game for Stanford, in an era when most *teams* didn't score fifty points. And Luisetti's fifty points, achieved before the three-point shot and bonus free throws, still is the Stanford record. San Francisco has produced a plethora of baseball heroes, such as Lefty O'Doul, Dominic and Vince DiMaggio, and Frankie Crosetti, plus Hall of Fame inductees in Joe DiMaggio, Tony Lazzeri, Harry Heilmann, and Joe Cronin. And San Francisco had not one, but two Triple-A baseball franchises—the Seals and Mission Reds—before the Mission Reds high-tailed it to Hollywood in 1938.

Even with its rich athletic heritage, San Francisco wasn't perceived as a football town on the eastern seaboard. The University of San Francisco played a major-college schedule, but it wasn't as recognized on the national scale in the 1940s as its neighboring Catholic rivals, St. Mary's and Santa Clara. "Those were booming days for the Catholic independents," said Lou Spadia, especially when facing one another at San Francisco's Kezar Stadium before capacity crowds of nearly 60,000.

But a homegrown San Franciscan and Santa Clara alumnus, wealthy lumberman Anthony J. "Tony" Morabito, had a similar vision—Kezar sell-outs supporting San Francisco's very own professional football team. So in 1940, then again in 1942, and continuing into 1944, Morabito hounded the National Football League about putting a franchise in the city by the bay. He was rebuffed every time.

"I'm sure the primary reason was because there was no other West Coast team," said Spadia. There wasn't an NFL team, at that time, west of the Mississippi River, the dividing line for Major League Baseball as well. (The National Basketball Association wasn't yet a reality.) But even though Morabito was rejected repeatedly, he had gained traction from a resource he hadn't envisioned: war.

"The big boom for football was during the war," said Spadia, "when college locations turned into military establishments, like St. Mary's Pre-Flight. The 49ers were born out of this environment, where admission to a game was the price of a war bond. Kezar Stadium was filled Saturdays and Sundays with this new kind of football."

But the NFL snubbed Morabito and other businessmen eager to see the league expand beyond 10 teams. It finally budged, approving the Cleveland Rams' move to Los Angeles shortly after the Rams edged Washington, 15–14, for the 1945 league title. Of course, it helped the Rams that their star quarterback, Bob Waterfield, was a Los Angeles hero as a UCLA alumnus.

If the NFL was thinking, at last, that it would be wise to toss Morabito a bone in order to establish a West Coast rivalry between San Francisco and Los Angeles, it had reacted too late. An exasperated Morabito grew tired of waiting.

"Tony was the type of person who never balked once he made up his mind to do something," his widow, Joephine, said 30 years later. "One night, out of the blue, he said he wanted to own a professional football team, and he just went ahead and did it."

Morabito joined a group described, not entirely truthfully, as "men of millionaire incomes" in tapping into the pro football market. Thus the All-America Football Conference was formed in Chicago on September 3, 1944. The announcement came from *Chicago Tribune* sports editor Arch Ward, an AAFC organizer and visionary who had previously created the Baseball All-Star Game and the College Football All-Star Game, which involved the reigning NFL champion.

Eight teams composed the initial AAFC, which commenced play in 1946: the San Francisco 49ers, Cleveland Browns, Los Angeles Dons, and Chicago Rockets in the Western Division, and the Miami Seahawks, Buffalo Bisons, Brooklyn Dodgers, and New York Yankees in the Eastern Division. The Rockets, Dons, Dodgers, and Yankees would compete against NFL teams in Chicago, Los Angeles, and New York.

Morabito had his coach handpicked. The same day the AAFC was established, he hired Lawrence T. "Buck" Shaw, a local, and logical, choice. Shaw, a star tackle for Knute Rockne at Notre Dame, coached Santa Clara to back-to-back Sugar Bowl victories in the late 1930s.

The AAFC's ownership group included actor Don Ameche (Los Angeles), trucking magnate J. L. Keeshin (Chicago), baseball Yankees owner Dan Topping (New York), oilman James F. Breuil (Buffalo), and cab company owner Arthur B. "Mickey" McBride (Cleveland), who hired future Hall of Famer Paul Brown as his coach.

But did Morabito, who succeeded in meshing political football with real-life football in San Francisco, play in the same league, financially, as the "men of millionaire incomes"? "No," Spadia said, emphatically, in 2012. "There wasn't that much money around. Two-hundred thousand dollars then would be ten million dollars today. You could buy a new car back then for $400. The All-America Football Conference entry fee was $20,000. NFL franchises now are worth billions."

Morabito didn't jump solo into this bold venture; lumber business partners Allen E. Sorrell and Ernest J. Turre joined him as 49ers' owners. The three men had been together since the 1930s, but their maiden voyage into pro football waters would capsize early.

"At one point, Tony controlled the lumber transporting business in California," said Spadia. "There was a need to move lumber, and Tony envisioned that; he had a very perceptive mind. The 49ers, initially, were a corporation called Consolidated Companies. The 49ers were a division of that corporation, though a small percentage. Tony and the other two men each had one-third ownership of the 49ers. In 1947, Sorrell and Turre divested themselves when things started going bad. They couldn't get out fast enough."

Lumberyards looked more sensible to Sorrell and Turre, especially when staring at a two-thirds-empty Kezar Stadium. "It was very tough at first," said Josephine Morabito. "Tony's partners took over the lumber business, and Tony devoted all his time to football." Morabito ended up with 100 percent of the 49ers, but he later gave a 10 percent share to his younger half-brother, Vic Morabito, a University of California, Berkeley alumnus.

Before Sorrell departed, he left his permanent mark on the franchise and the city: for it was Sorrell who picked "49ers" as the team's nickname. "It's obvious," he explained at the time. "San Francisco was born in the gold rush."

The gold miners of 1849 liked their booze, obviously, because the 49ers' permanent logo reflected those inebriated times. "Sorrell saw a cartoon of a [drunken] '49er shooting off guns," said Spadia. "And that became our opening game program cover, our nickname, and our logo."

Was the 49ers' nickname received favorably publicly? "There was no public reaction," said Spadia. Big league or otherwise, there remained a wait-and-see attitude in San Francisco.

But who was this Tony Morabito, and why did he persist in his undaunted quest to bring pro football to his hometown? "Tony was always a great football fan," said Spadia, who was one of Morabito's first hires. "It was his great love of the game. He was a supporter of Santa Clara, and he attended their football practices. He just had a heart for the game."

Morabito would have loved to become a 49er player, but he settled for owner instead. "Tony tried to play football at Santa Clara for Buck Shaw in the 1930s. He was a pudgy guard who wasn't good enough to make the team," said Spadia. "He and Vic weren't football prospects; they had two left feet. Later on, Tony always gave summer jobs to Santa Clara's players. Tony's dad had a ship-scaling business, cleaning the bottoms of ships on the San Francisco waterfront. It was a dirty job, but it paid well."

Tony Morabito didn't grow up poor. Or timid. He had an explosive temper that he had difficulty controlling. "He wasn't that big physically, but he would throw a punch," said Spadia. "I've seen Tony go after someone in a restaurant if something negative was said about his team or his coach.

Tony could be very acerbic, tough. When he got angry, he blew. But if he was your friend, he was your friend. Disloyalty bothered him. So did betrayal. He kept grudges."

He especially held grudges against sportswriters—some of whom he banned from team practices, team flights, and even home games if he resented their coverage. He wore a hearing aid, which, his newspaper critics contended, was fitted for rabbit ears.

But he believed that fairness crossed all cultures. "Tony was completely color-blind," said Spadia. "Not just skin color, but race. It didn't matter to Tony if you were Filipino, Italian, Irish, or Mexican. If you were good, you were good. If you were bad, you were bad."

A prime example of Morabito's color-blindness was his close relationship with Joe Perry, the 49ers' first African American player and employee. Perry joined the 49ers in 1948, before professional sports fully embraced integration. Not every team had a black player, but Perry became like a son to Morabito. "Tony went in person to sign Joe at the Alameda Naval Air Station," said Spadia. "After that, Tony took care of Joe's finances, and gave him money whenever he needed it. I don't think Joe ever had a salary with Tony."

Perry would sign a contract, and Morabito filled in the amount. No 49er ever had a day in his honor to match Joe Perry Day. Perry was the first NFL player to rush for a thousand yards back-to-back, in 1953 and '54 during twelve-game seasons. At a Kezar preseason game in 1955, Perry was lavished with gifts, from a new automobile to home furnishings. Morabito didn't mind spending his money if it meant rewarding his favorite 49er.

"Tony wasn't frugal at all," said Spadia. "He followed the policy of going first class, whether it was a restaurant or staying in a hotel. He always drove a Lincoln. But he was a loyal person, and if you were loyal to him, he would stand by you to the end."

Morabito had the same fondness for Spadia, whom he also treated as family (Morabito had two daughters, but no sons). Spadia was hired even though his favorite sport was baseball. "I wanted to be a shortstop for the New York Yankees," he said. "There was a point where I was serious. I had a chance after the Navy to sign a contract with the Sacramento Solons of the [AAA] Pacific Coast League. But, by then, I had a family. I was always practical. My wife, Maggie, would have gone along with whatever I chose, but it would have been a big drop in pay [from his 49ers salary] to play pro baseball. My mom wanted me to be a hairdresser or a sheet metal worker."

Spadia had the good fortune to serve in the Navy under Lieutenant Commander John R. Blackinger, who had attended Santa Clara with Morabito

The original 49ers board a plane for their first football game, an August 24, 1946, exhibition against the Los Angeles Dons in San Diego. Coach Buck Shaw is in the light suit (center, front). Norm Standlee is standing at the far left, Frankie Albert third from the left, and Joe Vetrano in front of Albert. The 49ers won, 17–7. (Dave Beronio collection)

before becoming the 49ers' first 49er general manager. Blackinger encouraged Morabito to hire Spadia as assistant general manager.

"I don't think I was ever told what my job responsibilities were," said Spadia. "Tony hired me in 1945 as someone who could type and take shorthand, since we were going to have an all-male organization. It wasn't the same being a woman back then as it is today. I was about 22, with one child, and one in the oven. The 49ers had budgeted $250 a month for my job. I was making $300 in the Navy. Tony said he'd split the difference and pay me $275. Thirteen days later, when the baby was born, I got a raise to $300.

"Jack Blackinger stayed only one year as general manager, then went to work for Marin-Dell Milk, owned by his wife's father. I was still assistant general manager—a title by default. I edited the game program, the yearbook, and all the press releases." That's what Spadia was paid to do, but not all that he did, which became clear to him when he flew with the 49ers to their inaugural game, an August 24, 1946, exhibition against the Los Angeles Dons in San Diego.

"I thought it was great; the team was doing me a favor by bringing me along on the plane," said Spadia. "But when the plane landed, the trainer hollered to me, 'Hey, kid, you stay with me.' I wound up under the plane unloading the players' duffle bags, putting them on the truck, and going out to old Balboa Stadium. One of our halfbacks, Ziggy Zamlynsky, hurt a knee in that game, and he was made the team's equipment man, a job he had for the next three years. Thank goodness."

The 49ers found additional work for their assistant general manager that made him feel even less important. "Against the New York Yankees in our (1946 regular season) opener," Spadia said, "we sold 2,000 tickets in advance. The other 33,000 were walkups. We didn't have enough ticket sellers in the stadium, so I wound up selling in the booth. So did our general manager, secretary, and switchboard operator—everybody we had. I did all sorts of errands. I passed out the jockstraps and towels, then picked them up after games."

The multitasking Spadia didn't ask for a raise. This was expansion football, where you only asked to survive. But the 49ers had found a dedicated, loyal employee. "Lou was extremely honest—the most honest man I've met in my life, straight down the middle," said Mario Basso, Spadia's friend of 75 years. "There was no hanky-panky with Lou; he's always been that way. He never did anything to shame the team or to be ashamed of himself."

Spadia and Basso had a beautiful, enduring friendship. Here were two Italian kids from a San Francisco world that no longer exists, regardless of Super Bowls and World Series championships. "I was born two months after Lou [in 1921]," Basso said. "We were 15 or 16 when we met. We used to go to Seals [Triple-A baseball] games all the time. Lou and I would climb up a tree across from Seals Stadium and watch Joe DiMaggio. We didn't have the money to get into the stadium. Lou and I came from poor families. My father was a ditch digger for PG&E [Pacific Gas & Electric], making a dollar a day. At night, he was a maintenance man for Ray Oil Burners. He made a buck there, too. Lou's mother and father sorted laundry at a cleaners named after a Sullivan. The Spadias had two flats on Missouri Street. They lived upstairs. Tony Lazzeri, the New York Yankees ballplayer, lived downstairs."

Spadia wasn't an only child. He had an older brother, Peter, who died at six months of age several years before Lou was born.

"Lou and I learned the value of money," said Basso. "We'd buy three large avocados at the Crystal Palace Market for 10 cents, and we'd split them for lunch. We didn't take the streetcar. Your feet did everything; you couldn't afford any other transportation. I walked or roller-skated to Seals Stadium, which was four miles away." For a San Francisco teenager in the decade before the 49ers arrived, having a good time didn't exact an exorbitant price.

"In the mid-1930s, there was a dance every night for kids during the summer," said Basso. "That's where I met Louie. He was a smooth dancer; we were both good dancers. I still have a medal that I won for doing the jitterbug. And there were always picnics everywhere—big picnics with big bands."

But back then, Italian teens in San Francisco gravitated toward baseball diamonds, not ballrooms. That was no surprise, given the city's strong tradition of Italian ballplayers. "Golf is for rich people; we played baseball," said Basso. "Louie played for Joe's Club at 25th and Valencia. I played for the Glen Park Merchants. Louie was a shortstop; I was a left fielder. He could have made the majors except for one problem—he couldn't hit a curve ball. I was about a .250 hitter; Louie was a little more than that. He was strong and could hit the ball pretty good. We played teams in Vallejo and Santa Cruz. I hit one home run; Louie hit a few more than that. Louie was strictly baseball. I was sixth man at City College of San Francisco in basketball. I was a guard—six feet, good shooter. But now I've shrunk.

"Louie and I both liked the same things, and we respected our parents. We lived five miles apart. I went to Lowell High School, Louie went to Mission High."

Then Louie met Maggie, his future bride.

"Oh, how he loved her," said Basso. "Louie was a typical Italian; he played the accordion. He was the greatest, playing at clubs and weddings. Know why he quit the accordion? He always took Maggie with him when he played. When she began to dance with others, he quit. Boom!"

Basso misses the San Francisco that he and Spadia knew as kids. Another Italian buddy, Pete Giannini, would become the 49ers' ticket manager. Spadia was loyal to his friends.

"Louie and I never felt poor," said Basso. "We had a wonderful life. The city was quiet back then. There was no television. If you had a radio, you listened to *Amos and Andy*. I remember the Macon dirigible flying over the city. They took us out of school to see it. There were two dirigibles, the Macon and Akron, which were built after the Hindenburg. You have no idea how big that was to watch a dirigible." There was no tweeting, no texting, no blogging. A dirigible flying overhead meant everything to a kid in the 1930s.

"There weren't many cars around," Basso continued. "When I got ready to drive, I practiced in front of my driveway. You'd wait forty-five minutes before another car came down the street. Now you can't wait two seconds before fifty cars come down the street. We had lots of parking spaces then. . . . God almighty!"

Basso and Spadia joined the Navy and went off to war. Spadia used his connections to get destroyer duty for Basso. "I saw the flag go up on Iwo Jima—the second flag," said Basso. "They arranged for Joe Rosenthal to take the second [Pulitzer Prize–winning] picture of the flag-raising on Mount Suribachi. I saw it through binoculars. Then I went to Okinawa and saw two destroyers hit by suicide bombers in six days. Lots of guys got killed on our ship. I was lucky; I was on the bridge. I saw planes shot down. I helped carry the dead to the fantail, and then covered them."

Does Basso have lingering nightmares about the war?

"No, I forgot them all," he said.

Spadia didn't see combat. "Louie's sea duty was on the *Delta Queen* in San Francisco Bay," said Basso.

When peace returned, there was a new game in town, a game played at a higher level in a new league, with new heroes, many of them swapping uniforms. Pro football had docked.

"Who was the left-handed quarterback? Yes, Frankie Albert," said Basso. "I played golf with John Brodie at the Sharon Heights club. Heavy drinker, heavy bettor. I saw Montana to Clark—The Catch. I saw the Alley Oop catches. I loved watching [Hugh] McElhenny run. Oh, God! He was so elusive; he'd get through spots you couldn't get through. He was wonderful to watch, so graceful. He'd make these cuts, they'd go to tackle him, and he was gone. Louie said he was the best runner they ever had. And he was a nice man." The 49ers started on a wing and a prayer, then required plenty of praying to keep winging on Albert's passing arm.

"Everyone was proud of the 49ers," Basso said. "Everyone wanted tickets, including my insurance business clients. I had requests for sixty-two tickets. Louie let me pick out the ones I wanted from the very beginning. Of course, I paid. Louie would do nothing that wasn't legal.

"I had the thrill—all Louie's doing—of sitting on the 49ers' bench in New York when they played the Yankees in 1949. After the 49ers won (24–3), we ran into a severe storm on the flight home. Those were the days of engine planes, not jets. Joe Perry, Tony Morabito, Louie, and I had our rosary beads out. We didn't think we'd make it, but we did, thank God."

That same frantic feeling hovered over the 49ers' future from the get-go. Would they stay above ground or crash land? Tony Morabito held tightly onto those rosary beads.

2 1946–47
The GI Joe League

Ken Casanega was a World War II hero, a Navy bomber pilot who flew over Germany, Africa, and the Pacific. On his last mission, near Okinawa, a Japanese kamikaze pilot blew a hole in the left wing of Casanega's plane. He managed to land the aircraft safely. "Otherwise, I wouldn't be talking to you today," he said, laughing, in June 2014, when, at 93, he was interviewed for this book.

After completing his football eligibility at Santa Clara Uiversity, Casanega was drafted by the Pittsburgh Steelers. But after the Japanese attack on Pearl Harbor, he was "steamed up" to defend his country, so he joined the Navy and served with distinction. When the war ended, the Steelers no longer were on his radar. "I had no interest in playing professional football," he said. "Then Buck Shaw called me, and said they were starting this new team [in San Francisco], and how would I like to play for them. So I went up to Lake Tahoe and ran around those hills for two weeks to get in shape."

Casanega played for Shaw at Santa Clara, but it had been five years since he had last worn a football uniform. Shaw's persuasiveness made Casanega an Original 49er. "Buck had those two Sugar Bowl wins in 1937 and 1938, both against LSU, the 'Scourge of the South,'" he said of Santa Clara's 21–14 and 6–0 victories over the Bayou Tigers. "Buck was a good gentleman, a good-looking guy, and a good coach."

The six-foot, 175-pound Casanega was a defensive specialist during the 49ers' first season in 1946, leading the team with eight interceptions, besides leading the All-America Football Conference in punt returns. "I was pretty instinctive," he said. "I played right halfback on offense behind [Len] Eshmont, then I replaced him on defense. I had played both ways in college, mostly on offense. I was a runner and a passer."

Casanega was, in a historic sense, clearly an original, joining a brand-new franchise in a brand-new league. But the National Football League snubbed its competition. Before the AAFC ever played a game, the relationship between the two leagues was frosty, even leading to an icy split between two of college football's legendary Four Horsemen of Notre Dame.

After Jim Crowley was named AAFC commissioner, NFL commissioner Elmer Layden, Crowley's Four Horsemen backfield mate, delivered thorns instead of a dozen roses to the new league. "They should first get a ball, then make a schedule, and then play a game," Layden said sarcastically.

If this flippant remark wasn't demeaning enough, George Preston Marshall, the Washington Redskins owner, fired his own zinger: "I didn't realize there was another league," he said, "although I did receive some literature telling about a WPA project."

The Works Progress Administration, or WPA, was a 1930s government project that created jobs during the Depression. The AAFC would discover soon enough that it also needed financial relief, for the public embraced it with mostly closed arms.

Marshall had his own issues. Critics branded him a racist; he was the last NFL owner to integrate his team, which still carries his handpicked nickname—"Redskins"—the most racist moniker in professional sports. The Redskins' name is defended by the team's present owner, Dan Snyder, and NFL commissioner Roger Goodell, who doesn't find it at all demeaning.

Defiantly, Marshall said, "We'll start signing Negroes when the Harlem Globetrotters start signing whites." Marshall, in fact, signed no African Americans over the first 25 years of his owning the franchise, which originated in Boston in 1932. He then changed the team's nickname from Braves to Redskins. Only after the federal government challenged his segregationist policy did Marshall make halfback-wide receiver Bobby Mitchell, a future Pro Football Hall of Fame inductee, his first African American player.

The AAFC, even as a rookie entity, was more innovative, and more color-blind, than the NFL, in spite of the 26-year difference in their backgrounds (the NFL began in 1920).

The AAFC was the first pro football league to play a 14-game schedule and the first league to travel by air (NFL teams still rode trains in 1946). The new league also popularized zone defenses at the professional level. The AAFC, unlike the NFL, also had a female executive—league vice-president Eleanor Gehrig, widow of baseball immortal Lou Gehrig.

But hurting the NFL, mostly, was its loss of 100 players to the AAFC, and the African American players the NFL didn't sign, including fullback

Marion Motley, center-linebacker Bill Willis and punter Horace Gillom of the Cleveland Browns, halfback Buddy Young of the New York Yankees, defensive end Len Ford and halfback George Taliaferro of the Los Angeles Dons, and fullback Joe Perry of San Francisco.

Despite its innovations, the AAFC was viewed with skepticism, like a circus fat man becoming a trapezist. Might the new league fall on its face? And with the NFL's own attendance issues, how much more pro football could the public digest, with two leagues from which to choose, especially when college football was king?

"There's this nut with a hearing aid in San Francisco who is putting his own money into his team," said sportscaster Harry Wismer, who would do the same thing with the New York Jets (née Titans) of the American Football League in 1960.

But Tony Morabito did the math and set a budget of a half-million dollars for 1946. The highest-paid 49ers were Frankie Albert and Norm Standlee, at $10,000 apiece. As the franchise's most marketable players, both men were deserving, having led Stanford to a Rose Bowl–winning season in 1940, the only undefeated, untied season in school history.

"I'd say the average 49er's pay in 1946 was $4,500," recalled Lou Spadia, "with the lowest-paid player at $2,500."

In the AAFC, only Cleveland's Paul Brown paid his players year-round, though he could afford to do so, as Browns' home attendance reached 80,000. Brown had coached many of those Cleveland players at the Great Lakes Naval Station in Illinois. He assembled a team of military men, some of whom served their country in football cleats, not combat boots.

San Francisco pursued local college talent. Besides Albert and Standlee, the 49ers signed guard Bruno Banducci and end Hank Norberg from Stanford, plus five Santa Clara players—end Alyn Beals, quarterback Jesse Freitas, halfback Casanega, and guards Visco Grgich and Dick Bassi. They also locked up end Bob Titchenal from San Jose State and halfback Pete Franceschi from the University of San Francisco.

Many of the new 49ers had NFL experience: Standlee (Chicago Bears), Banducci (Philadelphia), Titchenal (Washington), Len Eshmont (New York Giants), Art "Dutch" Elston (Cleveland Rams), and end Bill Fisk, center Gerry Conlee and tackle Bob Bryant (Detroit). So the AAFC pilfered its competition, the NFL, in order to build rosters.

"I spoke with Norm recently," Bears owner and coach George Halas said of Standlee in 1946, "and I agreed to top any [AAFC] offer. He promised to call me, but never did." Standlee had been a rookie standout for the

Bears. He scored two touchdowns as Chicago beat the New York Giants, 37–9, for the 1941 NFL title, then he went into the military. Albert had no previous pro experience, but his image alone was worth $10,000.

The AAFC provided Standlee, Albert, and other returning war veterans a rare opportunity to sign as free agents with the team of their own choosing, rather than the team that drafted them. A number of these players chose home cooking. "Standlee was an outstanding player, big and strong," said Spadia. "He played offense or defense; he could play today. So could Frankie, who was an excellent punter."

Casanega felt the Original 49ers had three marquee players: Albert, Standlee, and Beals. Albert was the 49ers' first, and smallest, superstar at five feet eight, 160 pounds. The cagey left-handed quarterback, inventor of the bootleg play, wasn't only a veritable bag of tricks, but he was vital to the 49ers' early existence as their biggest box-office draw.

Freitas, Albert's backup in 1946 and '47, was a war hero who earned the Bronze Star for valor in Germany during World War II. After playing for San Francisco, he started for Chicago and Buffalo in the AAFC; overall he passed for 21 touchdowns and 1,884 yards in four seasons, while throwing 27 interceptions. "Nobody got much playing time," Freitas recalled of his reserve role in San Francisco. "There wasn't much competition. The team tried to sell the public on the backfield of Frankie Albert, Norm Standlee, Johnny Strzykalski, and Len Eshmont. The only time I got in, we were way ahead or way behind."

Shaw brought a Hollywood image as the 49ers head coach. He was tall, trim, gray-haired, and impeccably dressed; he resembled an aging movie star. Bill Walsh would have that identical mien on the 49ers sideline 30 years later. "Walsh had the same pixie-like sense of humor as Shaw did," said Spadia. "Both are Irish, and both are football geniuses."

Dave Beronio was among the last journalists left who covered the 49ers during their first season. A former professional boxer who sparred against Joe Louis and Archie Moore—Beronio was a welterweight—during World War II, Beronio then became sports editor of the *Vallejo Times-Herald.* He retained a vivid picture of Shaw. "You would have thought Buck was a matinee idol," he said. "He was very handsome with a shock of gray hair. He was a gentleman. I never once heard him raise his voice. As a coach, he was a good tactician. He turned down Tony Morabito's offer to hire more assistant coaches, like Paul Brown had done in Cleveland."

Shaw, who also turned down the head coaching job at Notre Dame in 1941, had two 49er assistants in '46: Jim Lawson and Al Ruffo. Lawson was a great end at Stanford in the 1920s. Ruffo starred as a lineman for Shaw at Santa Clara in the 1930s.

How different was pro football in those days? Well, Ruffo wore three hats. While he was a 49ers' assistant coach, he practiced law in San Jose and also served as that city's mayor. "Ruffo was a remarkable man, really a genius," said Spadia. "When you walked into his office, you had to tippy-toe around stacks of papers spread on the floor. He introduced Tony to Josie, and sparks flew. Ruffo coached for us for a couple of years, then later became a 49er minority owner. The other assistant, Jim Lawson, almost lost his job because of drinking."

Shaw coached with a dignified bearing that was so unlike midcentury football coaches, with their screaming, demeaning, denying-players-water-during-practice, military approach. "I looked at Buck as bigger than life," said Beronio. "He was so calm. He made me think that he never had a worry on his mind, that he wouldn't win the game. He didn't show you that, but you got that feeling."

Tackle Bob St. Clair spoke of Shaw as "a real gentleman. He was a stickler for cleanliness. We wore coats and ties on road trips. During the game, he might say 'Darn it to hell' if you didn't do your job. Those were the harshest words he spoke. He never yelled at you. I respected him a great deal."

"Buck was intelligent and had a nice way about him," added center-linebacker Pete Wismann. "All the players liked and respected him. He was a model coach."

Shaw had one serious flaw, of which the public was generally unaware. "He didn't see very well," said Spadia. "But he never wore glasses." How could Shaw coach if he couldn't see? "He could memorize a game plan," Spadia pointed out. "His only problem was reading the scoreboard."

The giant scoreboard clock at Kezar and other aging stadiums had a minute and a second hand, denoting how much time was left in a quarter. And when those old clocks wound down to the final minute, with the two hands converging, Shaw had difficulty determining how much time remained.

Of course, he had Albert, his eyes on the field. "Frankie was the brightest football mind around," said Paul Salata.

Those early 49er teams were instant winners. Morabito and Shaw had built competitive rosters. The 49ers' only problem was that the Cleveland juggernaut was even stronger. "The Browns were pretty well organized from the start," said Wismann, "with all that depth." And the Browns had a top-notch defense—the primary difference between the two franchises. The 49ers were stacked on offense, but defense hampered them in the AAFC, and for decades beyond.

The 49ers' very first game in 1946 was an exhibition in San Diego against the Los Angeles Dons, partly owned by the flamboyant former St. Mary's coach Slip Madigan, and coached by onetime San Jose State coach Dud DeGroot.

Before a measly turnout of 8,000, the 49ers beat the Dons, 17–7. Standlee scored the franchise's first touchdown on a one-yard plunge. At 235 pounds, he was huge for a running back of that era; he outweighed his entire line—center Elston at 190, guards Banducci and Bassi at 215, and tackles John Mellus and John Woudenberg at 218 and 225. Standlee wasn't called the "Big Chief" by accident.

On September 2, the 49ers made their San Francisco debut at Kezar Stadium, a 21-year-old facility with wooden benches throughout, by defeating the Chicago Rockets, 34–14, before 35,000, 25,000 short of capacity, thereby concluding the Niners' two-game preseason schedule.

The sporting press had difficulty seeing the action. "The second quarter was still warm enough," wrote Bruce Lee of the *San Francisco Chronicle,* "but the first wispy trailers of fog began sneaking into the stadium. By the time the third quarter started, the fog was whirling across the gridiron."

Football in the fog, a San Francisco tradition, like cable cars and sourdough bread.

The 49ers felt confident before their first season opener. Too confident, as it turned out. The New York Yankees and their talented single-wing tailback, Orban "Spec" Sanders, dealt the Niners a 21–7 setback before 35,698 disappointed fans. The home club's only touchdown involved some razzle-dazzle. Albert passed to Strzykalski, who lateraled to Eshmont, who completed the 68-yard play. "It was a hard and, at times, viciously played game," wrote *Chronicle* sports editor Bill Leiser, "but the finesse and niftiness that is supposed to be the trademark of major-league professional football was apparent only in spots."

San Francisco now had pro football, but the 49ers weren't an instant attraction. Only 20,000 fans showed up the next week as the Niners slipped past visiting Miami, 21–14. Shaw alternated Albert and Freitas at quarterback; the mild-mannered coach wanted results, even if it meant sitting down his No. 1 star. Fullback Dick Renfro of Washington State, filling in for an injured Standlee, scored all three touchdowns.

After beating the Brooklyn Dodgers, 32–13, at Kezar, the 49ers set off on a five-game road trip. The first stop was Chicago, where Rockets ownership already had fired coach Dick Hanley. Three players—Bob Dove, Ned Matthews, and Wilbur "Wee Willie" Wilkin—assumed the coaching duties, and the fragmented Rockets still humiliated the 49ers, 24–7. Later on that first season, Pat Boland and Stanford legend Ernie Nevers coached Chicago, making it *six* coaches in one year. The Rockets somehow finished 5–6–3, last in the Western Division.

Off to a disappointing 2–2 start, the 49ers came alive in Miami with a 34–7 win as tackle John Kuzman returned a fumble 24 yards for a touchdown. Earle Parsons then ran 65 yards for a score in a 23–14 win in Los Angeles; the disciplined 49ers were penalized only once. The Niners managed three wins and two losses on the trip, which ended with a surprising 34–20 victory in Cleveland as Albert outplayed the great Otto Graham. Cleveland coach Brown was furious, and the Browns caught his fury. They would dominate the 49ers thereafter in the AAFC.

Eshmont picked up a fumble and scored from 20 yards away as the 49ers beat the visiting Buffalo Bisons, 27–14. The Bisons would change their name to "Bills" before the '47 season. The Browns then exacted revenge at Kezar, 14–7. "Any time Cleveland needed yardage," said Freitas, "Otto Graham would throw that down-and-out to Dante Lavelli or Mac Speedie. Or they'd run traps for Marion Motley, who was a big kid for a running back in those days [at 240 pounds]. They had a system that nobody could defend against."

The 49ers' longest play that first season occurred in a 14–0 win over Chicago. Casanega intercepted a pass and ran 68 yards, then lateraled to Ed Balatti, who ran the last 22 on a 90-yard scoring play at Kezar. The 49ers had a rougher time with the Yankees than against the Browns, dropping both games to New York, 10–9 in the rematch at Yankee Stadium. Cleveland then beat New York, 14–9, in the AAFC's first championship game.

The 49ers wound up 9–5, highlighted by the tandem of Albert to Beals, who had an AAFC-high 10 touchdown catches. Standlee, with 683 yards rushing, finished second to Sanders's 709 yards, though the Big Chief scored just twice. Banducci, at guard, was the 49ers' only all-league player. Cleveland dominated with 6 of the 11 selections, including Graham, the AAFC's Most Valuable Player. Back then, there was one all-league team as most players went both ways, shifting back and forth between offense and defense.

The 49ers fielded the same two rough-and-tumble guards from 1946 to 1952: Bruno Banducci and Visco Grgich. The 49er franchise, and possibly pro football in general, hasn't ever had a more colorfully named pair, regardless of position.

Morabito estimated the 49ers' financial losses for 1946 at "just short of $150,000. But we didn't expect to make any money this year, and we aren't counting on a profit next season."

If the team hoped to better itself by the first AAFC draft, following the '46 season, it was mistaken. None of its 20 selections worked out. Make that 22 selections, as the 49ers had league approval to put together a package deal for West Point's dynamic Heisman Trophy backfield mates, Glenn "Mr. Outside" Davis and Felix "Doc" or "Mr. Inside" Blanchard.

Davis and Blanchard had post-academy military commitments, but they sought four-month furloughs to play for the 49ers at contracts rumored in the $25,000 to $40,000 range. The War Department refused, and the two resumed military service—at considerably lower pay. Davis eventually would play for the Los Angeles Rams in the 1950s, while Blanchard made the military his career, becoming a decorated combat pilot.

With Albert and Standlee the highest-paid 49ers, each at $10,000, the extraordinary money offered Davis and Blanchard would have set a record for either league. In sharp contrast, two 49ers, Woudenberg and Balatti, each picked up an extra $5,000 by playing under aliases in a semi-pro Pacific Coast League football game. Shaw found out about that January 1947 contest in Los Angeles and fined them $236.36 apiece. Nice profit, nonetheless.

"We'll have a more experienced team," Shaw predicted before the 1947 season. "We fear nobody."

Not even Cleveland or New York.

By 1947, the AAFC already was coming apart. Miami folded after one season, replaced by Baltimore. Commissioner Crowley resigned and was succeeded by Admiral Jonas H. Ingram, former Atlantic Fleet commander in chief. Ingram's first mission: keep the AAFC afloat.

Albert received a $2,500 raise, and the 49ers crushed visiting Brooklyn, 23–7, in the '47 season opener. The Niners then edged visiting Los Angeles, 17–14, on Joe "The Toe" Vetrano's 12-yard field goal in the fourth quarter. Only 25,787 attended the 49ers' third straight home game, a 14–7 win over Baltimore as Standlee scored on two plunges. Morabito was curious about whether the 49ers had sufficient public traction. His answer came the following week as 57,000 showed up at Kezar, only to see Spec Sanders and the Yankees dump the Niners again, 21–16. Albert threw scoring passes to Beals and Balatti, but the lefty's three interceptions led to three New York touchdowns.

The bootlegging Albert ran for three touchdowns in a 41–24 victory at Buffalo. San Francisco's Ned Mathews, not to be confused with Chicago's Ned Matthews, returned an interception 52 yards in a 42–28 win over the Rockets, hiking the 49ers' record to 5–1–1, including a 28–28 tie at Baltimore.

Then the 49ers lost to the visiting Browns, 14–7, before falling to them again three weeks later along the banks of Lake Erie, a 37–14 stomping played before 76,504. Cleveland remained the only AAFC franchise without attendance issues.

Mathews picked off two more passes, returning them a combined 77 yards, in a 21–21 tie with Buffalo. Eddie Carr had a 49-yard interception return in a 41–16 win over Chicago. Those first 49ers were opportunists, by getting turnovers and making them pay off.

The season's one harrowing moment came against Los Angeles. Standlee had a wad of chewing tobacco in one cheek. On a line plunge, two Dons slammed into him, and the chew disappeared down his throat, along with his tongue. Standlee's jaw was locked, and he couldn't breathe. Dr. Wilbur Cox, the team physician, grabbed a scalpel and was about to perform an emergency tracheotomy. Just in time, Standlee's teeth came unclenched, his tongue was pulled from his throat, and his breathing resumed. But a frightening moment, nonetheless.

The 49ers ended their second season at 8–4–2. Graham was named the AAFC's Most Valuable Player, a huge snub of Sanders, who accounted for 2,874 yards and thirty-three touchdowns. He was named All-AAFC halfback, with Graham the first-team quarterback. Only one 49er, guard Banducci once again, was selected all-league, even though Beals had another 10-touchdown catch season. Albert, who threw for 14 touchdowns and 14 interceptions the year before, had 18 touchdown passes and 14 picks in '47, while his completion percentage stayed at 52.9, barely acceptable despite his theatrics.

With Sorrell and Turre having bolted, the Morabito brothers owned the team exclusively. However, Tony Morabito needed to borrow $50,000 to keep the franchise operating. "If I had known then how really precarious things were," said Spadia, "I think I'd have gone after a civil service job."

But what Spadia didn't know then worked out best for him in the long run. He discovered, in the process, that while the Morabitos were brothers, their personalities were quite different. "Tony was more aggressive in business and in person," said Spadia. "Vic was a little more . . . I won't say timid, but more reluctant to take a shot. He was 10 years younger than Tony, and Tony's half-brother. When Tony was about 10, his mother died. Tony's aunt, who was single, moved in to take care of Tony. Then she married Tony's father and they had Vic.

"I liked both Tony and Vic immensely, but Vic and I were closer in age. We worked side by side, and we always got into arguments about sports.

Vic thought golf was a tougher game to play, and I thought baseball was a tougher game. But we were friends who worked well together."

Both Morabitos impacted Spadia's life, but he was more loyal to Tony. "Tony never did anything but help me," he said. "He always impressed me by treating people fairly and honestly. He was really a role model for me. Vic never treated me as an underling. He was always my superior, but he treated me as a coworker, while Tony treated me as an employee. Vic looked for my opinion whereas Tony did not." The Morabitos, unintentionally or otherwise, prepared Spadia to replace them one day in running the team.

Following the 1947 season, Ruffo reduced his considerable workload by resigning as assistant coach. Shaw picked Eddie Erdelatz, a former St. Mary's end and future Naval Academy and Oakland Raiders head coach, as Ruffo's replacement.

Then a battle for home turf ensued. St. Mary's, Santa Clara, and USF played at Kezar on Sundays, declining to challenge California's and Stanford's firm local grip on Saturday football. The 49ers also coveted Kezar for their Sunday games and thus were accused of forcing the "independents" out of the football business. The truth was that the three independents were driving themselves out of the football business. Since the 1930s, all three had played in front of declining crowds. The city's Parks and Recreation Committee, which controlled Kezar Stadium, awarded Tony Morabito seven Sunday home dates for the 1948 season. The 49ers now had a stronger foothold in San Francisco, which meant slippery sliding for the three Catholic schools.

Freitas went on to a successful coaching career at Serra High School, just downwind from San Francisco in San Mateo. His 17-year record at Serra was 101–49–3, including seven league championships. Freitas, whose son, Jesse Jr., was a San Diego Chargers quarterback in 1974 and '75, groomed Pro Football Hall of Fame wide receiver Lynn Swann.

Would Freitas Sr. have believed in 1946 that it would take the 49ers 35 years to win their first league championship? "There are a lot of good football teams and good football players out there," he noted. "So it's just a question of the chemistry of the teams making a difference."

Some chemistry lessons take longer to figure out, but does Freitas take special pride in being an Original 49er? "There were 36 of us that first year," he replied, "and there are four of us left—Ken Casanega, Earle Parsons, myself, and a wide receiver named Alford. Earle has Alzheimer's. I think Alford's first name is Al, and I believe he went to Cal." Research failed to locate an Alford, by any first name, on the 49ers' all-time roster or having lettered in Cal football.

Meanwhile, Freitas was zipping along in March 2014. "I'm 93," he said then. "I'm in good health, and I hope to live a while longer."

Not only were Freitas and Casanega two of the oldest living 49ers in 2014, they were two of the oldest living professional football players.

"That doesn't make me feel too good," said Casanega. "At 93, I can't talk too good."

Quite the contrary.

3 1948

Racism on the Gridiron

The 49ers resembled wallflowers at a high school dance. Cleveland was the class of the Western Division, while New York controlled the Eastern Division. Then the Browns dusted the Yankees once again in the 1947 AAFC championship game 14–3. So how would the Niners, without a full dance card, get by the Browns in 1948, let alone those damn Yankees? The 49ers were 1–3 against the two, waltzing in place while the Browns and Yankees were doing the samba.

Someone of superstar magnitude was needed to improve the 49ers. And so they signed fullback Joe Perry, the franchise's first African American and its first contracted Pro Football Hall of Fame inductee. Now the team seemed legitimate. "Joe Perry was the team's first star," said Jesse Freitas.

Signing a black player, though groundbreaking for the 49ers, wasn't revolutionary for the AAFC, which had signed other African Americans prior to Perry's arrival. Therefore, Perry wasn't quite San Francisco's Jackie Robinson, although their experiences in different sports sounded similar.

"It was no picnic," Perry said. "I can never remember a season where I didn't hear a racial slur. Someone would say, 'Nigger, don't come through here again.' And I'd tell him, 'I'm coming through again, and you better bring your family.' Look at my nose: Ed Sprinkle of the Chicago Bears got me. If someone speared me, I'd find some way to jump into his face, even with my two feet. I could do that, and I have done that. I didn't hear racial slurs from every team, but I heard them until I got respect. Then it was like, 'This guy can play. I can't intimidate him.' After that, we got along."

Jackie Robinson deliberately reined in his temper early on, despite the racial invectives hurled at him on the baseball diamond and from the stands. Perry didn't hesitate a second to get even. "My MO," said Perry, "is,

'I won't take no shit.' Larry Brink of the Los Angeles Rams broke my jaw when I was blocking on a punt. I'm spitting out teeth and Y. A. Tittle told me, 'You're not going back in there.' I told Y.A., 'I'm going in there.' The next time Brink came in, I kneed him as hard as I could in the groin. They carried him out. Years later, he told me, 'You son-of-a-gun, you're the cause of my not having children.' I said to him, 'I tried to kill you.'"

The Chicago Bears didn't become the "Monsters of the Midway" by accident. Malevolence lived in their hearts. The first time Perry played against them, defensive tackle George Connor cracked the 49er fullback's ribs on a sweep, after the whistle had blown. Perry threw off his helmet and chased after Connor, but was restrained. After the game, Perry waited for Connor in the Kezar tunnel, outside the teams' locker rooms. Connor was escorted away, safely, through another exit.

Perry's teammates found out quickly that he had a hair-trigger temper along with unlimited athletic ability. And when he merged the two, he was unstoppable. "Could Joe Perry play today?" wondered Dave Beronio. "Sure he could. He'd walk on the field and say, 'That's my ball.' Frankie wouldn't dare take the ball from him. Joe had 9.5-second speed in the 100, but he was strong. Big size. He enjoyed the rough stuff."

Perry's first official game as a 49er, against the Buffalo Bills, set the tone for a Hall of Fame career. Bills owner Jim Breuil chastised Tony Morabito in the Kezar press box for having signed a black player. "It makes it tough on all of us who don't sign a Negro," Breuil said to Morabito. "Besides, they're troublemakers. Why did you do it, Tony?"

Breuil was seated next to Morabito when Perry took a pitchout from Frankie Albert on his first carry as a 49er and jetted 58 yards into the end zone. "That's why, Jim," Morabito replied.

Though Perry felt freedom on that run, he was punched, kneed, and gouged at the bottom of piles by AAFC foes. The Brooklyn Dodgers really got nasty at Ebbets Field. "They had me down and were beating the crap out of me in full view of one official, who stood there watching," said Perry. "Norm Standlee, my teammate, came up to the official and said, 'Can't you see what they're doing?' The official said, 'They ain't hurting that nigger.' Norm grabbed the official by the collar and punched the shit out of him. When I got the chance, I got back at the Dodgers. I gave them both feet or a John Henry [Johnson's vicious forearm blow] alongside their heads. I wouldn't play dirty unless I had no choice."

Perry had other racial barriers to break through in his early years as a 49er. He wasn't allowed to stay at the same hotel as the rest of the team; he either stayed with a black family or at a segregated hotel. Finally, he received the same hotel accommodations as his teammates. Then came yet another hurdle, his being allowed to eat with them. "At the Lord Baltimore, they wouldn't serve me," he said. "Now there were black people working in the dining room, but black people couldn't eat there. If they were like me, then they had fought for their country. So I started turning over tables until I got my way."

The system didn't change Perry; he changed the system. Eventually, his fight for equality broke down every barrier. He was a freedom-fighter for fairness. His parents were that way, and they reared him in their image. He survived all of this racism, somehow, without becoming militant. "Joe and Jackie Robinson went through the same thing," said Lou Spadia. "In my 35 years with the 49ers, I received one gift from a player—a necktie from Joe Perry."

Perry was built from a much stronger fiber than hatred. The color of his skin, as Dr. King would say, wasn't as noticeable as the content of his character. That's why Tony Morabito liked him immediately; they were so alike in character. Perry had a short fuse; so did Morabito. Neither of them took any crap. "Tony loved Joe," said Spadia.

Perry instantly made the 49ers faster. At the Fresno Relays, he raced against USC's Mel Patton, who would set the world record in the 100-yard dash at 9.3 seconds. In Fresno, Patton was timed at 9.4 and Perry at 9.5. "And I had the tape in my hand," said Perry. "Go figure."

Perry arrived in San Francisco to find the same backfield set: Frankie Albert at quarterback, Johnny Strzykalski and Len Eshmont at halfback, Standlee at fullback. Buck Shaw worked Perry in slowly—too slowly, considering which back was the most explosive. "If I'm the only one in Canton, shouldn't I have played more?" Perry reflected.

Would you ask Fred Astaire to work on his dance moves? "I guess it was a dilemma for Buck—who did he want to take out?" said Perry. "So I played more on defense. I'd go from cornerback to linebacker. I had no problem tackling, but I wasn't enamored with defense. The excitement for me was running over people."

The 49ers, in 1948, added another productive back in Verl Lillywhite, enabling Shaw to move Standlee to linebacker, where the Niners were deficient. "Standlee was an all-purpose player, a good athlete," said Beronio. "He'd be a linebacker today, but he'd have to be meaner."

The 49ers signed a second black player in '48, tackle Bob Mike of UCLA, who lasted only two years because "he was easily trapped," said Perry. Those two were the team's only black players in the 1940s, even though the AAFC carried more African Americans than the NFL during that decade.

Paying African Americans to play football originated at the start of the twentieth century, when the sport was semi-professional. Charles Follis, "The Black Cyclone," became the first black semi-pro in 1904, playing for the Shelby (Ohio) Athletic Club, known as the Shelby Blues. Other black gridders in that era were Charles "Doc" Baker, who played for the Akron Indians from 1907 to 1911; Jenry McDonald, who suited up for the Rochester Jeffersons in 1911; and Gideon Smith, who got in one game for a Canton team in 1915.

The most celebrated black football players then were two collegians—halfback Fritz Pollard of Brown University and lineman Paul Robeson of Rutgers. Their gridiron talents were immense and timeless; they could play today easily. Pollard led Brown to the 1916 Rose Bowl, a 14–0 loss to Washington State. He was named to legendary sportswriter Grantland Rice's all-time backfield with Jim Thorpe, Red Grange, and Ernie Nevers. Pollard joined the Akron Pros in 1919 before becoming the NFL's first black head coach, in 1922, with the Milwaukee Badgers. Robeson was a first-team All-America selection, the first black to achieve that distinction. He played professionally for Akron and Milwaukee between 1920 and 1922, then became a famous opera singer, a dramatic actor on stage and in film, a public orator, and a social activist.

Though the All-America Football Conference was a work in progress, it fostered racial integration in modern-day professional football. In sharp contrast, from the time it was formed in 1920 until 1933, the NFL had only 13 black players. Then it refused to sign any more blacks until 1946. The Washington Redskins' George Preston Marshall, adverse to social progress, was the last NFL owner to sign a black player, in 1962.

Ken Casanega rejoined the 49ers in 1948 after Buck Shaw asked if he might like to play quarterback, since he had thrown the ball in college. Casanega wasn't interested, initially.

"I asked Dad about that later," said his son, Len Casanega. "I asked him if he could pass better than Frankie Albert. And he said, 'Oh, yeah.' I asked him if he could run better than Albert. And he said, 'Oh, yeah.' I knew he was faster than Albert, so I asked him why he didn't play quarterback. And he said, 'I don't know.' He did play one game for the 49ers in '48, and then told them his heart wasn't in it."

Ken Casanega became a high school principal in Napa, California. After earning a doctorate at the University of California at Berkeley, he served as school superintendant in Hollister, California. Ken and Helen Casanega had their 71st wedding anniversary in 2014.

Casanega takes special pride in being an Original 49er. "It's wonderful," he said. "The team we started in 1946 is still going." Looking back, he said, wistfully, "I wish I had played three or four more years." With Perry a needed weapon, the 49ers shot out of the gates in 1948 with their best start in history, a 10-game winning streak. They crushed Buffalo in the opener, 35–14. Albert passed to Hal Shoener and Jim Cason for touchdowns, Strzykalski bolted 48 yards for a score, and Perry added that 58-yard run to pay dirt. Eddie Carr also returned an interception 57 yards. And Albert got off an 82-yard punt—was there anything he couldn't do?

Cason was a most interesting study. He could pass effectively with both his right and left hands. But if he had to throw a halfback pass in a game, which hand would he use? "My right," he replied. "It's stronger with a football, but I pitched as a southpaw at LSU. I batted left-handed, too, but I play golf right-handed. And I punt left-footed." The ambidextrous Cason was the 49ers' most versatile player during his six-year career in San Francisco. Play him anywhere, and he was comfortable.

The second Sunday of the '48 season, Albert passed for two touchdowns and ran for two more, and Joe Vetrano kicked a 33-yard field goal, during a 36–20 win over Brooklyn. With Perry spotting the other backs, the 49ers amassed 485 yards of offense.

The Niners were rolling. They dominated New York, 41–0, in front of 60,927 at Kezar, finally controlling Orban "Spec" Sanders. A Yankees coach said of the 49ers' aggressive play, "Those guys are mad dogs."

San Francisco next walloped Los Angeles, 36–14, as Albert passed for three touchdowns and Perry scored on a four-yard run. The 49ers made it five in a row in Buffalo, overcoming a 21–17 halftime deficit to beat the Bills, 38–28. Albert's 20-yard touchdown run off the bootleg was the decider. Then it was on to Chicago, where Standlee, Strzykalski, and Perry all scored, and Vetrano kicked a 17-yard field goal, in a 31–14 victory.

The 49ers exploded in Baltimore, 56–14, as Albert connected on 13 of 15 passes (86.7 percent) for two touchdowns. Feinting Frankie added three more touchdowns on the ground—a five-touchdown day. A booming punter as well, he had emerged as a bona fide triple threat.

Forrest "Scooter" Hall of hometown USF provided the 49ers additional speed by scooting 57 yards with a punt as the Niners ended the four-week road odyssey with a 21–7 win in New York, continuing their new-found mastery of the Yankees.

Albert was playing better than even the celebrated Otto Graham, a two-sport star at Northwestern who was an All-American in basketball. "Frankie was the best ball-handling quarterback," said Beronio, "and the greatest ad-libber. He had a quirkiness; he would call one play in the huddle, then run a different play. He was adventurous, doing everything wrong at the right time."

There was no stopping the 49ers after a 21–10 victory over the Colts at Kezar. The best passer that day, however, was the Colts' Tittle, who was 21 of 33 for 266 yards. Albert was 8 of 21 for 108 yards, though he iced the victory with an end zone flip to Nick Susoeff, another Original 49er.

The 49ers improved to 10–0 after shellacking visiting Chicago, 44–21, before a shallow turnout of 25,306. The 49er Faithful resembled the 49er Faithless, reluctant to support one of the franchise's all-time unstoppable offenses. Hall had a 65-yard touchdown run that afternoon. Standlee rumbled 57 yards for another tally. Perry and Eshmont scored on plunges.

But the 49ers hadn't yet played Cleveland and now would face the Browns twice over the last four weeks of the season. Anticipation in Cleveland reached a fever pitch for the first match-up as 82,768, the largest crowd ever to see a pro football game, crammed into Municipal Stadium. The 49ers then self-destructed. Hall fumbled away the opening kickoff at his 10-yard line. Two plays later, Graham faked a pass and scrambled for a touchdown. Perry tied the score before halftime after an 80-yard drive. Then Edgar "Special Delivery" Jones delivered a 14–7 Browns victory on a short run. Albert had a horrible day, hitting on 6 of 15 pass attempts for a measly 32 yards.

The 49ers then showed no aftereffects, winning by a basketball score, 63–40, over the Dodgers in Brooklyn. Albert rebounded like a true competitor, connecting on 16 of 23 passes for 219 yards and four touchdowns—three to Alyn Beals and one to Strzykalski. Albert added a fifth touchdown on a four-yard run as the disruptive 49er offense scored twice in each quarter.

The 49ers and the AAFC were discovering together that you didn't know which Albert would show up on any given Sunday: the phenomenal Frankie or the feckless Frankie. Either way, he was worth the price of admission.

Tempers flew the following week as San Francisco and Cleveland met up again, this time before 61,000 at Kezar. Three Browns roughed up Perry on one play before he flattened several tacklers in scoring for the eighth straight week. Standlee and Mike squared off with Lou Rymkus. Finally, Browns captain Lou Saban resorted to lecturing his own players, ordering them to knock off the cheap shots.

The game itself was rip-roaring. Graham played valiantly on a gimpy leg; he kept the Browns offense moving all day long. Albert threw three scoring strikes—two to Beals and one to Perry. Vetrano drop-kicked an extra point through the uprights after a bad snap. Try that, Adam Vinatieri! But the day's featured play was an incredible 29-yard run by Strzykalski. He was knocked down twice but got up each time and fought his way into the end zone. Back then, a player had to be pinned to the ground to be considered tackled. Even with all those 49ers' highlights, Cleveland slipped out of town with a 31–28 win and another division crown.

With one game left, the 49ers dominated the Dons, 38–21, in Los Angeles as Vetrano kicked a career-long 47-yard field goal. Albert ended the year with 29 touchdown passes—a pro football single-season record, surpassing the 28 thrown by Sid Luckman of the Chicago Bears. Albert had only 10 interceptions, completed 58.3 percent of his passes, and came within 10 yards of passing for 2,000 yards. His favorite target, Beals, had two more touchdown catches against the Dons, giving him a league-high 14.

Perry rushed for 562 yards and an AAFC-best 7.3 yards per carry. He led all 49er backs with 11 touchdowns, 10 on rushes. As a backup! He combined with Standlee, Strzykalski, Eshmont, Albert, and Lillywhite for a pro-football–record 3,663 yards rushing. The 49ers averaged 261 yards a game on the ground, 6.5 yards a carry, while amassing 495 points—35.3 points a game. Shaw was the offensive-minded Bill Walsh of his day.

An awesome season, but the 12–2 Niners still finished second in the Western Division to the 14–0 Browns, who were responsible for both San Francisco losses. Cleveland then steamrolled Eastern champion Buffalo, 49–7, for the AAFC title.

Albert and Graham were co-league MVPs. Graham, with 25 touchdown throws, four fewer than Albert, and 723 more passing yards than Albert, was named All-AAFC quarterback. But Albert was *SPORT* magazine's Pro Player of the Year—a slap in the face of the NFL, and a slap on the back for little folk. Albert, at five feet eight, was five inches shorter than Graham.

The 1948 all-league selections once again slighted the 49ers. After setting a pro football record for rushing yardage, none of their offensive linemen—center Bill Johnson, guards Banducci and Grgich, or tackles Bob Bryant and John Woudenberg—was named All-AAFC. Huh! Only two 49ers were voted all-league: Beals and Strzykalski. Johnny Strike finished second in AAFC rushing—just as he had in 1947—with 915 yards, right behind the massive Motley's 964 yards.

But the AAFC took on a terminally sick appearance in its third season. More owners jumped ship, more coaches were canned, chaos abounded, and league attendance dropped 30 percent. In New York, where the baseball Yankees and Dodgers existed as mortal enemies, the football Yankees and Dodgers merged their financially stricken franchises rather than have both teams wave the white flag of surrender.

The AAFC would have one more year of flag-waving, although its flag, at the end, would be waving at half-staff.

4 1949

The Maestro

Among the 49ers' great quarterbacks, there was no one more important than Frankie Albert. Not Y. A. Tittle, not John Brodie, not Joe Montana, not Steve Young, and not yet Colin Kaepernick. For Albert was the franchise's first gate attraction, the one player responsible for making the 49ers an attractive entry in a neophyte league that lacked staying power from the first day it collectively pulled on its shoulder pads.

The 49ers might not even exist today except for Albert, for he was their sustaining force at an important juncture, when San Francisco finally could call itself big-league. "We wouldn't be having this conversation if it wasn't for Frankie Albert," emphasized Paul Salata, who caught the little lefthander's passes in two leagues. Albert was that vital, although his memory gets lost today, because the 49ers of the 1940s now seem like ancient history.

But in the post–World War II period, when sports helped heal a nation's wounds, the National Football League needed a West Coast rival for the Los Angeles Rams, and San Francisco already had a team in place. Albert gave the 49ers star appeal from the start, which the NFL also took into consideration as it began contemplating a merger with the AAFC.

Those early 49ers wouldn't have been nearly as entertaining or productive without Albert. With early inconsistencies in their attendance, the 49ers easily could have gone belly up without someone of Albert's magnitude: a charismatic Stanford star, a two-time consensus All-America, and a Rose Bowl hero who played himself in a movie about himself when he was just out of college. Albert was central pro football casting at its finest.

After their first season, the 49ers had endured an ownership upheaval.

To get operating capital, Tony Morabito borrowed against his debt. The team was all he owned after selling his lumber business share. He looked upon Albert as his golden child.

Morabito's friends thought he was crazy when, in 1949, he hiked Albert's salary to $20,000, making Albert the highest-paid player in *both* leagues—the Joe Namath of his time. Morabito defended that business decision quickly. "I don't think Frankie can be beaten," he said. "He has great imagination and is a born leader. He is the best ball-handler I've ever seen. He is an outstanding passer and kicker. I wouldn't trade him for Otto Graham of Cleveland."

The only negatives about Albert were his size and his difficulty throwing the deep ball with accuracy, which was seldom an issue with Graham, though he had a better supporting cast. But Albert ignited the 49ers' franchise with a style of quarterbacking wizardy that surpassed all succeeding Niner quarterbacks, spanning the team's seven-plus decades. The 49ers have three quarterbacks in the Pro Football Hall of Fame—Tittle, Montana, and Young—and a fourth, Brodie, who certainly is deserving. But none of the four had Albert's bag of tricks.

In the 1940s, there were two sorcerers of note: Mandrake the Magician in the comic pages, and Albert on the football field. They both made things disappear—in Albert's clever hands, that would be the pigskin. Nobody was sure what he might do from one moment to the next, not even Albert, as he often overruled himself after calling a play in the huddle. He would fake a handoff and take off on one of his patented bootleg runs. Or if he decided on a running play to, instead, throw a pass, his teammates had better stay alert. He might even throw a jump pass—a relic play in which he took the snap from center, then quickly leaped up and fired the ball to a crossing receiver. Albert also ad-libbed as a punter, often deciding to run instead.

There was no telling what Albert might do next, but whatever he chose, he was successful much of the time. "He was the brightest football mind around," said Salata. "He told me to catch a pass and stumble back to the huddle, like I was hurt. He'd tell me to stumble back to the line of scrimmage. Then I'd shoot past a fooled defensive back, and Frankie would hit me for six points. Frankie loved to confuse defensive linemen. He would tell them that we were coming after them. Sometimes he would, sometimes he wouldn't. He was a great faker and ball-handler and miles apart as a leader."

Salata joined the 49ers in 1949 along with center-linebacker Pete Wismann, who still shows up at his masonry business in Mountain View,

California, even though he turned 91 in 2014. "Frankie had talent, but he outsmarted a lot of people," said Wismann. "He had a good head on his shoulders. He'd call a play, and he wouldn't hand off, but run around the end on a bootleg. He scored a lot of touchdowns that way. Everyone liked Frankie; he was a good guy."

End Gordy Soltau became a 49er in 1950 and was instantly captivated by Albert's diversity. "He was a phenomenal quarterback," said Soltau. "He was left-handed with great skills. He was very fast, and he had the right temperament for a quarterback. He was very capable of doing the unusual. Buck Shaw let him do pretty much what he wanted to do"—such as calling the plays. Then the defense would have to find him, at five feet eight. Standing next to a modern-day pro quarterback, he'd look like a dwarf.

Sportswriter and caricaturist Dave Beronio, who saw Albert in action often, is convinced that he could play today in some capacity. "He was a beautiful player. His brain was worth a year's salary," said Beronio. "He was the master of the hidden ball. He was a nifty ballplayer and a sure tackler. And don't forget, quarterback Eddie LeBaron played twelve years in the NFL, and he was five feet seven. Eddie modeled his game after Frankie, who certainly could be a punter today."

Punting might be Albert's only possibility in the twenty-first century; he didn't have the strongest throwing arm. But in six years as the 49ers punter, he averaged between 41.0 and 48.2 yards a season. He was an effective free safety, too, with his speed, smarts, and tackling ability. In the military, he brought down the fast, elusive Buddy Young in the open field.

And with today's concept of a more mobile quarterback, Albert might be worth a look. Seattle Seahawks quarterback Russell Wilson, at 5 feet 10, is only two inches taller than Albert, and he was the Super Bowl MVP in 2014.

As magical as Albert was for the 49ers, there was only so much magic to his game. He couldn't make the Cleveland Browns disappear, and he couldn't make the AAFC reappear. The Browns dominated the 49ers and the AAFC, which was headed for the same ultimate dead end as those other instant leagues that tried, and failed, to challenge the NFL.

Besides the AAFC, there have been four different versions of the American Football League. The first version lasted only the 1926 season, after being formed to showcase legendary running back Harold "Red" Grange. The three other AFLs existed from 1937 to 1938, 1940 to 1941, and 1960 to 1969. The fourth, emulating the AAFC, forced a merger with the NFL.

Two other entities, the World Football League and the United States Football League, had relatively short lives in the 1970s and 1980s. So did

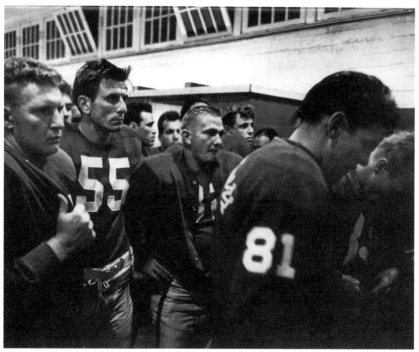

Two early 49ers, center-linebacker Pete Wismann (far left) and end Paul Salata (55) leave
the locker room for a 1949 game. Wismann and Salata played for the 49ers in the AAFC and
NFL. Salata later created the "Mr. Irrelevant" award, honoring the last man taken in the
NFL draft. (Paul Salata collection)

the United Football League, which lasted from 2009 to 2012. A boxing
match between Woody Allen and Mike Tyson makes more sense than most
of these fly-by-night football leagues, which have tried to knock out, but
failed to earn a draw with, the NFL bully.

The struggling AAFC returned for its fourth season in 1949, having cut
down from eight teams to seven following the Yankees–Dodgers merger.
The Eastern and Western Divisions were done away with; the AAFC now
was one league, barely standing on one leg. With the reduction of franchises, the regular season also was shortened, from 14 to 12 games. For
the 49ers, there was one positive change: They no longer had a division
obstacle in the Browns, which meant they might play each other in the
AAFC championship game—if the AAFC managed to last long enough.

"What we were talking about was survival," recalled Salata. Even the
ever-stubborn Tony Morabito must have realized that the end was near,
but he acted as if the AAFC was in the driver's seat. "They have asked for
a battle, and they're going to get it," he said. "We won't go to them again.
They'll have to come to us." The NFL's reaction? Don't drive off the road,

Tony. One of the AAFC's marquee talents was Buddy Young, an NCAA sprint champion at Illinois who played brilliantly for the consolidated Yankees-Dodgers, which was called the Yankees, in 1949. Built like a bowling ball, he was nobody's buddy when it came to being tackled. Young, a future NFL front-office employee, assessed the deteriorating AAFC thusly: "The weakness was in overall coaching and player depth. Some of the coaches had never been associated with pro football and didn't realize the necessity of having more than eleven or fifteen good players. In college, you could get by that way, but in the pros you must have depth."

Young pinpointed Cleveland's loaded roster. The 49ers' confidence grew somewhat by holding the mighty Browns to a 21–21 preseason tie in Cleveland, though exhibitions were nothing more than mirages in the calculating mind of Paul Brown.

The Niners' training camp in '49 featured an interesting kicking duel between Joe "The Toe" Vetrano and Bill "The Knee" Pacheco, a ukulele-strumming, barefoot specialist from Hawaii. The Toe prevailed, and The Knee went back to the islands.

Heading into the regular season, Salata believed the 49ers had enough firepower to challenge Cleveland. He also was convinced the Niners had the right coach in Shaw. "Some of the coaches I had in college couldn't carry Buck's jockstrap," he said. "Everybody worked hard for him, a terrific guy and a gentleman."

Salata also believes some of his 49er teammates could play for the current 49ers: "Joe Perry was a sprinter, a big enough guy who could fly. He would be a first [draft] pick in my time. Norm Standlee was really good carrying for short yardage, and he was a stud at middle linebacker. He was as good as it gets. Johnny Strzykalski was a tough back, willing to block, a good guy to have on the team. Jim Cason was more of an all-around back; he could catch the ball. Len Eshmont was a gentleman, a good player with wonderful character."

The 49ers eventually named an award after the inspiring Eshmont, honoring their most inspirational player annually. But the 49ers should also have an overachieving award, for players like Alyn Beals. "Beals wasn't that big or fast, but it was his faking that brought all those touchdown catches," said Salata. "He and Frankie worked a lot on the side. Beals wasn't that good on defense; he and I were a shade toward offense."

Another 49er teammate led Salata to filmland. "Bob Bryant, our offensive tackle, was a stunt man in the movies, and he'd get me parts," said Salata. "In *The Joker Is Wild,* I slit Frank Sinatra's throat. I had a part in

Angels in the Outfield; I was the first baseman. You didn't think I'd be working in some foreign movie or something, did you? I was in movies like *The Kid from Left Field.*"

"And," the affable Salata added, "I helped Pete Wismann with his masonry during the season. Movies I did in the off-season." Most of the 49ers looked for extra income, even during the season. Players would practice in the morning, then sell Oldsmobiles in the afternoon, or Granny Goose potato chips, which the great Hugh McElhenny peddled all around the Bay Area. Today's NFL player *spends* more in one day than what he makes in practice.

Masonry was passed down from Wismann's grandfather to his son and, finally, to Wismann, who started his own business in 1952. After retiring from football, he put in a barbecue and swimming pool at Tony Morabito's residence. Lou Spadia even helped Wismann paint the player's house, before Wismann then showed Spadia how to lay brick at his home.

"When I was drafted by the 49ers [in the 15th round in 1949 out of St. Louis University], they had nine centers," said Wismann. "They cut the center, Dutch Elston, who had been there since 1946, and kept three others: Bill Johnson, Tino Sabuco, and myself. I started on defense, but I snapped the ball on punts and field goals. I was a good tackler. I got a lot of tackles at inside linebacker. I never gave up. I never quit."

Some current NFL quarterbacks are bigger than Wismann. "I was six foot two, 218 pounds," he said. "Guards were 220 back then, tackles 240. I intercepted Otto Graham twice in one game, and I intercepted Sammy Baugh. The 49ers' stars were Frankie Albert, Alyn Beals, and Joe Perry. Joe was exceptional. Beals had good fakes and would come open. Bill Johnson was exceptional. He should be in the Pro Football Hall of Fame. On defense, we were above average, that's all."

The Niners opened the 1949 season with three home games. They whomped Baltimore, 31–17. A strong 49er pass rush thwarted Tittle, and Colts receivers dropped his passes. Albert tossed touchdowns to Beals, Eddie Carr, and Verl Lillywhite. Free-agent rookie Sam Cathcart returned a punt 57 yards. Cathcart was from Santa Barbara State, which later became the University of California at Santa Barbara, the 49ers' summer training site from 1968 to 1975.

Spadia's son, Lou Jr., hasn't forgotten those early years. "Bud Foster, the 49ers' radio man, was going to interview me with my father," said Spadia Jr. "I was six. Bud was in a tent above Kezar Stadium; that was his radio booth. He asked me about my favorite sport, and I said, 'Baseball.' My dad was shaking his head. The next day, Tony Morabito told my father, 'You have to tell your son to straighten up. Football has to be his favorite sport.' Kids say the silliest things, but when I said it, it went out live.

"When I was in college, I talked to Dad about working for the 49ers. Dad's good friend was Jim Finks, who was with the Calgary Stampeders in Canada. I worked two summers in Calgary. After Jim went to the Minnesota Vikings, he told me he was thinking of hiring me but didn't think I'd want to be there because my dad was the 49ers president. I said, 'You should have asked me, I'd have been there in an hour.' And so I became a special education teacher for dyslexic students."

The AAFC underwent further change in 1949. Chicago, once the Rockets, now was called the Hornets, with their fourth set of owners in four years. After losing 42–7 to the Niners, their coach, Ray Flaherty, accused Albert of kicking a Hornet. "I've seen Frankie provoke attacks," said Flaherty, "yet I've never seen him penalized for it."

The 49ers improved to 3–0 by drubbing Los Angeles, 42–14. Dick Woodard picked off an Albert-to-Salata pass, and it returned 40 yards for six points. After that, 49er backs shredded the Dons' defense. Perry had a 59-yard touchdown run, while Carr scored from 55 yards, Verl Lillywhite from 24, Standlee from 23, and Albert on a 7-yard bootleg.

Carr returned a fumble 35 yards for a touchdown during a 28–17 loss at Buffalo, after which Albert was accused of punching a Bills rooter. A fan entered the press box to show a bruised cheek, contending an Albert left hook had caused it. A 49er official said the fan had thrown the first punch before Albert's teammate, Bob Mike, broke it up. Albert had completed 9 of 22 passes for 97 yards, while Buffalo's George Ratterman outplayed him: 15 of 20 for 224 yards and two scores.

But kick an opponent, punch an opposing fan? Albert's erratic personality was a well-kept secret on the 49ers. "Frankie was a manic depressive," Beronio said. "He battled it all of his life."

Ken Flower, who became one of Spadia's closest friends, confirmed Albert's condition. "Lou roomed with Frankie on the road," said Flower. "Because of Frankie's situation, if he stayed out too late or had other problems and considerations, Lou would have to be his chaperone. One time in Chicago, the night before the game, Lou walked with Frankie to be with him and calm him down."

Albert was pro football's cat on a hot tin roof—flitting about nervously, light on his feet, improvising, talking trash. He was flighty, fidgety, a noted prankster.

The 49ers won their next game in Chicago, thumping the Hornets, 42–24. If this was the particular weekend where Spadia calmed down Albert, it worked beautifully. He threw for four touchdowns that day, three to the clever Beals.

The Niners followed up with their signature AAFC moment, a 56–28 whipping of the stunned Browns before 59,790 fans at Kezar. Albert was spectacular, throwing five touchdown passes, an AAFC record, to Strzykalski, Beals, Perry, Nick Susoeff, and Carr. Shoener harassed Graham all day. Perry shot up the middle for a 49-yard score and finished with 155 rushing yards and a 9.69-yard average. The 49ers were unstoppable with 561 yards of total offense. "On this day, the 49ers were the greatest football team I have ever seen," coaching icon Glenn S. "Pop" Warner observed from his press box seat.

One week later, Strzykalski broke a leg in a 51–7 home victory over visiting Buffalo, ending his season. Carr was lost, too, with a knee injury. Albert hit Beals for one score and Salata for two. Perry tallied three times. Cason returned punts, played both ways, and had a 20-yard fumble return. Forty-Niner fans booed the officials for allowing Buffalo to roughhouse.

Albert was off-target in New York as the Yankees won, 24–3. He connected on 13 of 30 passes and was intercepted four times. Perry gained 16 yards in nine carries. "They didn't have to worry about Strike [Strzykalski] and were able to gang up on Joe," analyzed Shaw.

The 49ers took the train to Baltimore and won, 28–10. Albert improved with a 9-of-19 passing day and touchdown passes to Beals and Salata.

Cleveland sought revenge from three weeks earlier, and won, 30–28, on Lou Groza's 38-yard field goal. Albert and Graham dueled evenly—two scoring passes and a touchdown sneak apiece. Albert threw a 48-yard pass to Eshmont and a 22-yarder to Beals, both six-pointers, plus a 72-yard pass to Cathcart to set up a third score. But the Browns regained their edge, though barely, on the 49ers.

San Francisco dominated in Baltimore, 28–10, and then flattened the Dons, 41–24. Albert was brilliant in Los Angeles, throwing for four touchdowns—two to Beals, one to Perry, and a combination play on which Salata caught a pass and lateraled to Eshmont, who then scored. Cason had three interceptions that Sunday, giving him nine for the season, while Cathcart had a 55-yard punt return.

Flower had grown up in San Francisco, where he was a high school basketball star. He attended Menlo Junior College in 1949, en route to the University of Southern California, where he was a Converse second-team All-American. At Menlo, he met Spadia while hashing meals for the players during summer camp. Then he served as ball boy during games at Kezar.

"Lou was executive secretary then," Flower said. "One night, there was a fire on campus near the 49ers' locker room. I reported it and got $100 from Lou and Tony Morabito for being alert. That was my first business encounter with Lou."

Flower was called upon in an emergency before the season-ending home game with the Yankees. Vetrano had left his kicking shoes back at Menlo JC. With kickoff rapidly approaching, Flower was assigned to fetch them. "Hal Shoener was a big end with a big Lincoln Continental convertible," said Flower. "So I said, 'I'll take Hal's car.' My whole thought process was 'Oh, boy, I'd love to get stopped for going too fast, so I can tell the cop that I'm on a mission for the San Francisco 49ers to get shoes.' It was 35 to 40 minutes to get down to Menlo, and 35 to 40 minutes to get back. I wasn't stopped. Vetrano got his shoes, and the 49ers won, 35–14. Flower wasn't ticketed for speeding, even though he cut that trip by a half-hour each way.

The 49ers' Lowell Wagner scored on a 66-yard interception return that day. A future NFL coach with a familiar fedora, Tom Landry, was impressive for the visitors, averaging 52.8 yards a punt. Albert got off a 72-yard punt; he finished the season with a club-record 48.2-yard average. Coaching the Yankees was Norman "Red" Strader, who would leave his imprint in San Francisco one day.

The Niners, who finished the regular season 9–3 to Cleveland's 9–1–2, didn't know where they would be playing in 1950, or even if they would be playing. "All I remember is that they weren't going to take all of the teams into the NFL," said Wismann. "But we didn't know [the AAFC] would fold until after that season. It was the [lack of] attendance and quality of the players that ended the league."

But, first, a four-team AAFC playoff. The 49ers, who drew New York in the first round, threatened to strike unless they received a playoff bonus. Morabito fired back at his players: "Read your contracts. You played only 12 league games instead of 14, and the contract specifies a playoff game, if necessary. If you're not on the field tomorrow morning at 10 o'clock, we'll forfeit the game. Furthermore, you'll be fined 25 percent of your salaries." The players caved in and reported.

The 49ers beat New York, 17–7, with Landry averaging 55 yards on 10 punts. Albert passed to Don Garlin and Lillywhite for touchdowns, Vetrano kicked a 37-yard field goal, and those Yankees soon would be history in the Big Apple.

The Niners finally got their wish, meeting the Browns for the title, but in Cleveland. They played in the snow and slush. Only 22,550 attended after reading two days earlier that the NFL and AAFC had entered into an agreement of sorts, and that the AAFC would be pared down to almost nothing. Which teams would survive; which teams would perish? No one could be sure.

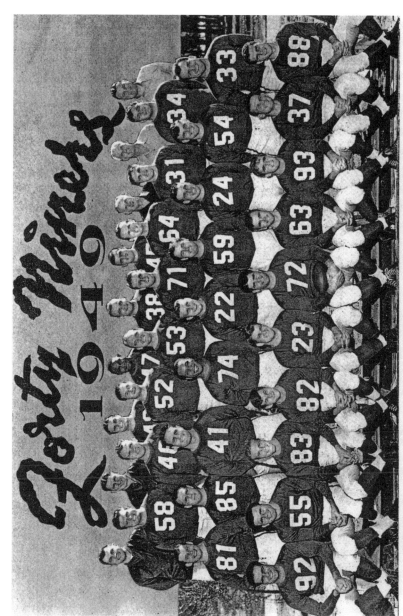

Team picture of the 1949 San Francisco 49ers, who reached the AAFC championship game but lost to Cleveland, 21–7, in the league's last official game. It was the 49ers' only league title game appearance in their first 35 years of existence. (San Francisco 49ers archives)

FIRST ROW, left to right: Wagner, Salata, Cathcart, Vetrano, Johnson, Standlee (captain), Albert, Cason, Hobbs, Garlin. SECOND ROW: Eshmont, Carr, Woudenberg, Perry, Wismann, Maloney, Sabuco, Bruce, Bernhardi. THIRD ROW: Susoeff, Evans, Shoener, Isnili, Lillywhite, Wallace, Clark, Grgich. REAR ROW: Zemlynsky (equip. mgr.), Kleckner (trainer), Morgan, Mike, Carpenter, Quilter, Lawson (ass't coach), Shaw (head coach), Erdelatz (ass't coach).

The Browns smacked the 49ers, 21–7. Marion Motley rumbled 63 yards for a touchdown. The Jones boys, Edgar and Dub, each scored. Albert passed 24 yards to Salata for the 49ers' only score. Vetrano kicked a pro record 107th consecutive extra point. Each Brown received $216.11; each 49er $172.61.

Then, implementing some weird logic, the AAFC staged what turned out to be a sayonara game, matching the Browns against a league all-star team in, of all places, Houston. The all-stars won, 12–7, before a small crowd.

Salata remains a trivia note in 49er history. "I made the last touchdown for the 49ers in the AAFC," he said, "and then I made the first touchdown for the 49ers in the NFL, an exhibition game against the Eagles or somebody."

Cleveland finished the AAFC with a 52–4–3 record, while the 49ers were 39–15–2. The final All-AAFC team accommodated Albert as a *halfback*. Graham was the all-league quarterback again, even though Albert threw for more touchdowns, 27 to 19. Albert's accuracy was down, 49.6 percent, and he had 16 interceptions along with his 1,862 passing yards. Beals was selected as an All-AAFC end; his 12 touchdown catches set the AAFC career scoring record of 278 points (46 touchdowns, two extra points). Perry won the league's last rushing title with 783 yards, a glittering 6.8 average, and eight touchdowns. He was the All-AAFC fullback.

"I idolized Frankie Albert," said Flower. "He was a star's star, so clever and so smart—bold, tricky and daring, a great achiever. He had the quick kick, the speed, and he could play safety. It's an injustice that he's not in the Pro Football Hall of Fame."

Memories, echoes of the past, linger.

"I also remember what neat guys those 49ers were for the most part," said Flower. "Strzykalski was a nice guy. Eshmont was very quiet. Woudenberg was intimidating with his size. Beals had great hands and great moves. I'd run pass patterns with them after practice. Then they'd take me to a drive-in and buy me a hamburger and Coke."

Flower has another 49er memory; the day he feared for his life. "Nick Susoeff told me to look after his car when the team went on the road," he said. "I'm dating my future wife, Alvina, and we go out riding in Susoeff's car when the rod broke. I didn't have the resources to fix it. I thought Susoeff would kill me. But he was very understanding."

It was during the 49ers' AAFC era that Spadia experienced early signs of deep depression. "My mother told my brother and me when we were very young," said Kate Spadia, "that the first episode of depression happened when Dad had just started with the Niners. When [John] Blackinger left the team, Dad wasn't sure what would happen to him. He thought, 'If he's getting fired, maybe I'm getting fired, too.' He couldn't get out of bed. This depression of his would only arise when there was a feeling of personal failure."

Blackinger wasn't fired; he left on his own. But before he managed to get himself out of bed, Spadia needed assurance that his position was secure. When he babysat Albert on the road, the quarterback was unaware that both of them suffered from some form of depression.

In 1949, Tony Morabito's patience was rewarded: twice. The 49ers showed a profit—a small one, but his belief in San Francisco as a pro football town was, at last, paying off. And the NFL was about to welcome San Francisco to the fold.

Then, as an NFL marketing ploy, the 1949 AAFC and NFL champions met in the 1950 season opener. Cleveland and Philadelphia played on a Saturday night, the day before everyone else opened. Eagles owner James Clark wouldn't give his consent for the game, as he vigorously protested the merger. But Redskins owner George Preston Marshall wasn't worried about the game's outcome. "The worst team in our league could beat the best team in theirs," he boasted.

The visiting Browns then drilled the Eagles, 35–10.

The AAFC's last hurrah.

5 1950

Stubbing Their Toe

Gordy Soltau and Joe "The Toe" Vetrano were on a collision course, though they didn't know it, or each other, until their gridiron careers came to a direct head in 1950. Vetrano was a placekicker, but that's all he was to the 49ers, even though he saw himself, first, as a football player. Soltau was a placekicker, too, but he played both offensive and defensive end. The 49ers viewed him as all three. And three-to-one odds didn't favor Vetrano.

Upon entering the NFL, 49ers' coach Buck Shaw figured he needed depth. He decided he no longer had the luxury to carry a player whom he perceived strictly as a placekicker. So he summoned Vetrano for a talk.

"This means, Joe, that we'll have to make every man count," the coach said. "We can't afford any extras. So that's how it is, Joe. How would you handle it?"

Vetrano gulped, realizing what was at stake.

The end.

"I'd ask Vetrano to quit," he said.

"Thanks, Joe," Shaw said. "I hoped you'd see it our way."

A professional career can be built or broken in a heartbeat, whether it's football or any other chosen path. Vetrano graciously accepted his demise rather than to try and convince Shaw that he was something more than a mere specialist.

"Dad thought of himself as an athlete, and he was a great athlete, which gets lost with 'Joe the Toe,'" said Joe Vetrano Jr. "Dad played minor league baseball with the Pittsburgh Pirates before his arm gave out. And he was really fast, running track in the Air Force. He grew up in New Jersey; he was a survivor. In a high school championship football game, he broke his arm so bad, the bone stuck out in two places. Dad came out of the game, they wrapped up the arm, and he went in for the last play, when he ran 90 yards for the winning touchdown. He was crying as he ran because he thought he was going to get hit."

Joe Vetrano Sr. was too small—five feet seven, 150 pounds—to supplant Johnny Strzykalski and Len Eshmont at halfback for the 49ers. Vetrano played some defensive back and returned punts for the 49ers before he was told to concentrate on his kicking. He accepted, obligingly. He was some kind of kicker, too, although the offense-minded 49ers didn't rely on placements. Besides a record-setting 107 consecutive points after touchdowns, he converted 16 of 27 career field-goal attempts, or 59.3 percent. Some future 49er placekickers had more opportunities and worse percentages.

Vetrano had no regrets, though, regarding his four-year pro career. After all, he met his wife, a stewardess, on a 49er flight, and together they raised a son and daughter. Joe the Toe later was a 49er assistant coach and chief scout before deciding to sell automobiles for a living.

"I never met anyone who enjoyed life more," Vetrano Jr. said of his father. "He loved his time with the 49ers, the camaraderie and the practical jokes. When Dad was going for his 100th straight PAT, [Frankie] Albert was the holder. As a joke, he pulled the ball away as Dad was kicking, and passed for the PAT, like a 'Charlie Brown' play. On another PAT, Albert fumbled the snap [unintentionally], and Dad picked up the ball, ran around, and dropkicked it through."

How many current NFL placekickers could do likewise?

"It was goofy back then," said Vetrano Jr. "The 49ers were in some city, and Dad's teammates held him over a bridge by the ankles. You'd get arrested for that today. Those old guys played without face masks. Look at all those guys; none of them have teeth."

Without Vetrano, the 49ers stubbed their toe that first NFL season. They clearly were overmatched, regardless of who was placekicking. The 49ers had made it into the NFL, but they clearly were out of their league.

Vetrano had, at least, surrendered his roster spot to a genuine hero. Soltau was a football hero and a World War II hero. "I volunteered to join the navy, and I was part of a new group known as the Underwater Demolition Team, a forerunner of the Navy Seals," said Soltau. "We were trained in handling explosives under the auspices of the OSS, which later became the CIA."

Soltau's joining the navy's first class of frogmen was more dangerous duty than running pass routes. "Five of us were selected for final training at Camp Pendleton in 1943," he said. "We were sent overseas for six months of additional training in England. Our mission was to attach explosives to German submarines, or U-boats, to blow them up. A pretty risky mission,

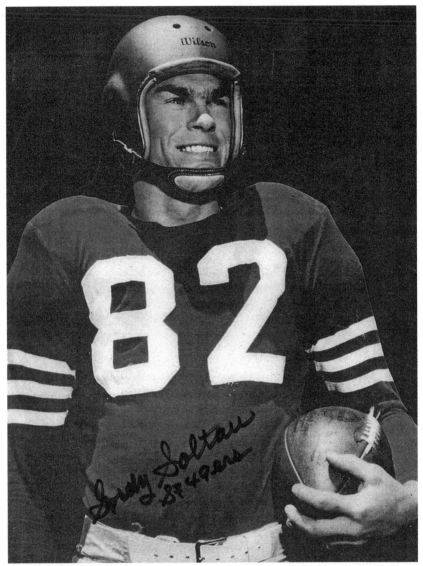

Gordy Soltau, shown here in 1954, was a premier receiver and placekicker for the 49ers in their NFL infancy, leading the NFL in scoring in 1952 and 1953, after serving his country heroically during World War II as a Navy Seals–like underwater demolition expert. (Gordy Soltau collection)

for there was no plan to get us out. Fortunately, the mission was scrubbed. We were sent to Ceylon for a year, where we did sabotage and rescue missions up and down the Malayan peninsula. We knocked out some Japanese outposts, got shot at a lot, but were never captured. We were on a British frigate when they dropped the bomb on Hiroshima."

Soltau made it home safely, returned to the University of Minnesota, married Nancy the Winter Carnival Ice Queen, and converted from frogman to flanker. He later was made an honorary member of the Green Berets because of his military record as a combat diver.

After graduating from college, he became a 49er in 1950, but only after taking a circuitous route. Drafted third by Green Bay in '50, he was traded to Cleveland. He reported to the Browns and saw that Dante Lavelli and Mac Speedie were entrenched as ends, and Lou Groza was the placekicker. Paul Brown told Soltau he could play right away in San Francisco. Brown worked out a deal, and Soltau got back in his car and headed west.

He wasn't happy, initially, as a 49er. "When I got there," he said, "it was like I was with the raggedy-ass cadets. Buck Shaw was a wonderful guy and a good coach, but he had only two assistants. There were a lot of things that never got covered. Paul Brown had a coach at every position. Things were very low-key with the 49ers. I played left end and [Alyn] Beals was the right end. He had good speed, but he only weighed 180, and he was 5 [feet] 10. But he and Frankie worked well together."

Soltau, a 25-year-old, war-tested rookie, was disappointed, additionally, with the team's insufficient manpower. "At some positions," he said, "we were outmanned, no question about it, especially in the offensive line. Our defense was pretty good. Leo Nomellini, my teammate at Minnesota, was a 49er rookie with me. He was big and strong, and he punished people."

The San Francisco 49ers of 1950 were punished more often than they punished others. An unnamed Los Angeles Rams coach assessed those 49ers in the most negative way: "They're not big enough or tough enough."

The 255-pound Nomellini and 270-pound Don Campora, both rookies, were the only 49er linemen who topped 230. Each halfback weighed below 200. Even Joe Perry, then 195 pounds, was small for a fullback, though he made up for it with speed and power. "We were outweighed by 30 to 40 pounds," said Soltau. "Our backs were OK. As the years went on, the 49ers didn't do too much to build up the defensive squad. They drafted for offense most of the time."

Teaming with Sam Cathcart on the 49ers in 1950 was his brother Royal, also a halfback from Santa Barbara State in California They were the first set of brothers to play for the 49ers prior to the Kruegers, Charlie and Rolf, in the 1970s and the Fahnhorsts, Keith and Jim, in the 1980s. Royal would play just that one season in San Francisco, rushing three times for five yards, before becoming a longtime NFL side and back judge, and later an instant replay official in the booth. Brother Sam had a longer, more productive, 49er career, from 1949 to 1950 and again in 1952, rushing 108 times for

509 yards (4.7-yard average) overall, while catching 21 passes for 296 yards, intercepting 7 passes, and returning kickoffs and punts.

Sam Cathcart was another World War II veteran who played for the 49ers. He fought in the Battle of the Bulge and then earned a Silver Star for bravery in the Colmar Pocket in southern France, serving with the 75th Division, I Company, 291st Infantry.

"I was an Army platoon sergeant, and we were trying to get to the walled city of Wolfgantzen," he said of that February 4, 1945, confrontation.

"Our division was with the French First Army when we encountered the German Nineteenth Army in a wide-open field. Unbeknownst to us, the Germans had crossed that field and set up a defensive line along the edge of the woods. We were facing an artillery barrage, and the Germans held us up.

Leo "The Lion" Nomellini, the 49ers' first NFL draft pick in 1950, became a Pro Football Hall of Fame defensive tackle as well as an off-season professional wrestler who grappled with heavyweight champion Lou Thesz. Drawing by Dave Beronio, 1982. (Dave Beronio collection)

"Then I did what I was trained to do, make the assault. So I just jumped up and yelled, 'C'mon, I Company, let's go.' I ran and jumped in a German machine gun nest with four of their guys, and battered those people around pretty good. Our whole line then moved across that open field, mowing them down like a bunch of sheep. It was a mess. But metal fragments from a blown tank hit me in the right arm, and also hit a good friend of mine in the belly. I couldn't use my arm [for combat], so I carried my friend back to the aid station, and then I went to a receiving hospital. I heard later that my friend died. Within three or four weeks, I was back with I Company, and moving toward the Rhine River, and the end of the war. But they didn't take the shrapnel out of my arm, thinking it would tear up the arm."

And so with metal fragments in his right arm, his passing arm, Sam Cathcart became a San Francisco 49er. "I never was a good passer anyway," he said, "so I became a running back. I hit the hole real good, but I wasn't quite fast enough to break it." His only pass attempt with the 49ers was an interception, but his all-around ability benefitted the team.

SAN FRANCISCO 49ERS 1950

During their first NFL season, in which they finished 3–9, the 1950 49ers were described as "not big enough or tough enough." A noticeable difference from the NFL of today: Joe Perry (fourth row from the front, left) was the team's only African American player. (San Francisco 49ers archives)

"I replaced Len Eshmont on the field," he said. "Jimmy Cason and I alternated at defensive back and running back. One game I'd start on defense, one game I'd start on offense. I was Joe Utility. I was good at being a team guy, having a good attitude, working hard, doing the right things. I wasn't Hugh McElhenny or Joe Perry. When we got down inside the 10-, 15-yard line, it was Joe all the way, or Norm Standlee or Johnny Strzykalski. They were really strong."

Sam Cathcart was six feet, 175 pounds, his brother Royal six feet, 185 pounds. Sam was called back to active duty during the Korean Conflict as an army officer, and though he remained stateside, he missed the 1951 NFL season. He finished his 49er career in 1952, then became a teacher and coach for 30 years at Santa Barbara High School; his football teams had a 143–56–9 record, with 10 league championships, during his 19 years as head coach. His brother, Royal, died at 85 in 2013. Sam was 90 when interviewed for this book in October 2014.

Sam is among the few 49ers left who played in the AAFC and NFL. He noticed the difference between the two leagues right away in 1950. "Organizational-wise, the NFL was way ahead," he said. "The Chicago Bears would have ten coaches; we had three. We were like a college team, still in that era."

Before the Niners' first NFL preseason game, Tony Morabito was cocky—too cocky. "Pour it on, Buck," he encouraged his head coach. "If you get 40 points, shoot for 80." Instead, Slingin' Sammy Baugh and Washington poured it on the Niners, 31–12.

Philadelphia followed up with a 28–10 clobbering. Morabito grew less cocky. The Niners' only preseason victory came against Y. A. Tittle and those pushover Colts, 27–14.

Shaw, with a year left on his contract, was given a new five-year deal. He welcomed that security, considering what lay ahead. He needed to replace both offensive tackles; John Woudenberg and Bob Bryant retired after the 1949 season. This meant Nomellini's first three NFL seasons would be spent on offense.

The revitalized New York Yankees rolled into town for the 49ers' first official NFL game and stunned the locals, 21–17, before a disappointing crowd of 29,600, a shocker because season tickets had doubled to 10,000. The 49ers still hadn't turned their fans into believers. And in Albert's NFL debut, he connected on 7 of 17 passes for 81 yards and one score, along with an interception. A bad start all the way around.

The schedule maker kindly handed the 49ers three consecutive home games to launch their NFL career. But it didn't matter; the team wasn't very good. George Blanda kicked three field goals as the Chicago Bears

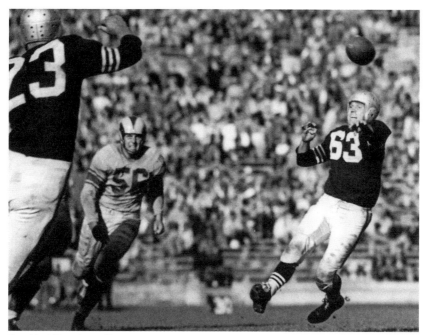

Frankie Albert fires off a pass against the Los Angeles Rams on October 1, 1950, the 49ers' first season in the National Football League after four in the All-America Football Conference. Albert wears No. 63, a carryover from the AAFC, where quarterbacks were numbered in the 60s. (San Francisco 49ers archives)

blasted the Niners, 32–20, before 35,558. Albert, facing bigger and quicker defenses, completed 11 of 25 passes for 109 yards, with two more interceptions. He was better as a runner with 59 yards (5.3 average).

Albert's once-effective passes to Beals were stifled by more-talented NFL secondaries. The 49ers looked hapless for the third straight week as the Rams pummeled them, 35–14, before 27,262. The seagulls took better aim than Albert that day, and Bay Area sportswriters accused the 49ers, specifically the shackled Beals, of loafing.

The reeling 49ers took to the road and lost twice more, 24–7 in Detroit and 29–24 to the Yankees, dropping to 0–5. Returning home, the Niners nipped Detroit, 28–27, as Albert hit Soltau and Beals for touchdowns. The 49ers made it two in a row, 17–14 over Baltimore, with Soltau kicking a game-winning field goal. Tittle completed 17 of 32 passes that day, while Albert was 7 of 16, though both men were picked off three times. But 49er backs controlled the football with a club-record 56 carries, and their defense stymied Colt rushers with just 21 yards.

A 49er turnaround? Hardly. The team dropped its next four games, all blowouts except for a 25–21 setback in Green Bay. For the season finale,

Norm Standlee Day was held at Kezar. The Niners beat the Packers, 30–14, though Standlee carried four times for a meager three yards. Perry rushed for 135 yards, including a 78-yard touchdown romp. The Big Chief did drive home in a new automobile.

The 49ers finished an embarrassing 3–9, without a single all-league selection. Meanwhile, the Browns became instant NFL champions as Lou Groza kicked a 16-yard field goal with 28 seconds left to nudge the Rams, 30–28, in Cleveland. Hoist the AAFC banner!

The Niners' NFL debut was an exercise in futility. They set club records for the fewest touchdowns (29), fewest points (213), and fewest first downs (201), plus the most penalties (93) and most yards penalized (851). No punch, no discipline, no hope.

Albert was pressured all season without a consistent ground attack, largely because of an ineffective offensive line. He threw a club-record 306 times, 50 in one game against the Rams. Verl Lillywhite did most of the punting, giving the beleaguered Albert a needed break.

Shaw and his assistants were accused of "lack of fire." The only NFL team with a record inferior to San Francisco's was Baltimore, at 1–11. The Colts were disbanded after that one season and their players placed in the regular draft pool. On January 16, 1951, the 49ers selected Tittle with the third pick after Lou Spadia won a coin flip with Green Bay and Washington, both teams with 3–9 records, identical to the 49ers.

Albert was instrumental in establishing the 49ers franchise in the 1940s, but the NFL proved a tougher challenge for his brand of wizardry. Cleverness only goes so far, he learned. At six feet, 200 pounds, Tittle was larger than Albert, with a stronger arm and better accuracy. "Frank was good at faking out the defense, but he was a lousy passer," Spadia said. "He would throw three-hoppers."

Searching hard for some glow in the gloom of 1950, Soltau said, "That still rates as my favorite 49er team. Everything seemed to go against us, but we never threw in the towel. We had wonderful esprit de corps, and most of us couldn't wait until we got organized for 1951, getting another shot at the clubs that were laughing at us."

The 49ers had no All-Pro selections in 1950. Albert, Nomellini, Strzykalski, Standlee, and Visco Grgich were picked for the Pro Bowl. Perry, who led the team in rushing with 647 yards, fifth in the NFL, wasn't selected. Go figure.

In 1953 Joe Vetrano Sr. returned to the 49ers as an assistant coach. He held that position for four seasons before moving into the team's scouting department. "He was very good at knowing talent," said Joe Vetrano Jr. "I remember as a high school kid watching Dad help Ray Guy with his punting. They both went to Southern Miss. The 49ers could have drafted Jim Brown, but the story was that Brown was only going to play a handful of years. So Dad recommended John Brodie because of the longevity factor."

Brown played 9 seasons in Cleveland, while Brodie lasted 17 years with San Francisco. But the relationship between Joe Vetrano Sr. and actor Jack Nicholson lasted a lifetime. "Dad was from Neptune, New Jersey," said Joe Jr. "When Jack was born, he didn't have a father's guidance. Dad knew the family and helped raise Jack, taught him how to play football. They bonded together and kept in contact."

Nicholson's favorite sport, though, was basketball, which the Los Angeles Lakers came to realize years later with Nicholson's regular court-side presence at their home games.

"As fate happens, Jack became a movie star," said Joe Jr. "He'd invite Dad to come down and stay with him twice a year. They'd play golf and go to 49ers-Rams games. Dad even started Jack playing golf. Every month, he sent Jack golf balls. Dad went to some parties with Hollywood celebrities and saw things he wasn't used to."

After Vetrano Sr. passed away, Nicholson received a best-acting Academy Award for *As Good As It Gets*. He thanked his mentor, Joe the Toe, in his Oscar acceptance speech. "They were extremely close," said Joe Jr. "Jack gave Dad things from his movies, like a Hoffa jacket and Hoffa shoes. When I buried Dad, he was wearing the Hoffa shoes. Jack thought that was funny. They wore the same-sized shoes."

Joe the Toe's two other closest friends were Lefty O'Doul and Joe DiMaggio, the most famous homegrown San Francisco baseball figures. "Lefty was the nicest guy," said Joe Jr. "He gave me my first set of golf clubs when I was four and a half. He cut them down in size, and got me started in golf. Joe DiMaggio was a good guy. He was known as 'Mr. Coffee,' but he was drinking Sanka."

Joe the Toe and Joltin' Joe stayed friends until the last putt dropped. "Dad had a heart condition as he grew older," said Joe Jr. "He came out of the hospital one time without knowing his heart was racing. He called Joe DiMaggio and said, 'Let's go down to Half Moon Bay and putt.' DiMaggio didn't like to drive, but he picked up Dad and they went down and putted for quarters. They got some ice cream on the way back, then sat in our garage on folding chairs, chatting with the door open. Dad looked at DiMaggio and said, 'Joe, I'm going.' DiMaggio looked at Dad and said, 'Where are we going? We just got here. We're not going anywhere.' And Dad said, 'Goddammit, Joe, I'm going.' Then he died in Joe DiMaggio's arms."

Both Joe DiMaggio and Jack Nicholson attended the funeral of Joe the Toe. Requiem for a placekicker.

6 1951

The Bald Eagle

Yelberton Abraham Tittle was a persistent passer, but he kept misfiring at that most important target: stability. He had been with one league that crashed, then with a franchise that folded. He was looking for a home that wasn't a trailer. Finally, he found a settled living situation in San Francisco. And he headed west with some Texas-sized swagger.

"I'm not coming out to California to sit on the bench," he said confidently. But upon his arrival, the prematurely balding Tittle, from Marshall, Texas, encountered something he hadn't experienced in the AAFC or with the NFL's Baltimore Colts: a quarterback controversy.

Frankie Albert was the 49ers' established quarterback, and prior to the 1951 season, he signed a new contract that maintained his status as the highest-paid Niner. Tony Morabito treated Albert as family, even though his sleight-of-hand magic and velvet-soft passes had proven less deceptive in the NFL.

Years later, Tittle recalled the difficult task he faced in bringing down a franchise idol. "Frankie was a great quarterback, the best T-formation quarterback I ever saw," said Tittle, nicknamed "The Bald Eagle." "Trickery was part of the T-formation, and Frankie was the master, the best that has ever been. He was a bootlegger, he was a great leader, he could make things happen, and he had that cocky flair about him. He could throw the slant and he could run. He was like Steve Young, running around and making things happen. But he wasn't in my league as far as being able to fling the ball."

Paul Salata echoed Tittle's evaluation of Albert. Halfway through the 1950 season, Salata was traded to Baltimore. He saw a remarkable difference in quarterbacking, going from Albert to Tittle. "Tittle was the best

The first of many 49ers' quarterbacking competitions: Y. A. Tittle and Frankie Albert in
1951, in a process that, eventually, elevated Tittle to No. 1 and forced Albert to run off to
Canada. (San Francisco 49ers archives)

quarterback I saw or knew of as far as throwing under pressure," he said.
"As a passer, Frankie was no Y. A. Tittle. I had five catches with the 49ers
in 1950. Then after I was traded to Baltimore, I caught 10 passes in one
game against Pittsburgh. And I finished the year with 50 receptions, tied
for third-best in the league. Look it up."

Salata then moved on to Canada, where he enjoyed further success in
Calgary before launching a lucrative sand and gravel business back home
in California. He's still actively involved with pro football with his annual
"Mr. Irrelevant" event, established in 1976. He honors the last player taken
in each NFL draft with a weeklong tribute in Newport Beach.

"We wanted to celebrate the underdog, and [NFL Commissioner] Pete Rozelle thought it was a pretty good idea," said Salata. "The first pick, the last pick, they're all picks."

Tittle felt like the underdog, at first, in San Francisco. Albert was the big dog in town, but he agreed to tutor Tittle. "I learned the bootleg from Frank," Tittle said. "I got three, four touchdowns a year doing that. Frankie taught me to be free, to make the game fun. He'd go back to punt, and 20 percent of the time, he would run for a first down. Or he would punt on the dead run. He was a nut."

Lou Spadia recalled that competition decades later. "Y. A. had great confidence," he said. "He thought there was nobody who could throw a football or run a club like he could. He loved to throw the football—the farther the better, the harder the better. He was a natural at the quarterback position, but it took a couple of years before the club was his."

The 49ers had gotten bigger in size and tougher, too, after their embarrassing NFL baptism. They hadn't forgotten the denigrating words of that Rams coach. "I think he was probably right," said Pete Wismann. "We were a little light, and we had to bolster our defensive line. So, then, we toughened up. Hardy Brown was tough at linebacker. We got him in 1951, and one year he KOed 42 players with his shoulder block. We didn't have face masks back then."

Still, these were the offensive-minded 49ers. And so they drafted Billy Wilson, a tall, gangly end known as "Goose." He was paired with Gordy Soltau as the less-involved Alyn Beals, with 22 catches and three touchdowns in 1950, faded into the shadows. But Soltau saw his own role reduced with Tittle's arrival.

"When Frankie was the quarterback, he threw to me," said Soltau. "When Y. A. became the quarterback, he threw to Billy. They ended up being a good combination, and they stuck with that. We had a good team in '51 and should have won the title. But we didn't have a good defense like the Rams and Bears."

Norm Standlee sensed a positiveness in the team's outlook and returned, at 32, for his seventh season, his fourth as team captain. Following a 4–1 preseason, the 49ers opened up against their nemesis, Cleveland, a perfect time to show that they had buried 1950's ugly memory—buried it in stone. "That's the game where I intercepted Otto Graham twice," said Wismann, the lifetime mason. "I caught the first one at their 20-yard line, and that set up the first touchdown."

The 49ers whipped Cleveland, 24–10, before 48,263 at Kezar, amassing 373 yards and 18 first downs to the Browns' 281 and 11. Verl Lillywhite,

Gordy Soltau scores a touchdown against the Chicago Cardinals in 1951, as a photographer is caught with his camera down. Soltau was a favorite target of Frankie Albert, but when Y. A. Tittle took over at quarterback, he preferred Billy Wilson as a receiver. (Gordy Soltau collection)

using a new trap play designed by Buck Shaw, rushed for 145 yards on 17 carries (8.3 average). Wilson caught his first touchdown pass, and Soltau kicked a 42-yard field goal. Shaw called it "the greatest game the 49ers have ever played"—even better than 56–28 over the Browns in '49.

But Albert injured his shoulder in the '51 curtain-raiser and could barely lob the ball. So Lillywhite got off a 75-yard punt. Shaw's blueprint was to utilize both Albert and Tittle, without creating acrimony. An improbable quest, but Shaw planned to play the hot hand regardless.

With Albert hurting, Tittle had his opportunity. But the 49ers laid an egg in Philadelphia, a 21–14 loss to the Eagles. Lillywhite ran 69 yards for one touchdown and caught an 11-yard pass from Tittle for San Francisco's other score.

The Niners continued to show a split personality. They won in Pittsburgh, 28–24, on Jim Cason's 65-yard interception return for a touchdown. Then they lost to the Bears in Chicago, 13–7. But the ever-optimistic Shaw said, "This team won't admit anyone else is better. They're playing for keeps—and the title."

The 49er Faithful had heard that same hollow title promise before, and 49ers' management would repeat that same unfulfilling chorus over the franchise's first four decades.

San Francisco played like a championship team at times in 1951, against Cleveland and again in shocking visiting Los Angeles, 44–17, picking off six Ram passes. Leo Nomellini blocked Norm Van Brocklin's punt at the Rams' 30-yard line, chased the ball into the end zone, and fell on it for six points. Rookie Pete Schabarum had a 67-yard run. But the hero was the frogman, Soltau, with a team record 26 points—three touchdown catches, a field goal, and five PATs; a record that lasted until Jerry Rice scored 30 (five touchdowns) against Atlanta in 1990.

Progress arrived that same afternoon in 1951: The 49ers-Rams game was televised live locally, a first-time happening, while 49,538 showed up at Kezar, 10,000 shy of capacity.

But Santa Clara University coach Dick Gallagher complained that TV had reduced the University of San Francisco–Santa Clara game attendance that same afternoon by 10,000. USF coach Joe Kuharich added that the NFL was "killing off the hands that feed them" by hurting the colleges. Kuharich was right. USF, Santa Clara, and St. Mary's would all discontinue football after the 1951 season.

The Rams did a turnabout the next week, winning the rematch with the 49ers, 23–16, in Los Angeles. Rams coach Joe Stydahar devised a "Bull Elephant" backfield of "Deacon" Dan Towler, Paul "Tank" Younger, and Dick Hoerner that overwhelmed the Niners' defense. Bob Waterfield made the biggest difference, however, with three field goals and a 76-yard touchdown pass to that former Chicago Rocket-Hornet, Elroy "Crazylegs" Hirsch. Albert had another rough day, completing 5 of 16 passes, though it wasn't his worst professional effort. He twice completed four passes in the AAFC. Albert had to be a magician to win as much as he did with an average arm.

Tittle's first victory as a 49er came in relief of Albert. Tittle pulled out a 19–14 home win over the Yankees by throwing a 47-yard touchdown pass to Schabarum and then drilling a seven-yard scoring strike to Wilson with 46 seconds left. Shaw complained afterward, "We were not high for the game." Tony Morabito next encouraged his team to "pour it on" against the visiting Chicago Cardinals, who then won, 27–21, making Morabito 0–2 with his pouring-it-on predictions.

By now, 49er fans were divided in their loyalties between Albert's midrange arm and Tittle's deep-threat possibilities. "I knew that, inevitably, we were going to get into this squeeze," said Shaw. "It's the same thing in Los Angeles, where they have Waterfield and Van Brocklin. One or the other is always on the pan with the fans and the press . . . or else the coaches are"—except that Waterfield and Van Brocklin would enter the Pro Football Hall of Fame along with Tittle, while Albert has been denied that same honor.

The 49ers then laid a stinker in New York, a 10–10 tie with the Yankees that was played before 10,184, assuring the Yankees that they would be playing elsewhere (Dallas) in 1952.

The yo-yoing Niners stood 4–4–1 with three games left and in danger of reverting to their 1950 status. Tittle then threw two touchdown passes as the 49ers won in Detroit, 20–10. He started the following week, but it was Albert who rescued the team in a 31–19 win over Green Bay before a paltry turnout of 15,121 at Kezar. Quarterback tensions aside, the bloom had come off the rose in San Francisco.

Meanwhile, game officials were keeping a close eye on Brown and his crunching shoulder block. On multiple occasions, opponents sent officials into the 49er locker room to see if he had metal reinforcements hidden in his shoulder pads. He didn't have, but did Ronnie Lott ever undergo such an inspection? "Hardy would pop that shoulder at his best friend," Tittle remarked, "if the guy was carrying a football."

Tittle started the last game against Detroit, when Brown knocked out Lions end Bill Swiacki with yet another shoulder pop. Defensive back Lowell Wagner intercepted three passes that day. Tittle threw for a pair of touchdowns. And Joe Arenas's electrifying 51-yard punt return to the Detroit nine set up Tittle's bootleg touchdown run that locked up a 21–17 win.

The fickle 49ers narrowly missed winning the National Conference. They tied with Detroit at 7–4–1, a half-game behind Los Angeles at 8–4. The Rams then beat Cleveland, 24–17, for the NFL title. The Niners were so close. So very close.

Nomellini was the 49ers' only All-Pro choice. Wagner failed to make the Pro Bowl despite nine interceptions; the 49ers set a team record with 33 pickoffs. Cason, who had 147 yards in interception returns, was chosen over Wagner for the Pro Bowl along with Soltau, Nomellini, and defensive tackle Ray Collins.

The 49ers had made great strides in 12 months, setting season records for most first downs rushing (134) and fewest touchdowns allowed (24). But 1951 marked the end of the line for Beals. An AAFC standout with 177 catches for 2,510 yards and 46 touchdowns, his second NFL season amounted to 12 catches and no scores. He was overmatched, though he wasn't alone in San Francisco.

Albert struggled, too, against better defenses. Receiving 60 percent of the playing time in 1951, he threw five touchdown passes and 10 interceptions. Tittle, with nine scoring throws and eight picks, had closed the gap between them. Soltau caught 59 of their passes, second in the NFL, and scored 90 points, fifth in the league.

Albert's biggest contribution, interestingly, happened after the season.

"Frank was over at the Hula Bowl, playing in an all-star game against some college stars, including this halfback, Hugh McElhenny," said Soltau. "After the game, Frank called Buck Shaw and told him, 'You have to draft McElhenny. He's the best thing that you will ever see.' Buck replied that he had heard McElhenny was too hard to handle. And Frank said, 'Buck, even if you have to room with him, you have to draft him.'"

Albert convinced Shaw, and the 49ers took McElhenny with the ninth pick of the first round of the 1952 NFL draft.

The 49ers would owe Albert their eternal thanks.

7 1952

The King

To fully appreciate how spellbinding Hugh McElhenny was for the San Francisco 49ers in the 1950s, one need only visualize Joe Montana's mesmerizing mojo in the 1980s.

McElhenny and Montana—two rock-star figures who had that certain something that separated them from football's mortals.

"When McElhenny got the football," Lou Spadia recalled, "the whole stadium stood up." McElhenny had that special magnetism. When Frankie Albert, Y. A. Tittle, or John Brodie pitched the ball to him, he pulled the fans at Kezar Stadium right up off their seats. They thought he would go all the way every time. Often he did, or nearly did.

Since the NFL launched itself in 1920, few broken-field runners have been more thrilling than McElhenny. "No. 1," Brodie believes. "Class, class, class." Others agree. "Mac was fantastic," said Bob St. Clair, who blocked for the elusive 49er halfback "He had this great peripheral vision to go either way quickly. The only one who looked close to Mac later on was [Barry] Sanders. No one else had moves like Mac."

McElhenny was like tackling a ghost. "He was like a cloud of smoke," said Pete Wismann. "He had the fakes, he was quick, and he was a [California high school state] hurdles champion. People couldn't get a hard hit on him. He'd be to their left or right before they knew it."

McElhenny's instincts were as impressive as his moves. "He was something special," said Bob Fouts, who then broadcast 49er games. "A guy would catch up to him from behind, and Hugh, even without eyes in the back of his head, would cut away from him at just the right moment."

McElhenny turned sprawled tacklers into an art form, much like pitcher Hoyt Wilhelm's baffling knuckleball that rendered batters helpless during

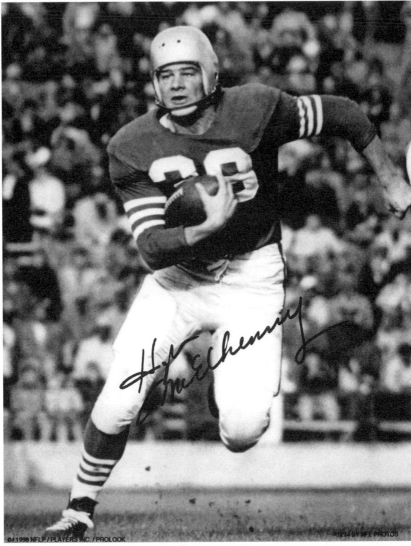

Hugh "The King" McElhenny, pictured here in 1956, is the greatest running back in 49ers history, a juking, elusive, swivel-hipped halfback who caused many a tackler to grab at air. He reportedly took a pay cut upon entering the NFL in 1952 from the University of Washington. (Nick Peters collection)

that same era. Big whiffs, either way. Quarterback Don Heinrich, a University of Washington teammate of McElhenny's, said he was the only back he had ever seen who could run in one direction, jump in the air, and come down running in the opposite direction.

Even McElhenny had difficulty describing his Houdini-ish manner of escape. "I don't think you can explain it," he said. "It's a gift. You don't

Hugh McElhenny jumps over and through some Los Angeles Rams on another of his break-away runs, in 1953. McElhenny, a California state high school hurdles champion, was equal-ly adept at catching the ball and leaving tacklers sprawling. (San Francisco 49ers archives)

teach a kid to be an open-field runner. I don't remember dodging people, but it's like something is coming down your back, and then you cut away. I could really sense someone on my butt."

No NFL rookie ever debuted more spectacularly than McElhenny in 1952. He was named first-team All-Pro, NFL Rookie of the Year, and *SPORT* magazine's NFL Player of the Year. And he was just getting started.

Albert, sensing the rookie's greatness, instantly named McElhenny "The King," which had a more lasting impact than "Hurryin' Hugh," his other sobriquet. He actually pictured himself, though, as hurryin' from trouble with a football under his arm. "I used to say that I ran scared, like I was being chased in an alley," he explained. " I had this fear of being tackled, the embarrassment of getting caught."

McElhenny was the embodiment of smooth, both on the field and off, with his suave manner. He carried himself with a special aura. He was as cool as Joe Cool.

He certainly wasn't the normal college kid who enters the NFL. He already had a reputation, and a growing myth. "Men," Albert said in introducing

McElhenny to his 49er teammates, "I want you to meet the only college star ever to take a salary cut to play pro football." Rumors persisted that McElhenny had been on the payroll at the University of Washington, where at the end of the century, he was selected as the school's greatest football player.

Albert may have been on to something. McElhenny was married in college; his wife, Peggy, a non-student, had two jobs—one at a Seattle jewelry store and the other at a medical center. McElhenny also had jobs, but an additional $300 check arrived monthly at their apartment, no questions asked. "I don't know where the check came from," he said years later. "Every month, it would have a new name on it. It was illegal to accept it, and I was investigated every year over what I was making. But they never caught me." College athletes weren't investigated as intensely then as now. McElhenny juked his way through Washington.

For the first time, the 49ers had a halfback with speed and size in the 198-pound McElhenny, "who has every requisite to become a great running back in this league," Buck Shaw predicted. Shaw was prophetic; McElhenny was headed for the Pro Football Hall of Fame.

With Joe "The Jet" Perry and McElhenny, the Niners' backfield firepower was unlike any other NFL team in the 1950s. But the 49ers' quarterback situation remained uncertain, as Shaw announced before the '52 season that he planned to platoon Albert and Tittle.

Tony Morabito was excited about the team's chances, regardless of who was playing quarterback. But in March 1952, he suffered a serious heart attack. Dr. Bill O'Grady examined him and told Morabito's wife, Josie, "it's 60–40 against him." A priest was summoned, and last rites were given. But Morabito, miraculously, recovered. And despite various groups of buyers who tried to convince him to sell the team, he resisted in spite of his heart condition. "I'll be worse off if I get out of football," he told O'Grady. "What the heck will I do with myself?"

Sportswriter Dave Beronio recalled speaking with Morabito at a cocktail party. The owner told him that football was in his heart, permanently, whether it was beating properly or otherwise. "He had a bad heart," said Beronio, "but he said, 'I'm not going to sell.' I told him that he had the most valuable franchise in the league, what with the 49ers being a colorful team, and everyone wanting to come to California. He agreed. That team was his life."

In '52, Shaw had three assistant coaches for the first time, as Red Strader joined Jim Lawson and Phil Bengtson. But McElhenny's first pro touchdown would be drawn up in the huddle, not on the sideline. On his first carry in the NFL, Albert pitched out to him, and he hurried 60 yards into the end zone during a 38–14 preseason win over the Chicago Cardinals.

The 49ers opened the regular season with a 17–3 victory over Detroit before 52,750 at Kezar. McElhenny was sensational, dodging Lions' tacklers. Another 49er rookie, defensive tackle Bob Toneff, disrupted Detroit's offense. Strader received huge credit for the win after scouting Detroit during the preseason. Morabito took notice of Strader's analytical expertise.

Also making his debut with the 49ers was a versatile and precocious athlete from San Diego, Charlie Powell, a defensive end who, at 19, became the youngest starter in NFL history.

Shaw started Tittle in the second game, at Dallas, where McElhenny stole the show with an 89-yard touchdown run. Albert added a touchdown pass in the 37–14 triumph.

The 49ers throttled the Lions again, 20–0, in Detroit. Then McElhenny's scintillating 94-yard punt return and his 114 yards rushing on 12 carries against the Bears in Chicago keyed the Niners' impressive 40–16 victory over the "Monsters of the Midway." "He's the best running back I have seen in a long, long time," said Bears quarterback Johnny Lujack.

McElhenny struck again the following week, burning Dallas once more with an 82-yard touchdown run. Perry jetted 78 yards for another score in that 48–21 win at Kezar. The 49ers used those explosive runs to average 10.96 yards a rush that day, a franchise record.

The 49ers were 5–0 despite their shaky quarterback rotation. Then Albert made a colossal error that altered the team's season. Back to punt on fourth-and-two from his 32-yard line against the visiting Bears, he opted to run for a first down. He didn't make it this time; Ed Sprinkle was waiting for him. Chicago got a gift touchdown as a result, then won, 20–17, on George Blanda's 48-yard field goal in the final minute.

It was the worst gamble of Albert's career, but Shaw defended him, regardless. "Frank has won a lot of games for us with his daring," the coach said. "He's gotten away with that same gamble many times. That's all I can say."

The difference this time: Tittle loomed larger as a threat.

The 49ers dropped to 5–2 in New York after a 23–14 loss to the Giants. Gordy Soltau had a career-high 196 receiving yards that day, and Tittle and McElhenny linked up on a 77-yard pass play, but the Giants stuffed the 49ers' rushers with 37 yards on 21 carries (1.76). Even worse, linemen Gail Bruce and Visco Grgich suffered career-ending ankle and knee injuries.

The fading Niners needed a spark badly, and Tittle and McElhenny delivered. Tittle threw a 32-yard touchdown pass to Billy Wilson, and McElhenny ran 46 yards for another score in a 23–17 win at Washington. Now 6–2 with four games left, the 49ers were in good shape for a playoff spot. Then the roof fell in as the Rams hammered them, 35–9, in Los Angeles. It was a double loss: Norm Standlee was stricken with polio after that game, ending his career.

Then reports of dissension appeared in Bay Area newspapers. McElhenny's teammates, according to rumors, resented his royal treatment, especially after Shaw compared the rookie to the "Gipper," George Gipp, Shaw's nearly mythical Notre Dame teammate.

Pittsburgh Steelers coach Joe Bach fanned the flames of discord by contending that Perry, not McElhenny, was the 49ers' main offensive threat. Regardless, where would the 49ers be without either of those two men, neither of whom was regarded by teammates as a locker-room cancer? The King, in truth, was no more regal than The Jet.

After the visiting Rams defeated the 49ers once again, 34–21, California attorney general and future governor Edmund G. "Pat" Brown denied a report that he was investigating whether the game had been fixed—with sufficient reason. Those 49ers couldn't beat the Rams to save their lives, so how could they be involved in a fix?

The nose-diving 49ers made it five defeats in six games, falling 24–7 to the harmless Pittsburgh Steelers as the fading Albert threw five interceptions, a career high. Watching the destruction at Kezar were 13,886 fans, fewer targets for the—bombs, away!—second-half seagulls' invasion, a Kezar tradition. The team's collapse didn't sit well in the owner's booth, which, at least, was protected from the seagulls.

Albert and Strzykalski announced their joint retirements. As they emerged from the Kezar tunnel together for the last time before the season finale against Green Bay, Joe McTigue's 49er band played "Frankie and Johnny," saluting these two important Original 49ers. Albert, at 32, said, "It's hard for me to play the way I should. Time marches on." Shaw, fittingly, let him start against the Packers. He came through with a 24–14 victory, completing 16 of 26 passes for 213 yards and a touchdown.

Albert finished fifth among NFL quarterbacks in his farewell season, although with eight touchdown passes and 10 interceptions, compared to Tittle's 11 scoring tosses and 12 pass thefts. But in their defense, they were harassed all year long, sacked for a combined 396 yards. No wonder that Albert punted 68 times, a career high, for a 42.6-yard average.

After the season ended, Albert unretired. He signed to play in Canada for the Calgary Stampeders. Now only guard Bruno Banducci was left from the class of 1946.

The 49ers had limped home 7–5 after their promising start. Soltau tied for third in NFL receptions with 55 and led the league in scoring with 94 points. Perry and McElhenny finished third and fourth in NFL rushing with 725 and 684 yards, though McElhenny led the league with a kingly 7.0 per-carry average.

Jim Cason also retired, with 25 career interceptions. Soltau joined McElhenny as an All-Pro. Soltau, McElhenny, Perry, Leo Nomellini, center Bill Johnson, and defensive end Ed Henke were chosen for the Pro Bowl.

There was a small season-ending celebration in the front office. Spadia was promoted to general manager, officially making him the third man in charge after chief executive officer Vic Morabito and a majority owner with a defective heart.

8 | 1953

Canadian Sunset

Y. A. Tittle's agonizing two-year apprenticeship with the 49ers was history. Opportunity had arrived. This now was his time, his team, and his future. No one had ever questioned his determination or toughness; quarterbacks didn't come any tougher than Tittle. But the ordeal with Frankie Albert had tested his mettle.

Those two years felt like a personal purgatory. "There was pressure on Buck Shaw to play us both," Tittle said. "So he alternated us. One would play the first and third quarters, the other the second and fourth. The next game, it would be just the opposite. It seemed to work out fine, because if one of us wasn't on, the other might be hot. But it was a stupid idea, really. You can't alternate, because you're not given a chance to build any kind of momentum."

Shaw's alternating plan led to hostility, which Tittle caught full blast from Albert one week when it was Tittle's turn to start. "Frank pouted that whole week in practice," Tittle recalled. "He was off by himself, punting to little kids. He wasn't even a part of the team. We didn't have much scouting in those days, so when I'd ask Frank if that was an odd-man front, he'd make some smart-ass remark like, 'Why don't you figure it out; you're trying to get my job.' Frank was a good guy, but he was resentful of me. It was hard for him to sit down."

But Albert was in Calgary, anticipating a glowing Canadian sunset to a flickering career. Tittle was in charge. The Bald Eagle was ready to fly, and he wasn't an easy target to bring down. "Nobody ever died harder than Tittle," said former Cleveland Browns' defensive end Paul Wiggin. "When you think of football—character, heart, personality—he was a classic. Tittle and Bobby Layne: They never lost, they just ran out of time."

"Y. A. was a competitor; he wanted to hang in there," said quarterback icon Johnny Unitas. "His idea of football was to throw it. He didn't care about running the ball. He was an aggressive guy who just loved the game, loved to play."

Meanwhile, up in Calgary, early returns indicated that things were going badly for Albert. The larger Canadian playing field didn't benefit aging legs and a weakened arm. Sadly, Albert had left his heart, and his talent, in San Francisco.

Conversely, his 49er successor was winning over the NFL. "Tittle was outstanding, one of the top three, four quarterbacks I've seen," recalled Philadelphia Eagles linebacker and ironman Chuck "60-Minute Man" Bednarik. "He stood in the pocket pretty good. That took some courage to hold the ball that long until he found a receiver open."

Forty-Niner teammates appreciated Tittle's pocket presence. "After a play, he'd come back fighting," said defensive tackle Leo Nomellini. "He didn't take bull from anybody."

But Tittle and his teammates weren't getting help from the 49ers' scouting department. The 1952 draft produced three solid players in Hugh McElhenny; Bob Toneff; and another defensive lineman, Marion Campbell. Conversely, the 1953 draft would have come up empty, if not for a tremendous third-round pick, Bob St. Clair.

San Francisco wasted a '53 bonus pick—a onetime additional selection awarded one NFL franchise per year before the actual draft—on end Harry Babcock of Georgia. He lasted three seasons, although he was a bust from the start. "He lacked certain abilities, like going aggressively after passes," said St. Clair. "He couldn't block worth a damn. We were all shocked that he was a bonus pick."

After taking Babcock, the 49ers drafted another end, Tom Stolhandske from Texas, but he opted to play in Canada. The 49ers already had Gordy Soltau and Billy Wilson at ends, so what was the team's thinking? "They drafted those two," Soltau said of Babcock and Stolhandske, "because [assistant coach] Jim Lawson said Billy and I weren't capable of lasting a full season. None of those guys could play."

The 49ers saved themselves from an overall draft-day disaster by taking St. Clair, a 6-foot-8½, 270-pound offensive tackle who finished his college career at Tulsa after USF dropped football—a blow to this native San Franciscan.

St. Clair became one of the greatest 49ers, a Pro Football Hall of Fame inductee as well as being the tallest 49er. And while blocking for Tittle, Joe Perry, and McElhenny, St. Clair was elected mayor of neighboring Daly

City and then served on the Board of Supervisors in San Mateo County. "I just kind of fell into it," he said of politics. "Then I moved back to San Francisco, and I didn't need any more of this junk."

One characteristic that truly set St. Clair apart from others was his dining habits. He preferred his steak raw, right out of the meat locker. Serve steak to him rare, and he'd send it back to the kitchen. Thus he earned the nickname "The Geek." "My diet consisted of raw eggs, raw liver, and various raw meats," he said. "Many players wouldn't eat with me. They would get sick watching me eat, especially raw liver. This kid from Nebraska saw me eat some dove hearts, uncooked. He turned three different colors."

St. Clair was elated to return home as a 49er. As an 11-year-old Boy Scout, he had carried a flag into Kezar Stadium before the annual East-West Shrine Football Game. Now he would be playing there on autumn Sundays, and for Tony Morabito, St. Clair's perception of an ideal owner. "Tony was like my father; he treated everyone as his son," he said. "He was a helluva players' owner. If you had troubles—financial, marriage, children, whatever—you'd go to Tony."

Morabito wasn't a newspaperman's ideal owner, however. Write something critical about the 49ers, and Morabito's hot temper boiled over like a volcano. "He loved the 49ers the way President Truman loved his daughter Margaret," said Lou Spadia. "Tony reacted just as Truman did when people criticized Margaret's piano-playing. He fired back. He had feuds. My orders from Tony were that no one from the *San Francisco Examiner* be allowed in anything controlled by the 49ers. That included our dressing room, our meeting rooms, our train and plane trips. Thank God the day that [*Examiner*] feud was over. It was wearing on everybody."

But Morabito would launch a feud with somebody else, which wasn't good for his weakened heart. He seemed at odds with his combustible nature, which hid a benevolent soul. "Tony hated publicity," said Spadia. "He'd never pose for a picture, and he never allowed a photograph of himself in the program. He felt the game belonged to the players, and he did everything he could for the players' benefit."

Prior to the 1953 season, Shaw called his team "the toughest gang I've ever had." He was commenting on their gridiron demeanor, and not the fact that he had a professional wrestler in Nomellini and a heavyweight boxer in Charlie Powell. Nomellini, in the off-season, wrestled Lou Thesz for the so-called world heavyweight title. They met several times. Thesz either won or he was awarded a draw. Mercifully, Nomellini never used his wrestling "flying tackle" on the football field.

Powell had a split career with the 49ers, playing in 1952 and 1953, then taking a year off to box professionally, and returning to the team from 1955 through 1957. But his pugilistic skills didn't impress 49er teammates, especially St. Clair, a former Golden Gloves boxer. "I was surprised Charlie was a pro boxer, because he didn't have that killer instinct," said St. Clair. "There was no way he could become a champion. I knew I could take him easy."

There was a fighting mood in the air when the 49ers and Eagles—who else?—squared off in a September 7 preseason night game in San Antonio, Texas. "Locusts were everywhere, even crawling through your fingers as you got in your stance," said St. Clair. "There were so many locusts that they got into the transformer and the lights went out. Everybody got upset. Charlie Powell whacked one of their players and put him out of the game—it was an unnecessary hit. Then everybody was fighting."

So, who do the 49ers meet in the season opener but their favorite sparring partners, the Eagles? And fisticuffs, naturally, broke out again. "They went after Charlie Powell, and all hell broke loose," said St. Clair. "Joe Perry came flying off the bench, and everybody started throwing punches. Even the [49ers] band got involved, hitting an Eagle with a trombone—the biggest fight you've ever seen."

Hardy Brown broke Toy Ledbetter's jaw. McElhenny had 235-pound Frank Wydo in a headlock while hitting Pete Pihos with his plastic helmet. Bill Johnson was punched in the face. Team captain Bruno Banducci had a black eye. After all that, the 49ers were declared winners at Kezar, 31–21. "For the first time, we got rough," said Banducci. "Best team effort I have ever seen this team put on," noted Tittle.

The 49ers had created a fighting spirit that would last all season. They trailed visiting Los Angeles, 20–0, in the second quarter, when the Rams' Norm Van Brocklin rubbed it in by passing on fourth down from his 28-yard-line. Fortunately for the 49ers, Dick "Night Train" Lane, standing alone at midfield, dropped the ball. But who did Van Brocklin think he was, Frankie Albert? The 49ers fought back, narrowing the Rams' lead to 20–7 at halftime. Then Lowell Wagner's fumble recovery led to a touchdown, and Rex Berry returned an interception for six points. Now the 49ers were up, 28–27. The Rams' Ben Agajanian kicked an apparent game-winning field goal from the Niners' 11-yard line with three minutes left. That's when The King ruled again. McElhenny took a swing pass from Tittle and weaved 71 yards, setting up a Soltau field goal that salted away a 31–30 win.

A week later, Detroit defensive back Jim David broke Tittle's cheekbone in three places during the Lions' 24–21 victory in the Motor City. The 49ers called upon Jim Powers, a quarterback–turned–defensive-back–then-returned–to–quarterback, and he passed the Niners to a 35–28 win over the Bears in Chicago. Detroit triumphed again at Kezar, 14–10, as Tittle made a cameo appearance, wearing a protective face mask. He threw two interceptions.

Tittle returned as a starter against the visiting Bears and passed for 304 yards, connecting on 24 of 43 attempts to spark a 24–14 win. He next threw for 301 yards, hitting Soltau on a 17-yard touchdown pass with a minute left to culminate an 80-yard drive and steal another nail-biter from the Rams, 31–27.

"Y. A. Tittle is one of my all-time favorite 49ers," said George Seifert, a San Francisco native who one day would coach the 49ers to two Super Bowl victories. "And Gordy Soltau was really accomplished as a 49er. You still shake his hand, and he'll break your fingers. He was quite a player as an end and placekicker. And he's quite a man."

The 49ers stumbled, momentarily, in Cleveland, losing 23–21 before 80,698. They won their last four games: 37–7 and 48–14 over Green Bay and 38–21 and 45–14 over Baltimore. Against the Colts, Tittle tied Albert's club record of five touchdown passes in one game, while also setting franchise single-game marks with 29 completions and 371 passing yards. His first full season as 49ers starter ended with 20 touchdown passes and 16 interceptions.

But Detroit, which dumped San Francisco twice and finished with a 10–2 record, edged the 9–3 Niners for the Western Conference title—another near miss for the 49ers. The Lions then nipped Cleveland, 17–16, for the NFL championship.

Perry, McElhenny, and Banducci were named All-Pro on offense and Nomellini on defense. Two running backs from one team as All-Pros in the same year—how often has that happened in the NFL? Soltau, who, with 114 points, led the league in scoring once again, somehow was omitted.

Perry topped all NFL rushers with 1,018 yards, making him the first 49er back to surpass 1,000 yards, and in 12 games. He also scored 13 touchdowns. After the season, Morabito called Perry into his office and gave him a check for $5,090—a bonus of $5 for every yard. Tony, indeed, loved Joe.

Seifert hasn't forgotten those days as a teenager watching the 49ers, long before Ronnie Lott and Jerry Rice were born. "I can close my eyes, like I'm there again," Seifert said. "I can envision Billy Wilson going high in the air and his being tackled from behind. As a kid, I wore a Joe Perry jersey. That was probably my first sense of the 49ers, when I was at James Lick Junior High School. People would still be amazed at the flexibility

Joe "The Jet" Perry breaks off a run against the Los Angeles Rams in 1953, the first of his two consecutive 1,000-yard seasons and the first by any NFL runner. Perry was the 49ers' first African American player, signed in 1948. (San Francisco 49ers archives)

and athleticism of McElhenny as a runner. After games, we'd go down to where the players dressed. Looking down that stairwell, McElhenny always seemed to be one of the more dapper players. He'd wear a dark charcoal suit with a pink shirt, what they used to call the 'Mr. B' collar [named after singer Billy Eckstine]. It was a wide, rolled collar, and you needed a full, wide Windsor tie knot to fill it up."

McElhenny hip-faked tacklers on the playing field, and he was one hip daddy in the parking lot, signing countless autographs. Here was The King, descending from his throne, and mixing with his admiring legion of commoners.

As a footnote to the 1953 season, Albert returned from Canada, convinced beyond a doubt, this time, that his playing days were over.

But he was unaware of the 49ers' tightening hold on him.

9 1954

Buck Stops Here

Though Tony Morabito was loyal to Buck Shaw, he was growing more impatient by the year. Shaw was starting his ninth season, in 1954, as the 49ers only head coach, and he hadn't yet won a league championship. Morabito was tired of waiting. He had signed Shaw to coach a full two years before the 49ers' first game. Cleveland had been too great an obstacle in the AAFC. But now the 49ers, in Morabito's mind, had caught up to the Browns, and the NFL, in talent.

Morabito wasn't the only one who felt this way. "The 49ers are the toughest team in the league," said Hampton Pool, coach of the rival Los Angeles Rams. Tough enough and now big enough—1950 was ancient history.

Morabito remained committed to Shaw, but that commitment was loosening. Something else about their relationship nagged at Morabito, and pushed his hot button. "Tony was always upset with Buck's not wanting to buy into the team when the 49ers started," said Pete Wismann. "Tony wanted Buck to give up part of his salary, but Buck wanted all of it. That was the foundation of it right there. When you do that to an Italian, you better watch out."

One more factor, though not necessarily Shaw's fault, conspired against him. The 49ers had another atrocious draft, with only one viable pick, guard Ted Connolly from Santa Clara and Tulsa, a ninth-round selection. Their first draft choice was quarterback Bernie Faloney of Maryland. "I don't know about Faloney," Gordy Soltau recalled. "We were all laughing about that one." Faloney never played a down for the 49ers; he chose Canadian football instead.

With Y. A. Tittle coming into his own, why would the 49ers even need another quarterback? A strange drafting pattern, focused on offense, was building in San Francisco.

Lawrence T. "Buck" Shaw, photographed in 1953, often was described as an aging "mati-nee idol" by the media. He coached the 49ers from their beginning, 1946, through 1954, when he was fired. Though it wasn't generally known, Shaw had difficulty seeing. He needed help reading the stadium clock. (San Francisco 49ers archives)

Meanwhile, Morabito pulled Frankie Albert back into the 49ers organization as the new director of promotions. Albert also joined Fred Hessler as an analyst in the radio booth after the 49ers' first play-by-play man, the respected Bud Foster, was let go.

Another 49er addition was a super-mean, super-equipped running back, John Henry Johnson, a local product from Pittsburg, California, who had attended St. Mary's and Arizona State before heading up to Canada. Johnson would have an immediate impact, despite early fumbling issues, but injuries decimated the team. Soltau separated a shoulder in mid-August and was lost for two months, the first indicator of a medical malaise.

Shaw anointed Tittle as "the No. 1 quarterback in the NFL" before the season opener. Tittle and Joe Perry then delivered a 41–7 victory over Washington, with The Jet scoring four touchdowns. A displeased Shaw called the team's effort "horrible." Would a score of 51–7 have altered his opinion?

Then Tittle broke his left, nonthrowing, hand against the Rams in Los Angeles. His chief backup, Arnold Galiffa of West Point fame, had incurred the same injury the week before. Middle guard Art Michalik and linebacker Don Burke suffered knee injuries against the Rams, both men requiring surgery. The banged-up 49ers happily settled for a 24–24 tie as Billy Wilson set a club record with 11 receptions. The NFL was years away from instituting overtime to break ties. An irritated Morabito accused the rival Rams of "dirty football."

A broken hand couldn't stop Tittle for long. After Jim Cason, back from a year's retirement, started as an emergency quarterback in Green Bay, Tittle relieved him in the fourth quarter and, wearing a cast, valiantly rallied the 49ers to a 23–17 victory.

Tittle still was in obvious distress in Chicago. But, an untested quarterback, rookie Maury Duncan, steadied the 49ers after the Bears took a 21–7 lead. Pete Brown set a 49er one-game record of 11 punts, but long runs by the reliables, Perry and Hugh McElhenny, sealed another comeback win, 31–24.

The 49ers edged Detroit in a Kezar shootout, 37–31, though injuries mounted. Defensive back Rex Berry broke his jaw. Cason damaged a knee. The 49ers had hit a crisis point. Wismann, who left the team in 1952 to do masonry, was re-signed. "The 49ers called me after three centers were hurt on the same weekend," he said. "I played three games, but it was very easy for me to come back, because I was in shape from doing physical work. And those three games helped my [NFL] pension, because I got a fifth year."

Resembling a hospital ward, the 49ers somehow were 4–0–1. Then came the crusher. The Bears' evil-spirited Ed Sprinkle chased McElhenny out of bounds at Kezar and separated his shoulder. McElhenny was lost for the season. An unknown Bears rookie, Harlon Hill, caught four touchdown passes that day, including a 66-yarder from USF product Ed Brown in the final minute for a 31–27 Chicago victory.

"All our defensive backs were hurt, and they had to put John Henry back there," said Bob St. Clair. The aggressive Johnson bit on the run, Hill zipped past him, and there went the ballgame—and the 49ers season.

The NFL was more lenient in those days about late hits following the whistle. Sprinkle wasn't punished for a clearly illegal tackle on McElhenny, but this baddest Bear upheld his image as the league's dirtiest player. "Yes, he was," said St. Clair. "He had the meanest heart. He'd bite you, kick you, step on your fingers. He had a target on him every game."

McElhenny's injury was devastating. He had rushed for 515 yards in 64 carries, a phenomenal 8.0 average. Tittle's six interceptions against Chicago didn't help matters. Then minus "The King," the 49ers lost four times in five weeks, including the Bears debacle. Tittle missed a 48–7 drubbing by Detroit with a bad knee.

Rumors circulated that Shaw's job was in jeopardy. "No comment," said a terse Morabito. Such speculation hadn't existed before during Shaw's long tenure with the 49ers.

The deflated 49ers won their last two games, both at Kezar. Tittle connected with Bill Jessup on a 68-yard touchdown hookup, while completing 15 of 18 passes, to beat Green Bay, 35–0. Then the Niners scraped by Baltimore, 10–7. Attendance dropped to 25,456 for the finale, which left the battered 49ers with a 7–4–1 record.

Shaw had coached remarkably, considering that this had been his worst season, by far, for injuries, including the devastating loss of McElhenny, the league's best halfback. But that wasn't the sentiment in the owner's office.

Two days after the season, a fed-up Morabito fired Shaw. "This ball club folded," Morabito charged. "We lost the big ones. It is time that we tried something new. Our decision to release Shaw was not based on the 1954 campaign alone, but rather on the last four years. I believe our record this year should have been better, even with all the injuries we had. I believe we could have won the title."

Morabito based his weak argument partly on Perry and Johnson finishing first and second in NFL rushing with 1,049 and 681 yards, respectively, and the 17 touchdowns between them. Perry achieved a milestone as the first NFL rusher to have consecutive 1,000-yard seasons. And Wilson tied Philadelphia's Pete Pihos for the pass-catching title with 60 receptions.

Morabito didn't concern himself with the 49ers' defense giving up 30-plus points twice, and 40-plus points twice, with just 12 interceptions in 12 games. Temperamental Tony's mind was made up, and that was that. Bye-bye, Buck.

Perry, Bruno Banducci, and Leo Nomellini were chosen All-Pro, but the big story remained Shaw's surprising termination. "When he was fired, I was shocked," said St. Clair. "I figured, 'Who are we going to get?'"

Bob Fouts, the 49ers' eventual play-by-play man, handled pre- and post-game radio interviews during the Shaw era. "[Morabito] didn't think Buck was strong enough," said Fouts. "Buck would call a play in practice, and Frankie Albert would say, 'We don't need to do that. We already know it.'"

Regardless, 49er players, the fans and the media were stunned by the news that Shaw was axed. "Frankly, I don't know where they are going to find a better man than Buck," Soltau said immediately.

Ten days later, Norman "Red" Strader—former St. Mary's College star, part-time NFL scout, onetime AAFC head coach, and a 49er assistant in 1952—succeeded Shaw. Strader gave up a construction job for this coaching opportunity. Perhaps Morabito viewed him as a builder.

"I wish him the best of luck," Shaw said graciously, "and luck is what you need most in this game." Shaw walked out a class act, while Strader walked into a housecleaning instead of a homecoming. Shaw's assistant, the tippling Jim Lawson, also was canned. Albert and newcomers Howard "Red" Hickey and Mark Duncan joined Phil Bengtson, the lone Shaw holdover, on Strader's staff.

Insiders were curious about Strader's hiring, as he once was Morabito's mortal enemy. When Strader coached the AAFC's New York franchise, Morabito accused him of having a former San Francisco player scout a 49er practice. The breezy, fast-talking Strader must have won over Morabito, unless the latter was so desperate to have a new coach, any coach, that he hired a hammer-and-nails guy.

With Strader and Hickey, the 49ers would be seeing plenty of "Red" in the near future. But that color would blind the team's ambitions into the 1960s.

10 1955

Worth a Million

The most honored backfield in pro football history greeted Red Strader when the 49ers reported to their new summer digs at St. Mary's College's quaint hilly campus in rural Moraga, California, an odd site for a training camp, for the 49ers had killed off football at St. Mary's. By choosing to practice there, was Tony Morabito begging for forgiveness? This turn of the worm seemed a bad omen for Strader, himself a St. Mary's alumnus.

But with Y. A. Tittle, Hugh McElhenny, John Henry Johnson, and Joe Perry—a complete backfield ready-made for the Pro Football Hall of Fame—the 49ers looked lethal offensively. Defensively, not so lethal.

Johnson brought a different running style than Perry, a speed-burner, and McElhenny, an open-field threat. Johnson offered a bruising counterpoint. "John was like a tank, a slugger," said Bob St. Clair. "He had speed, but he would purposely go after you, including his blockers. I'd be leading him around end, and he'd have his hand on me. When I'd knock the guy backwards, John would run over the top of me. He left cleat marks all over my back."

The 49ers' only problem offensively was that there was just one football. Billy Wilson and Gordy Soltau were weapons, too, as receivers. Tittle's unenviable task was to make everybody happy. "It wasn't an easy job," he recalled. "I had three backs to please. They all wanted to carry the ball, and they all pouted a little bit if they didn't get the ball. Joe was the workhorse. Mac didn't have quite the stamina of the others; he worked everything in his body when he ran with the ball. John Henry was the best athlete of the three. If he had been a boxer, he'd have been heavyweight champion of the world. He could run as fast as the other two, if he wanted to. He could dog it a little bit. You'd have to light a fire under him."

The 49ers' Million Dollar Backfield—Hugh McElhenny, Joe Perry, Y. A. Tittle, and John Henry Johnson (from left)—is the only complete full house backfield ever inducted into the Pro Football Hall of Fame. 1979 Drawing by Dave Beronio. (Dave Beronio collection)

This foursome became known as the Million Dollar Backfield—a name created by the 49ers' publicist, Dan McGuire—even though their combined salaries topped off at $70,000.

Geography aside, the 1955 training camp had a very different feel. There was no Buck Shaw, and the players discovered instantly that Strader was a poor substitute. He patrolled the halls from 10:30 to 11:00 each night, making sure the players were in their rooms. "We're being led around by the hand like a bunch of children," one veteran complained anonymously. "This minute-by-minute scheduling every day makes me feel as though I'm in military school."

This was exactly the tougher approach, and the tighter control, that Tony Morabito wanted from his new coach. The 49ers reported in top shape, because even the veterans feared that they wouldn't fit into Strader's plans, whatever they may be.

"Red Strader was a nice man, but a disaster," said Soltau. "His coaching wasn't simpatico with pro football, which had gone past him."

"Red was a real nice guy, but I can't remember him being forceful," said St. Clair, defusing Morabito's post-Shaw expectations. "He wore a nightcap and a cotton nightgown in training camp. He'd come down to talk to Tittle that way."

Nonetheless, the training camp–wise veterans recognized that Strader couldn't patrol the halls all night long. "The 49ers wanted a disciplinarian as head coach," Bob Fouts remembered. "Red Strader wouldn't even give the players water in training camp, when it was hot and guys were keeling over. But Red worked himself so hard that when he went to bed, he snored. He was out. The players could hear him snoring, and Bob St. Clair would lead the group into town."

Bruno Banducci wasn't given an opportunity to break curfew. After back-to-back All-Pro seasons, the team captain and the last holdover from the Original 49ers, was waived. Pro football had changed drastically from 1946: 220-pound guards such as Banducci were becoming extinct.

Linebacker Don Burke retired to open a bowling alley; perhaps knocking down pins was safer than being knocked down by blockers. Unless he foresaw the 49ers' season as a gutter ball.

The Niners, for a change, had a solid draft, selecting defensive back Dicky Moegle, lineman Frank Morze, linebacker Matt Hazeltine, and utilityman George Maderos.

Charlie Powell gave up his boxing career, temporarily, after being knocked out by Charlie Norkus and John Summerlin. Powell, who did knock out No. 2–ranked heavyweight Nino Valdes, rejoined the 49ers, preferring sacking over being socked.

The versatile Jim Cason was traded to the Rams. McElhenny's shoulder was sound again, but he injured a foot in an August 13 exhibition against Pittsburgh. The 49ers held their collective breath again, but The King made it back for the September 25 opener and caught a 42-yard scoring pass from Tittle, although Los Angeles prevailed, 23–14, before 58,772 at Kezar.

McElhenny's touchdown was misleading; his foot hadn't responded to treatment. He was sent to specialists at Johns Hopkins in Baltimore, but they couldn't pinpoint the problem. Finally, it was determined that the injury was related to a mishap he had at age 11, when he cut his foot on a broken bottle and spent nearly a year on crutches. For the rest of the 1955 season—another bad omen for Strader—McElhenny would play on one good leg.

Cleveland then clobbered the 49ers, 38–3. Possibly, Morabito silently regretted ousting Shaw. The 49ers traveled to the Windy City and edged the Bears, 20–19, for Strader's first victory. Meanwhile, Morabito denied that finger-pointing, and team dissension, were happening.

Fingers were being pointed *at* the 49ers for sure. Walter Wolfner, the Chicago Cardinals managing director, said he wouldn't ever play the 49ers again if it were his choice. He cited John Henry Johnson's vicious blow to the face of the Cardinals' great halfback, Charley Trippi, breaking his cheekbone and nose and knocking out some teeth in a pre-season game. "It looked like someone had butchered a hog," said Pat Summerall, Trippi's teammate. "Charlie never looked the same after that. It changed his whole facial look."

Johnson also hit Cleveland's Ed Modzelewski with sledgehammer force, splitting the two bars on "Mighty Mo"'s face mask and breaking his nose. His face swelled up and, according to teammate Paul Wiggin, didn't return to its previous form either.

John Henry was a face-busting man. "I was no dirty player," he reflected. "I was a player, a good player. But you've got to love contact. I'd pop up like a snake. Or if I wanted to get even, I'd use my head in their chest or gut. Or if I really got mad, I'd put a helmet on their knees. It was survival; that's a good word for it."

The 49ers rode a roller coaster all season long. They edged Detroit, 27–24, on Tittle's 78-yard touchdown bomb to rookie halfback Carroll Hardy and Rex Berry's 44-yard interception return for another six-pointer.

Tittle hit Wilson with a 72-yard scoring strike, but the 49ers lost to the visiting Bears, 34–23. The unpredictable 49ers then beat the Lions, 38–21, at Kezar to even their record, at 3–3.

But all hopes of a midseason booster shot, and job security for Strader, evaporated with a five-game losing streak. Johnson separated a shoulder during a 27–14 loss in Los Angeles. Three visibly upset Rams chased after Johnson earlier in the game, but he grabbed a first-down marker and fended them off. His shoulder injury wasn't the result of any personal revenge, though his enemies weren't about to send him get-well cards.

Forty-Niner fans then hung Strader *and* Morabito in effigy, a rare coach-owner "hanging," and occurring in the same week. Meanwhile, 49er veterans missed Shaw more than ever. And so did their owner, finally, for the franchise was stuck horribly in reverse.

The multitalented Hardy played just one season with the 49ers, then he spent eight seasons as a major-league outfielder. Against the Redskins in Washington, Tittle hit Hardy with a 64-yard completion, but Hardy was tackled well short of the goal line, and the 49ers lost, 7–0.

Perry rushed for 133 yards on 16 carries (9.56 average) as Green Bay beat the 49ers, 27–21. Two weeks later, those same Packers completed San

Francisco's five-game skid, 28–7. Afterward, Green Bay's coach, Lisle Blackbourn, criticized the Niners' "weaker" offensive front. McElhenny had his best game of the season that afternoon, with 83 yards on 13 carries, then complained, "I still can't cut properly."

The 49ers staggered to a 4–8 record after beating Baltimore, 35–24, to close out the failed season. "I'd say we were lucky to win four games," said Strader, not exactly the year-end statement Tony Morabito had expected to hear from his head coach. Vic Morabito, speaking for his older brother, called rumors of Strader's ouster "ridiculous."

Perry slipped from 1,049 yards to 701, with only two touchdowns, but he still finished fifth among NFL backs. McElhenny had his worst season—327 rushing yards and a 3.6 average. No 49ers' offense hadn't ever gained fewer yards (3,651) or had fewer plays (711). Defensively, the 49ers surrendered 308 points and 250 first downs, both team records. Three of Bobby Luna's punts were blocked. Not a good coaching start.

Wilson finished second in NFL receptions with 53, including seven scores. Tittle wound up fourth in league passing, albeit with 17 touchdowns and 28 interceptions. Perhaps that explained why the defensively lacking 49ers drafted Michigan State quarterback Earl Morrall with their next No. 1 pick. Morabito couldn't draft enough quarterbacks, because he believed that they represented box office. He wanted an attractive team, but attractiveness doesn't win championships, not like defense wins championships.

Wilson, St. Clair and defensive tackle Bob Toneff were chosen All-Pro. Then the first branch of a famous football tree was trimmed when 49er defensive end Clay Matthews, the father and grandfather of future NFL stars, retired.

Eight days after the season, Strader was fired.

Tony Morabito described Strader and the 49er players as "incompatible." Incompatibility hadn't ever been an issue with Shaw; Morabito's temper simply had gotten the best of him.

At that same press conference announcing Strader's removal, Morabito reaffirmed that the 49ers were not for sale. "I have no desire to sell this club anymore," he said. "I'm going to stay in football and take my chances [medically]."

Morabito struggled to bring pro football to San Francisco, to convert it into a major-league city. He now faced a bigger challenge—his own mortality—in his race against time to give his city an NFL championship.

But he had a hidden ace up his sleeve.

11 1956

Favorite Son

Frankie Albert didn't ride in on a white charger or even in a white Cadillac, but Tony Morabito, who appointed him as the 49ers' new head coach, perceived him as a conquering hero, a savior.

The only flaw in the popular hiring of a local hero: Albert hadn't ever been a head coach. Buck Shaw and Red Strader had previous head-coaching experience; Albert had been an assistant coach all of one season. Was Morabito thinking with his heart, and not his head, in bringing back a favorite son? And why would Albert take this nerve-wracking job, especially with his medical situation?

"Tony made the mistake of hiring Frankie," said Gordy Soltau. "He didn't want to coach; he wanted to play. He wasn't cut out to be a coach. His temperament wasn't to coach. He told me he only took the job because Tony wanted him to. Tony always felt Frankie was the franchise. But other assistants wouldn't come to San Francisco because they knew he wouldn't last."

But some 49ers embraced Albert's flamboyance and his familiarity, believing he *was* the perfect hire. "He was one of us. Everybody knew him," said St. Clair. "He was an automatic motivator. He was a fireplug when he played, and he projected that image to the players. His philosophy was 'Show me a good loser, and you've showed me a loser.' His attitude was 'win, win, win' every game."

Would Albert's inspirational qualities outweigh his coaching inexperience? The answer lay in the 1956 season and in his ability to handle Y. A. Tittle, his former adversary. Earl Morrall was a threat to Tittle, but Albert had been part of one quarterbacking controversy, and he didn't need another as a coach. He showed his allegiance to Tittle by keeping Morrall around for one season, then trading him to Pittsburgh. Under the Morabito ownership, quarterbacks came and went, or sometimes didn't even show up.

Even though unchallenged, Tittle registered so-so numbers in 1956—seven touchdown passes and 12 interceptions. But his importance, unlike many quarterbacks, can't fully be measured by statistics. His leadership, his gamesmanship, and his late-game clutch throws outweighed other evaluations. And though he started slowly in '56, he closed with a flourish.

Albert, after a 3–3 preseason record, lost his official debut as a head coach, 38–21, to the visiting New York Giants. He earned his first victory the next week, 33–30, over Los Angeles, getting five fumble recoveries from an opportunistic defense and four field goals from Rams-killer Soltau.

Frankie Albert evolved from the 49ers' first superstar to their head coach from 1956 to 1958. According to some players, he didn't want to coach but acquiesced to owner Tony Morabito. Ugly comments directed at his family forced him to resign. 1961 drawing by Dave Beronio. (Dave Beronio collection)

Albert then experienced his first coaching nightmare; the 49ers dropped five in a row to drop into the cellar with a 1–6 record. Somehow, he kept a sense of humor during this slump. "Bill 'Tiger' Johnson, one of our assistant coaches, was cussing this official out," remembered Bob Fouts. "So the official came over to the 49ers' bench and said, 'Do any of you coaches know this guy?' Frankie said, 'I never saw him before in my life.' So they called the cops and threw Tiger off the field."

Fouts, who broadcast 49ers' games on radio and television for 13 years, worked with Ernie Nevers, a Stanford legend and holder of the NFL record for points scored (40) in one game. "Joe Perry was 'Zoom,'" said Fouts. "The quarterbacks had trouble handing the ball to him because he was so fast. But Ernie didn't think much of Joe as a fullback, because he wasn't like Ernie in carrying the ball. Ernie had this set of pills in front of him in the booth. He had pills to get him up, pills to slow him down. He asked me if I wanted some. I said no. But he was a good guy.

Y.A. TITTLE '51-60   ALBERT '56-58

Bob Fouts (right) was the 49ers' broadcaster when Y. A. Tittle and Frankie Albert were reunited as player and coach. In 1957, the year this photograph was taken, the three participated in the 49ers' most disastrous defeat, a 30–27 conference title tie-breaker loss against Detroit, when the Lions overcame a 27–7 second-half deficit. (Bob Fouts collection)

"Traveling with the team was the most fun I ever had as a broadcaster. We'd go to Chicago and then spend three weeks on the road, playing in Detroit and Green Bay. We practiced on a field in Chicago that [Enrico] Fermi had worked on in developing the atomic bomb. Some sections of the seating there were discolored because of it."

From bombs to bugging, those were memorable times. "The team," said Fouts, "would practice at the University of Chicago, across the street from these tenements. We all thought [Bears coach George] Halas had a camera in one of those tenements. Maybe he did. Red Hickey later told me that when he played for the Rams, then coached by Clark Shaughnessy, they planned in the locker room to return the kickoff to the right against the Bears. Instead they ran it back to the left, and all the Bears were on the left. Those were great days, all right. The equipment man took care of your luggage on the road. I was never a homer; I always gave credit to the opponent. Naturally, I was happy when our team won because I was making a nice living."

Winning makes a broadcaster's life more enjoyable, but the 49ers weren't exactly kind to Fouts. They were 63–54–3 in the 1950s, with one postseason showing, of sorts, a conference tiebreaking loss. Why weren't those 49ers more successful? "What stood out in my mind were the cornerbacks," said Fouts.

Ah, defense.

Long-time 49er fans remember the "Red Dog" alerts coming from Fouts's microphone; his reference to blitzing linebackers. "Nobody paid much attention to the linebacker," he said. "When Hickey played with the Rams, whenever a linebacker came after [Rams quarterback Bob] Waterfield, Hickey would call out, 'Red Dog!' So I said on the air, "The 'Red Dog' is on." That was fun. Today, they call it the blitz, after Adolf Hitler."

Despite the 49ers' snaillike start in 1956, Albert kept his players scrapping. Joe Arenas scored on a 90-yard kickoff return in a 17–12 loss to Detroit. The 49ers then emerged from their five-game tailspin with a 17–16 win in Green Bay. Hugh McElhenny's 86-yard touchdown run made the difference. Mac was back.

The 49ers preserved a 10–10 tie in Philadelphia by stopping the Eagles on the one-yard line as time expired. No major blows were exchanged between the two adversaries this time. The 49ers continued on to Baltimore, where Tittle's 77-yard touchdown pass to Billy Wilson, with the Goose hurdling three Colts' tacklers, gave the 49ers a 20–17 victory.

The 49ers finished strong, with four wins and a tie, for a 5–6–1 record. Arenas finished, too, brilliantly—a 67-yard punt runback for a touchdown, and a 96-yard nonscoring kickoff return—in a 30–17 victory over the Colts. Arenas remains one of the 49ers' greatest, yet unsung, return specialists.

From the beginning to the end of 1956, the 49ers' hero was McElhenny. Sound of body again, he raced 80 yards for a score in the first preseason game, against Cleveland, and then had a career-best 916 rushing yards, third in the NFL

Soltau kicked a career-high 13 field goals. Wilson set a team record with 889 receiving yards. But no 49er was more disruptive in '56 than St. Clair, who blocked 10 kicks, including field goals, extra points, and punts. "I played right over the center. I'd bull-charge him and run over him," he said. "The next time, he'd go down on all fours and I'd jump over him. With my height, I'd block the ball."

The Million Dollar Backfield was disassembled three years after it came together. Johnson was traded to Detroit for defensive back Bill Stits. Morabito wanted Johnson off the team, regardless of who showed up in exchange; he hadn't gotten over John Henry's bludgeoning of Trippi—a fellow Italian. But Johnson was a future Hall of Famer; Stits wasn't.

No 49er was voted All-Pro in '56—not McElhenny, St. Clair, Leo No-mellini, or Wilson, who led the NFL with 60 catches. Those four settled for the Pro Bowl.

But the 49ers were about to reinvent the art of catching a football.

12 1957

Alley Oop

Raleigh Climon "R. C." Owens had no idea that he would revolutionize football after joining the 49ers in 1957. But it didn't take long for the springy Owens to make the game grow taller.

At the College of Idaho, he was a scorer and rebounder in basketball, a Little All-America end in football, and—sis boom bah!—a campus cheerleader in his free time. It's no wonder that he was known in college as R. C. "Overdrive" Owens, for he always was on the move. But with the 49ers, he would take on a new, permanent nickname.

Alley Oop.

The 49ers drafted Owens in the 14th round in 1956, then waited a year for his rookie season, as he had a basketball commitment to fulfill with an Amateur Athletic Union team in Seattle. He averaged 27.6 points one year in college, but was just as impressive with his double-figure rebounding numbers.

Owens was a leaper who would lift pro football, literally, to new heights. In a preseason game in Seattle against the Chicago Cardinals, Y. A. Tittle heaved a wild pass into the end zone. Owens soared high and caught it for a touchdown. Something new was happening, but it wasn't yet exactly clear.

But the NFL, and perhaps the 49ers, didn't know that Owens already was *dunking* the football in college. In 1954, he pulled out a 20–18 comeback victory over Linfield College of Oregon with two touchdown catches plucked above the defensive backs. Dennis Anderson, a Linfield player and future journalist, watched agog from the sideline. "I thought the quarterback had put up a duck, but Owens jumped high, reached down over the

R. C. Owens, shown here in 1957, revolutionized pro football with his leaping touchdown catches, which earned him the nickname "Alley Oop." Owens was a college basketball star, and he *rebounded* a number of late-game throws that sealed comeback victories. (San Francisco 49ers archives)

defender, and took the ball away for a touchdown," said Anderson. "I hadn't ever seen that done before, and I didn't see it done again until he played for the 49ers."

The 49ers dropped their '57 season opener to the Cardinals, 20–10, at Kezar. A 49er rookie, Larry Barnes, set a club record with an 86-yard punt. Hugh McElhenny darted and dashed 61 yards for a touchdown. Gordy Soltau hit a 33-yard field goal. But the 49ers were outplayed, and team morale was low.

The 49ers needed some inspiration for their next opponent, the Los Angeles Rams, who owned them. Tittle and his backup, rookie John Brodie, were simulating Rams plays in practice when an accident suddenly turned into a trend. "Y. A. and John were throwing short passes," Owens said. "Red Hickey, our offensive coach, said, 'Throw the ball down the field to give the defense a picture of the Ram offense.' They threw some long passes, and I caught a couple in the air against double coverage. Someone said, 'Let's put that in for the Rams.' Someone else said, 'Yeah, but what do we call it?' And Hickey shouted, 'Hey, that's our Alley Oop play!'"

Alley Oop was a comic book character, a prehistoric figure with a caveman's demeanor. But the 49ers' new innovation was more sophisticated, and it would soon prove quite unnerving for perplexed NFL secondaries.

Wally Willis of the *Oakland Tribune,* who had covered the 49ers since their inception in 1946, described what occurred against the Rams in his Monday reportage of the game. "Time was running out on Tittle at the close of the second quarter," Willis wrote, "when he sent out Owens on what has become known to his teammates as an Alley Oop pass pattern."

Owens leaped over some Rams defenders to make the catch. Once singed, twice burned? He repeated the same pattern late in the fourth quarter, plucking another Tittle pass out of the ozone, and in the end zone, to secure a 23–20 win at Kezar.

Football's aerial game, which had been played closer to the ground up to that point, would never be the same. But Owens was just getting started with his scoring theatrics. One week later, Tittle hit him for a touchdown, this time on his knees—Alley Stoop?—against the Bears as the 49ers slipped out of Chicago with another last-gasp victory, 21–17. "I call that my 'prayer pass,'" Owens said afterward. Prayer answered. Owens had become an inviting target, leaping or kneeling, plus a welcomed weapon for the 49ers.

Invigorated and inventive, the 49ers were off on a five-game winning streak, pounding the Packers in Green Bay, 24–14. When the Bears hit town, hunting for revenge, tragedy struck.

Tony Morabito, 47, died of a heart attack at halftime.

"The day he died, we were having a sandwich on the upper level at Kezar Stadium," said Dave Beronio. "The weather wasn't very good, and Tony said, 'We've got to win for them, the fans.' After I went back to my seat in the press box, there was a call on the public address system for Father [William] McGuire. Everyone knew Tony had a bad heart."

There wasn't enough time to save him. Father McGuire showed up and gave Final Absolution. Morabito whispered his last words: "Thank you, Father." And the man who changed San Francisco sports forever was gone.

Josephine Ann "Midge" Morabito Tassi was 20 when her father died on November 3, 1957. She was away on that day, attending Los Angeles's Marymount College, an all-girls school that later went coed as Loyola Marymount. "My dad was really gruff sometimes, but he really wasn't. He was very caring at home," said Tassi. "He would say of sportswriters, 'You can read their stories, and then divide them in half, and you could get the truth.' It was a shock to lose my father. As my sister, Grace, and I stood outside the church at the funeral, she said, 'They're all vultures,' about the newspapermen who were there. They were trying to get their stories."

Not every newspaperman was Morabito's sworn enemy. "I would have liked to have had ten just like him, with his attitude of wanting to win," said Beronio. "I found him to be a fair man. I was the *Vallejo Times-Herald* sports editor when I covered my first 49ers game in 1946. I had to sit in the stands because businessmen and politicians had taken over the press box. It was raining, and my notebook leaked. I went to Tony and said, 'You're giving free tickets to the politicians, and we're giving you free publicity.' So I got to sit in the press box. Maybe it helped that my name was Italian."

When Morabito died, the Bears were leading, 17–7. The 49ers heard the devastating news in the locker room during halftime. "It gave us that little extra incentive," said Tittle. The 49ers rallied to beat Chicago, 21–17, on Tittle's 11-yard pass to Billy Wilson. Linebacker Marv Matuszak, acquired in the Earl Morrall trade, was instrumental in shutting out the Bears in the second half. Dicky Moegle had three interceptions that mournful day. Leo Nomellini, in tears, rushed Bears quarterback Ed Brown so hard, the ball popped into the air, and 49er lineman Bill Herchman grabbed it and lurched 46 yards into the end zone, a definite morale boost for the grief-stricken Niners.

Reminiscing about that game rekindled a memory for Soltau—the day he sought a new contract from Morabito. "I had a Stetson hat that I put on Tony's desk," he said. "Tony was a stylish dresser, and he kept looking at my hat. I asked for a thousand-dollar raise, and he wasn't happy with that, so he grabbed my hat and sailed it out the window. We looked down from Tony's ninth-floor office and saw a bum pick up my hat, try it on, but it didn't fit. The bum hung it on a post. By the time I got down there, the hat was gone."

Soltau's top salary as a 49er was $10,000. "I didn't really think about the money," he said. "I just played because I liked to play." One of Tony Morabito's last benevolent gestures was to support a group of 49ers in their pursuit of a players' union. Soltau, Tittle, McElhenny, Joe Perry, and

Bob St. Clair protested the NFL owners' antiunion stance. Morabito paid Tittle's expenses to New York to attend a players' meeting. The union was created, Soltau became the 49ers' first player representative, and Morabito proved once again that he was a player's owner.

After Tony's death, Vic Morabito was elevated to team president. There wasn't any doubt that Vic was different from Tony. "Vic was more relaxed," said Tassi. Vic had Tony's temper, but Vic's didn't reach boiling point as often. Vic, for instance, didn't slug his critics.

Owens struck again a week after the emotional win over the Bears. He sealed a 35–31 win against Detroit in the waning seconds by catching Tittle's 41-yard touchdown pass above secondary men Jim David and Jack Christiansen, who couldn't jump as high as this rocket man. The two Lions pounded the Kezar turf in frustration.

"The Alley Oop wasn't ever a play that was stopped," Owens reflected 40 years later. "It just became harder to make. Guys would cut me down, knock me out of bounds, and try to keep me from getting downfield. It was tough duty, but I kept my wits, and I improvised."

After winning five straight, San Francisco lost its way, dropping its next three, all on the road—37–24 to Los Angeles, 31–10 to Detroit, and 27–21 to Baltimore. The 49ers were reeling at 5–4 and confused about their true identity.

St. Clair, who had suffered a shoulder injury eight weeks earlier against the Rams, returned to action with three games left. He announced to the team, "Moses has returned from the desert." But which 49er team would show up for the final three games? Fortunately, it was the gang that had won five straight, although some rookie relief would be required in a pinch.

Facing the Giants in New York, Tittle passed to Billy Wilson for a touchdown. The Bald Eagle then became The Bold Eagle, with some daring first-down runs as the 49ers won, 27–17.

The visiting Colts then knocked Tittle out of the game at Kezar with two minutes left and the 49ers trailing, 13–10. Brodie, mainly a rookie bystander that year, was called upon. Shaking off the cobwebs, he found McElhenny in the end zone for a dramatic 17–13 victory.

If the 49ers beat Green Bay in the season finale, there could be playoff ramifications. Perry had a career-high 27 carries, and Brodie and Tittle teamed up to produce a 27–20 win over the visiting Pack, leaving San Francisco and Detroit tied for the Western Conference title at 8–4.

A deadlock-breaking game between the 49ers and Lions would determine which team would meet Cleveland for the NFL championship. Could this be the 49ers' first league title, a rose atop Tony Morabito's grave? And with the tie-breaker set for Kezar, the 49ers believed they had a home-field advantage. It certainly appeared that way early. Owens made another Alley Oop touchdown grab of 34 yards. McElhenny scored on a 47-yard pass. Wilson made a circus catch of a third Tittle touchdown throw. And Soltau's 25-yard field goal gave the 49ers a 24–7 halftime lead.

San Francisco was dominating; then early in the third quarter, it was McElhenny once again, racing 71 yards to the Detroit 9 before he was dragged out of bounds. Soltau's ensuing field goal gave the 49ers a commanding 27–7 lead. The 49ers could smell the title game.

It proved a foul smell.

The Lions clawed back like jungle beasts. Tobin Rote staged a second-half passing clinic. Tom "The Bomb" Tracy, a third-string fullback, lumbered 58 yards for a touchdown. Detroit kept coming back until it pulled off an unbelievable 31–27 victory. Kezar Stadium had turned into a giant tomb. "Devastating," remembered Brodie. "Big time," added St. Clair. "This was our first chance at a championship game. But all our defensive backs got hurt that day, and we had to put a running back, J. D. Smith, back there. He didn't know how to play the position, and Tobin Rote had a field day in the second half. So did Tom the Bomb."

Afterward, Detroit accused the 49ers of celebrating too early. The Lions contended that through an adjoining locker-room wall they heard the 49ers growing overconfident at halftime. Not so, said the Niners. "We were confident at halftime," said St. Clair, "but with guys hurt, we were struggling."

"We weren't celebrating in the locker room," Soltau said. "Frankie got us together just before we went back on the field and tried to get us going. And we roared out there. But Tittle had four interceptions in the second half. Two of Tom the Bomb's runs occurred when our linebackers knocked each other off [Tracy]. Tom the Bomb didn't have a good game all year until then. That was my toughest loss—by far."

George Seifert watched that game with two football teammates from Polytechnic High School, located across the street from Kezar Stadium in Golden Gate Park. "It was the big downer," he said. "The second half was like the movie *Forrest Gump;* I was there for the best of times, and then the worst of times, all in one day."

Detroit then crushed Cleveland, 59–14, for the NFL title. That demoralizing defeat to the Lions lingered on, indelibly, as the *signature* game of the 49ers' first three decades.

13 1958
Club Hangover

Charlie Powell left the 49ers again to resume his checkered boxing career. He climbed in and out of the ring almost as a lark. After playing for the expansion Oakland Raiders in 1960 and 1961, he put on the gloves once more.

His one glaring weakness as a boxer: a glass jaw. His ring record was 25–11–3. He fought two heavyweight champions. Cassius Clay knocked him out in the third round in 1963 during Clay's ascendance to his championship reign as Muhammad Ali. Floyd Patterson knocked out Powell in the sixth round in 1964, after Patterson no longer was champion.

Like Powell, no matter how hard the 49ers trained, they kept taking it on the chin. And getting up off the deck following the devastating collapse against Detroit would take them a whole lot longer. They had that same canvasback appearance as their pugilistic defensive end.

Looking for positives, any positives, from the 1957 season, the 49ers produced four All-Pros: Y. A. Tittle; Leo Nomellini; Marv Matuszak; and Billy Wilson, who led the NFL again with 52 catches. And Tittle was chosen as United Press International's NFL Player of the Year. So there was *something* to celebrate, though, strangely, no honors were forthcoming for R. C. Owens, only the league's most exciting discovery. Not even Rookie of the Year. How high, and how often, does someone have to jump to be recognized?

In the wake of Tony Morabito's death, his 30 percent ownership share was transferred to his widow, Josephine. Vic Morabito now owned 25 percent of the team, and Lou Spadia and Frankie Albert each received a 5 percent share. Three others, including future NBA Warriors basketball franchise owner Franklin Mieuli, also owned stock.

"My dad went to his mother and asked for $5,000 to invest in the team," said Kate Spadia. "And my grandmother said, 'You're asking an immigrant mother and father for $5,000, so adult men can run up and down the grass with a ball? I'm not giving you that money.' Then my grandfather said, 'You will do this for your son.' And that was it. My dad paid it back as fast as he could."

Bob St. Clair and Nomellini were named cocaptains in 1958, the same year the 49ers drafted two keepers: Defensive tackle Charlie Krueger from Texas A&M in the first round and defensive back Jerry Mertens from Drake in the 20th. But Krueger broke his arm in the fourth exhibition game and was gone for the year. Halfback Jim Pace from Michigan, taken above Krueger as a No. 1, would last only one year, the latest example of the 49ers' draft-day miscues.

Albert had his own issues. Not cut out to be a head coach in the first place, he became upset when his wife informed him of ugly comments directed toward her by 49er fans while she was grocery shopping. Albert was protective of his family, and with his allegiance to the 49ers shattered by Morabito's passing, he contemplated resigning as head coach.

The season opened with John Brodie, and not Tittle, getting the most playing time at quarterback. Owens caught 9 passes for 103 yards as the 49ers beat Pittsburgh, 23–20, before 51,856 at Kezar. Trying to validate the John Henry Johnson trade, Bill Stits had three interceptions that day. But it was Gordy Soltau's 22-yard field goal with three minutes left that made the difference.

Tittle disliked being upstaged, noting, "I just wasn't a good sport when I wasn't playing." So which of the two should have been playing, the NFL Player of the Year or his '57 backup? "Y. A. stayed in the pocket better than John, who had a more fragile build, while Y. A. was sturdy," said St. Clair. "But John was a helluva passer; his accuracy was unsurpassed."

Regardless, the offense stagnated the next two weeks. The Niners lost, 33–3, to the Rams and, 28–6, to the Bears. The 49ers didn't win consecutively until their final two games, beating the Packers, 48–21, and the Colts, 21–12. The 49ers seemed in a stupor all season, like they were still hung over from 1957.

With 758 yards (6.1 average), Joe Perry ranked third in NFL rushing. Clyde Conner, having replaced Soltau as a regular, finished fifth in the league with 49 catches. That was it for post-season highlights. The 49ers had not one All-Pro pick.

There was one bit of humor to the season, occurring October 26 during a 27–14 loss to the Bears. A 49er fan, William Dunn, 33, came out of the

Kezar stands to take a swing at legendary Chicago coach-owner George Halas as the two teams left the field at halftime. He swung and missed, but Bears assistant Phil Handler didn't miss, punching Dunn several times. Former middleweight champion Tony Zale, a Bears rooter, later wired Halas: "Will provide free boxing lessons upon your return to Chicago."

"I do remember that incident," said St. Clair. "I hit George Halas once myself. It was a pitchout with [Hugh] McElhenny running behind me. Mac got tackled near the Chicago bench, and I see some guy with a coat, glasses, and hat kick Mac in the head. It was Halas. So I whacked him with an elbow, and the hat and glasses went everywhere. After that, he tried to trade for me."

St. Clair would have been the tallest "Monster of the Midway," but he was too valuable a monster to the 49ers. Besides blocking for Perry and McElhenny, he blocked kicks, and he ran fast for a big man. He once chased down and tackled the Giants' Hall of Fame defensive back, Emlen Tunnell, following an interception. Raw meat must work.

But the '58 Niners couldn't win for losing, though they managed to beat nemesis Detroit at Kezar, 24–21. No Tom the Bomb Tracy that day. Perry rushed for 174 yards on 13 attempts (13.23), including a 73-yard touchdown burst. McElhenny scored the winning touchdown on a 32-yard run that, typically, included his zigging and zagging. The Jet and The King remained an exciting one-two punch, but their team was running in place.

A week later, the Rams humiliated the 49ers, 56–7, in Los Angeles. Tittle located Perry on a 64-yard touchdown pass for the Niners' only score. The boyish Albert aged after that loss. His hair turned gray and pouches formed under his eyes. He felt even more out of place. The Kezar fans, rowdy to begin with, grew rowdier. And there was no place for him to hide.

After the Lions got even in Detroit, 35–21, Albert approached Vic Morabito and told him that he planned to resign after the season. "Think it over, Frank," Morabito responded. "There still are four games to go."

With Albert's manic difficulties, losing didn't help. "Frankie would have tremendous times of depression where he didn't want to deal with anybody," said Lon Simmons, who, in '58, was in his first season as the 49ers' radio play-by-play announcer, a relationship that would last 26 years. "Frankie would be going great, then he'd drop into this thing where he didn't want anybody around him. He didn't want to do anything, then he'd snap out of it. It was a killing blow for him for most of his life, I guess."

Simmons admired Albert as a coach, finding him clever and innovative, akin to his quick-thinking reputation as a player. "Frankie had a lot of great ideas," said the broadcaster, "if he only had the players to complete those ideas. He was all for having an onside kick to start the game, then his team would mess it up. He was sort of a loose cannon, but he knew a lot about football. He just needed a more solid team."

Just when things were falling apart for the 49ers, McElhenny piled up 159 yards on 22 rushes (7.23 average) in a 33–12 win over Green Bay. Then in an instant rematch, J. D. Smith raced 80 yards for a score, and Abe Woodson had a 44-yard interception return, in a 40–21 stoning of the Packers.

The 49ers won three of the last four games to finish 6–6. Brodie had a better completion percentage than Tittle, 59.9 to 57.7, but Tittle had more touchdowns (9) and interceptions (15) than Brodie (4 and 13). Nonetheless, Brodie had become more of a threat to Tittle.

Albert couldn't wait for the season to end. He resigned before the December 14 finale with Baltimore. Vic Morabito then blasted the team in a closed-door session, threatening "a new policy." He didn't take long to implement it. On December 16, he named Red Hickey as the 49ers' fourth head coach, their third in four years. Hickey received a three-year contract.

"This is the top," Hickey said. "I have no place to go but down, and I don't intend to do that. This club has the nucleus to be a winner." A winner? The 49ers yielded 324 points, or 26 points a game, in '58, their worst-ever defensive output. The offense scored 257 points in '58, or 23 points a game, a telling three-point win-loss imbalance.

Club Hangover, indeed.

The 49er players were about to discover Hickey's turbulent motivational skills, his inability to properly evaluate talent, and his harebrained attempt to reinvent the game.

"Dumb son of a bitch," said St. Clair.

14 1959
Red Alert

It was easier for a prospectin' 49er, digging for ore during the California gold rush of 1849, to strike it rich than it was getting a footballin' 49er in 1959 to speak well of Red Hickey.

There hasn't ever been a 49er head coach who upset his players quite like Hickey, the tongue-lashing, morale-busting, offense-tinkering innovator who angered nearly an entire roster.

"He tore that team apart," said Gordy Soltau. "He traded away good players. He called me in and said, 'I want you to retire, but I want you to be one of my coaches.' I told him, 'I don't mind you retiring me, but I could never coach for you.'"

And so Soltau retired after nine seasons with 644 points, the third highest total in NFL history at that juncture. He was the first 49er to play in 100 games, and he was one of only three NFL players to have 25 touchdowns and 70 field goals. Besides being the 49ers' first player representative, Soltau was a pioneer in establishing benefits for NFL players, including a pension plan and compensation for playing in exhibition games. He later helped establish the northern California chapter of the NFL Alumni Association, serving as its president for 29 years. Hickey was cutting loose someone who not only played the game, and played it well, but *was* the game.

Don't get Bob St. Clair started on Hickey either. "I had absolutely no respect for him," said St. Clair. "He'd yell and scream at you and everyone else. It was awful. I remember Joe Perry chasing Hickey around the locker room; Joe was going to beat the hell out of him. I remember that distinctly. Joe had a terrible temper. Red didn't like me because the guys wanted me as captain. He didn't want that because I wasn't one of his guys. I stood up to him. He got me in the dressing room in Washington after I was named in some paternity suit. She was an actress, and kind of wild. Hickey held up a newspaper and said, 'St. Clair, you're a disgrace to the 49ers, and you don't respect me.' And I said, 'You got half of it right.'"

In fairness, not everyone in the 49er locker room regarded Hickey as Caligula with a chalkboard. The pro-Red bloc, however, took up roughly eight lockers. "He had his favorites who kowtowed to him," said St. Clair.

Charlie Krueger attempted to speak kindly of Hickey, though it took one mighty effort. "Red was a pretty smart coach, the first guy to come along with the Shotgun," said Krueger. "It's still here, basically, so it must have been a good offense. But you didn't clash with Red; you'd find a Greyhound bus ticket in your locker if you did. He treated me fairly, though I didn't care for him. I just didn't go around yelling about it. A lot of people did."

Hickey didn't hesitate to make changes, irritating his players in the process. He proclaimed that John Brodie, not Y. A. Tittle, was his quarterback. Hickey then moved Hugh McElhenny to flanker and inserted Jim Pace at running back. Pace over Hugh McElhenny—really? Then Pace broke his hand and was replaced by J. D. Smith, a Hickey favorite who emerged, deservedly, as a primary rusher. "A beautiful runner," Brodie said of Smith.

Hickey brought in Lions defensive great Jack Christiansen as an assistant and handed the dual punting and placekicking responsibilities to newcomer Tommy Davis. The older 49ers wished for a calmer climate, but Buck Shaw now was in Philadelphia, coaching the Eagles.

Hickey debuted officially with a 24–14 victory over those same Eagles at Kezar, ruining Shaw's homecoming before 41,697 wait-and-see fans. The 49ers also won the important field-position battle as Abe Woodson returned a punt 65 yards, and rookie Eddie Dove brought back another punt 62 yards.

The following week, 56,028 showed up for the Los Angeles game at Kezar, partly because of Hickey's bravado. "We're going to beat the Rams," he predicted, "and you can quote me on that. Let them put it on their bulletin board if they like." The 49ers routed the Rams for a change, 34–0. Perry tallied on a 32-yard burst, and Smith scored twice, including a 20-yard run.

Traveling to Green Bay, Tittle hit a wide-open R. C. Owens on a 75-yard touchdown hookup, but the Packers won a squeaker, 20–19, under new coach Vince Lombardi. Smith and Perry teamed up in Detroit to spark a 34–13 win; Smith busted loose for 152 yards and Perry for 145, while linebacker Matt Hazeltine returned a fumble 40 yards for a touchdown.

The Alley Oop play worked again as Tittle hit Owens from 45 yards to ice a 20–17 win over the visiting Chicago Bears. Then Smith ran 73 yards for a touchdown in a 33–7 home win over Detroit; a huge lead over the Lions that the 49ers held onto this time.

The visiting 49ers swept the Rams, 24–16, as Tittle threw a 57-yard touchdown pass to Billy Wilson, and the explosive Woodson returned a kickoff a franchise-record 105 yards.

The revitalized 49ers won six of their first seven games, losing only in Packertown. Despite locker-room turmoil, Hickey appeared saintly to an unsuspecting Faithful. Then the bottom dropped out; the 49ers dropped four of their last five games. The one win came after Tittle hurt a knee in Cleveland, and Brodie threw scoring strikes to Smith and Wilson for a 21–20 win.

Smith had a spectacular year, carrying a club-record 209 times for 1,036 yards and 10 touchdowns; he was the NFL runner-up to the great Jim Brown in all three categories. Smith, Leo Nomellini, and Woodson were selected All-Pro.

Though Hickey went with Brodie to start the season, Tittle received the bulk of work at quarterback. His 10 touchdown passes balanced against 15 interceptions didn't sit well with Hickey, but what could he do, bench him? For Brodie had only two touchdown passes and seven interceptions. Maybe the coach was thinking that to shake things up a new offense was needed.

Meanwhile, reports of team dissent finally reached the media. Vic Morabito squashed those rumors as if they were bothersome mosquitos. "If you complained about Hickey," said St. Clair, "Vic would chastise you tremendously."

15 1960

Heir, Apparently

Y. A. Tittle had waited patiently to supplant Frankie Albert. Then John Brodie served his apprenticeship under Tittle. Now all Brodie desired was a fair shot to become San Francisco's No. 1 quarterback. "If I am better than Tittle, it will show," he said at the beginning of 49ers' summer training camp in 1960. "And I'm not saying I am, and I'm not saying I'm not." What Brodie *was* saying: let the better man prove himself. It was becoming apparent that one of the two quarterbacks would have to go, eventually, to separate them. But which one?

Albert had to leave so that Tittle could take over, just as Bob Waterfield left the Rams so that Norm Van Brocklin could become a full-time quarterback. Controversies aren't healthy. The 49ers witnessed this same dynamic in the 1990s, when Joe "I'm going to Kansas City" Montana departed so that Steve Young could become No. 1 without having to look over his shoulder. Of course, these decisions aren't ever easy: Tittle, Waterfield, Van Brocklin, Montana, and Young all wound up in the Pro Football Hall of Fame.

Perhaps the 1960 season would settle the Tittle versus Brodie argument once and for all. But it couldn't be a 49er season, it seemed, without another Eagles brawl. The latest was a wild one during an August 21 exhibition. Boxing gloves should have been distributed beforehand. Bob St. Clair and Ed Khayat came to blows. R. C. Owens and Tom Brookshier duked it out. Fists flew all over Kezar Stadium. Smelling salts would be needed. Abe Woodson and the Eagles' Billy Barnes and Jerry Wilson were ejected. Oh, yes, the 49ers scored a knockout win, 45–28. "I was right in the middle of it," said Dan Colchico, then an eager 49er rookie defensive end. "I loved it."

"They were that kind of team," Charlie Krueger said of the Eagles. "Monty Stickles clocked one of their linebackers from the blind side. The linebacker chased Stickles down to the end zone and then back up the field. I tried to stay out of fights. Good idea, because the best you could do was get your ass kicked, and the worst was breaking your hand."

That win made the 49ers 3–1 against Shaw, including a pair of exhibitions. But old Buck was saving the last laugh for the end of the season.

Stickles, a mouthy tight end from Notre Dame, was the 49ers' No. 1 pick in 1960. Len Rohde (ROAD-ee), a more reserved offensive tackle from Utah State, was drafted No. 4.

Photographed here in 1971, Len Rohde, a 49er offensive tackle from 1960 to 1976, is the franchise's consecutive game record-holder. At six feet four inches, 250 pounds, he held his own against bigger linemen. In a training camp tiff, he also held his own against 49er teammate and tight end Monty Stickles. (Len Rohde collection)

They were training camp roommates at St. Mary's College. One afternoon, following torrid two-a-day drills and just before dinner, Stickles and Rohde squeezed in a few beers at the Rheem Valley Bowl near the Moraga campus, when they found out which one of them was the toughest.

"I usually don't have a temper, but it was a crappy day, I guess, and I was short," said Rohde. "Monty said something to me the wrong way, and I threw a dice cup at him. And he said, 'OK, Rohde, we're outside.' So now we're out in the parking lot. Monty had kind of a rough reputation, but it was more of a wrestling match. I'm not much of a boxer. We both lived through it, although we got different rides back to camp." Rohde is modest. His teammates said he whipped Stickles. The outcome? Rohde was a 49er for 15 years, while Stickles was gone after 8.

Rohde drove from his Illinois farm to his first 49er camp, thinking the entire way about Leo Nomellini and St. Clair, both of them growing bigger in his mind the closer he got to Moraga. "I read in this football magazine that Nomellini is wrestling bears, and that St. Clair is six foot nine and eats raw meat," said Rohde. "I thought it would be a long trip to nowhere. I was just trying to find a spot."

Then during punt coverage, Rohde found himself lined up next to Nomellini, by then entering his 11th season. "I told myself, 'I know I can beat
this guy,'" Rohde said. "But every time, he'd get a step and a half on me
before I could get going. He was amazingly quick for a big guy."

Did Rohde ever catch up to Nomellini? "Much later," he said. Rohde
didn't realize that Nomellini, as big as he was, had run on the college mile
relay team at Minnesota.

Besides Nomellini and St. Clair, Rohde was teammates with three other
future Canton inductees: Tittle, Joe Perry, and Hugh McElhenny. "They were
all still fantastic players, though in the last few years of their careers," said
Rohde. "It was really an honor to play with them, and with R. C. Owens
and Billy Wilson. McElhenny was smooth, man, he was smooth."

Rohde started off as a defensive end. Then St. Clair was injured, and
Rohde moved to right offensive tackle. His second year, he shifted to left
tackle, and there he stayed.

Rohde, as a rookie, already had sized up Red Hickey. "He was kind of
a tyrant," he said.

The 1960 season opened with a 21–19 loss to the Giants at Kezar as
44,598 watched Tittle play the entire game. Brodie continued to play the
disatisfying role of heir apparent.

Hickey then benched Nomellini, 36, even though he had been named
All-Pro the previous year for the sixth time. Other Niners couldn't believe
the cruel demotion of Leo the Lion. "Leo had a lot of leadership," said Colchico. "I didn't like the way he was being handled at the end. He was so
strong. The thing around the league was 'Don't get him mad.'"

The 49ers beat the troublesome Rams once again, 13–9, at Kezar. Hickey
then alternated Tittle and Brodie against Detroit, with Brodie starting and
finishing off an exciting 14–10 win with an 18-yard touchdown pass to Owens as time ran out. Both 49er quarterbacks knew to look for Alley Oop in
moments of crisis.

Brodie started the next week against the Bears, but neither he nor
Tittle generated much offense during a 27–10 whipping in Chicago. J. D.
Smith pounded out 93 yards that day, while McElhenny showed his ageless breakaway ability with 122 rushing yards. Brodie then started against
Green Bay but fared miserably, missing on all 13 pass first-half attempts,
minus one interception. Tittle relieved him with two touchdown passes,
but Vince Lombardi's Packers steamrolled the visiting Niners, 41–14.

Hickey was full of surprises, but they weren't working. "He'd always have
a trick play for the opening offensive series," said Lon Simmons. "The 49ers

practiced it all week, then they'd screw it up. Bob Fouts always wanted to know what the trick play would be, but the 49ers would fumble the ball or something. I don't think they ever made it work."

The Morabito Bench was dedicated at Kezar on October 30 before the 49ers–Bears game—fittingly, as these two teams played each other the day Tony Morabito died three years earlier. Tittle started, injured his groin, and Brodie directed a 25–7 victory. Smith had 95 rushing yards, McElhenny 71, and Perry 53 as the 49ers dominated on the ground.

A week later, Brodie threw three interceptions as visiting Detroit won easily, 24–0. The Kezar turf was taking a double-pounding, as the 49ers shared Kezar Stadium with the Oakland Raiders of the first-year American Football League, for there wasn't a football facility in Oakland bigger than a high school field.

The 49ers suddenly sprang to life. They beat expansion Dallas, 26–14, before intercepting the iconic Johnny Unitas five times in a 30–22 win at Baltimore, during which Owens made yet another Alley Oop touchdown grab.

On the 49er sideline that day in Baltimore was a very young future Pro Football Hall of Fame quarterback, Dan Fouts, the son of 49ers' broadcaster Bob Fouts. "I was the fourth of five children, and Dad would take one of us back to Baltimore every year, so we could see the nation's capital," said Fouts, today an NFL broadcaster himself. "I remember being in the Georgetown gym watching the team practice the Shotgun offense in secret. It was awesome." Hickey was experimenting with the innovative Shotgun, which he used sparingly in Baltimore.

Defensive back Dave Baker picked off four Rams passes as the 49ers prevailed in Los Angeles, 23–7, for their third straight win. The Niners now had the Rams' number. Hickey had brought *some* positive change.

Under Lombardi, Green Bay no longer was an NFL patsy. The Packers scored a 13–0 victory at Kezar, with Paul Hornung scoring all 13 points. A future sign: McElhenny and Perry had no carries. Hickey clearly didn't want them around.

Before the season-ender, Hickey once again predicted a victory, this time against Baltimore. "We did it before and we can do it again," he said. His word was gospel as the 49ers trampled the Colts, 34–10, at Kezar.

Hickey posted a second straight 7–5 record. He received a new contract through 1963, much to his players' chagrin. But fan interest was high. The 49ers attracted 312,382 customers in six home games, a 52,063 average. In contrast, the Raiders drew 65,756 in seven home games, a 9,395 average. The 6–8 Raiders moved to San Francisco's Candlestick Park the following year.

Billy Wilson, the Goose, retired after the 1960 season with three NFL receiving titles and 407 catches, second only to Green Bay Packers legend Don Hutson at the time. Yet Wilson, who would join Hickey's coaching staff the following year, remains a forgotten entity with Pro Football Hall of Fame electors.

Hickey took early aim on 1961 by squeezing the trigger on the Shotgun. He experimented with his innovative offense over the 49ers' last four games in '60.

Dan Fouts had watched it all develop. "My mother carried me in her womb into Kezar," he said of his family's long involvement with the team. "Back then, there was a family section in the press box, and we had two seats. I sat there often with my mom. Hugh McElhenny is still her favorite player. We got to know so many of the 49ers. It wasn't all that unusual to have them over for dinner—Tittle, St. Clair, Nomellini. The players were with the 49ers forever. They hardly traded anybody."

That dynamic would be shortened under Hickey.

Meanwhile, in Philadelphia, Shaw showed 49ers' ownership the error of its ways by coaching the Eagles to the NFL championship, 17–13, over Green Bay. The Buck then stopped permanently after that title game, as the gentlemanly Shaw retired from coaching.

He went out on top. The 49ers still hadn't reached the top.

16 1961

Ring Out the Old

With a proverbial broom, Red Hickey swept away three 49er icons during a dramatic spring cleaning. He traded Joe Perry to Baltimore and Y. A. Tittle to the New York Giants, and he exposed Hugh McElhenny to the expansion draft, where the Minnesota Vikings gobbled him up.

The King, The Jet, The Bald Eagle: all gone.

Hickey's message: this was his team now.

Bruising linebacker Ed Henke, not wanting to feel excluded, asked to be traded, and got his wish. To "find some peace, " he was sent to the St. Louis Cardinals.

Pro Bowl center Bruce Bosley also made his feelings known. "If they want to trade me, it won't hurt my feelings," he said. But Hickey held onto Bosley; he needed someone to snap the ball, and he couldn't do much better than Bosley.

But even Henry Schmidt, picked on Paul Zimmerman's All-Century Team for *Sports Illustrated* as a "wedge-buster" on kickoffs, was let go, playing next for the San Diego Chargers.

Anti-Hickey sentiment by then had crested among the players; those who challenged him, he branded as malcontents. Vic Morabito denied any "personality conflict," maintaining, "I know his treatment of all the players has been fair and just." Hear no evil, see no evil: the Morabito way.

Meanwhile, the Congress of Racial Equality (CORE) approached nine black 49ers to boycott the season opener against Washington, because the Redskins hadn't ever had a black player. The nine 49ers refused. "This is different from situations where there are segregated audiences and things like that," said Abe Woodson. "We have been treated wonderfully by the

49ers' organization and must consider our loyalty to this organization, too." Treated wonderfully? Woodson wasn't referring to his head coach.

The 1961 season began without further interruptions, albeit with the NFL's new 14-game schedule. Knowing the quarterback job was his, finally, John Brodie threw for four touchdowns in a 35–3 walloping of visiting Washington, prompting Hickey to say, "He was as good as any quarterback I have ever seen." Hickey, obviously, was justifying his trading of Tittle. But Brodie was on fire in the opener, hitting on 16 of 22 passes for 237 yards, with one interception.

The following week was a different story, a 31–10 blowout by the Packers in Green Bay. With Vince Lombardi running the show, the Pack was evolving into the league's dominant team. The 49ers appeared to be heading in the opposite direction after that weak effort.

Fancying himself the Thomas Edison of football, Hickey then unleashed his creative masterpiece: The Shotgun. The 49ers riddled the unsuspecting Lions, 49–0, in Detroit. Brodie, Billy Kilmer, and Bobby Waters alternated at quarterback. They stood five or six yards behind the center alongside a running back. A lot of spinning and faking then ensued, with the quarterback either passing or becoming a featured runner, mostly on carries up the middle. Brodie was the lesser runner of the three, but he acquiesced. He had no choice. Hickey believed he had revolutionized the game of football.

The 49er Faithful shared that belief, as 59,000 showed up at Kezar Stadium the next week to see the Niners bamboozle the Rams, 35–0. There was much celebrating, before and after, at the nearby Kezar Club. The 49ers, suddenly, seemed invincible.

"For a while, the Shotgun was working well, and I thought maybe [Hickey] had something," said Bob St. Clair. "It was great blocking for it. Hickey would tell us the guard had to be a yard away from the center, and the tackle two yards away from the guard. One time in practice, he blew the whistle and came out with a measuring tape, shouting 'Don't move. Don't move.' Then he'd tell us that we weren't the right distance apart."

The 49ers continued having fun in Minnesota. Kilmer rushed for 100 yards and four touchdowns in a 38–24 victory. "Billy was a good football player," said Charlie Krueger. "He could run the ball; he had the feel. Wonderful athlete."

Against the Vikings, the Niners faced former teammate McElhenny. The King showed them, and Hickey, that he hadn't yet abdicated his throne. On the old Statue of Liberty play, Fran Tarkenton reached back to throw, and McElhenny took the ball out of his hand, then faked, swerved, and danced through nine 49ers on a spectacular 32-yard touchdown run. Even those

Niners standing on the sideline were awed. "We started applauding," said Brodie. "We didn't know what else to do."

Minnesota's rookie head coach, Norm Van Brocklin, bragged about that McElhenny highlight-reel run for years afterward. "It was the greatest run I ever saw," he said. "Whenever I think something is impossible, I put that film on the projector and watch it again."

Three straight victories with a radical offense had the 49ers feeling unstoppable. Then it all blew up in Chicago. Bears defensive coach Clark Shaughnessy, who introduced the modern T-formation at Stanford with Frankie Albert and Norm Standlee in 1940, figured out how to stop the Shotgun. "Shaughnessy decided to put two guys over the center, and two guys over the guard," said St. Clair, "With the Shotgun, you were one blocker shy, and one of the Bears' linemen would always get through because there was no one to block him."

The Bears held the 49er offense to an anemic 132 yards in a 31–0 clobbering. Thanks to the wily Shaughnessy, the NFL knew how to make the Shotgun misfire. The 49ers, exposed, suffered three losses and a tie over the next four weeks.

Hickey then ditched the Shotgun, except for four plays in a November 19 rematch with the Bears. Brodie, comfortably back in a pro-set offense, went all the way, completing 11 of 19 passes for 322 yards, three scores, and no interceptions in a 41–31 win. Chicago's defense, and Shaughnessy, had no answers that day. "I'm not stubborn about sticking with the Shotgun," Hickey said, weakly. He lacked the patience to rework the Shotgun and give it the lasting impact it later achieved. Hickey's concept wasn't as harebrained as his giving up on it too early.

The 49ers ended up 7–6–1 by winning three of their last five games. Brodie carved up the Packers, completing 19 of 29 passes for 328 yards in a 22–21 Niners' upset. Owens caught 7 passes for 127 yards and a touchdown. Tommy Davis nailed down the win by booting a 14-yard field goal with 11 seconds left.

Owens had his best overall season with 55 catches for 1,032 yards. He became the first 49er receiver to surpass 1,000 yards, and his 18.8-yards-per-catch average also was the 49ers' high-water mark over their first twenty-four seasons. Owens wasn't enamored with Hickey either; he played without a contract in 1961, then escaped to Baltimore. With his departure, two creative chapters of 49ers' history exited together: the Shotgun, temporarily, and the Alley Oop.

Another 49er left the team, though not because of Hickey. Dave Baker, the team's best defensive back, had 10 interceptions in '61, and 21 over three seasons in San Francisco. But the friendly skies, to Baker, were most unfriendly. "He hated flying; it killed him to fly," said St. Clair. "He'd have to be sedated, even on a calm flight. One time we flew from Detroit to Chicago through a big storm with lightning. Sparks were coming off the plane, which was shaking. When we landed, Dave got off, kissed the ground, and swore he'd never take another flight. He quit right there."

Baker promptly retired from the NFL and became a minister. But did this All-American at Oklahoma, who made the Pro Bowl as an NFL rookie, have Hall of Fame potential if not for his fear of flying? "He was a damn good player with all the attributes to have a great career," said St. Clair, himself a Hall of Famer.

"Dave Baker was one of those people who could do a helluva lot with somewhat limited ability," Krueger said. "That's because he was smart and instinctive. He wasn't very fast, but he was very intense."

Unfortunately for the 49ers, he was most intense when shaking at 30,000 feet.

17 1962

The Dark Ages

George Seifert was a senior at the University of Utah when the phone rang at his college residence. Lou Spadia, the San Francisco 49ers' general manager, was calling about Seifert's roommate, linebacker Ed Pine, the 49ers' No. 2 draft pick in 1962.

"This was the early 1960s when the two leagues, the NFL and AFL, were battling over players. Spadia asked me if I could help get Pine to the 49ers," Seifert recalled. "Spadia wasn't calling about me playing football—I was pretty unsuccessful as a linebacker and end—but his call was a thrill for me at the time. I was aware of Lou Spadia, his background, and we started talking about the city. I lived on Noe Street, and he lived in the Noe Valley growing up."

Seifert has all kinds of 49ers' moments to remember. "At Polytechnic High School, our coach, Milt Axt, got us into 49er games as ushers," he said. "We helped people to their seats, and I saw any number of games. The first Alley Oop catch I ever saw, though, happened when I was standing on a roof across the street from the stadium. It was like that pass was thrown to me. I also remember being on the field after games, trying to get chinstraps from the 49ers and sizing myself up with the players. I walked next to [linebacker] Matt Hazeltine because I was almost as tall. Bob St. Clair was too tall for me but a focal point because he also went to Poly.

"You didn't want the 49ers to lose; those players were your idols. But you still loved them even when they lost, and what great idols they were. Most of them had to work other jobs besides playing football. Watching Leo Nomellini flying around . . . it was a special time. I mean, who had an entire backfield elected to the Pro Football Hall of Fame?"

Had Seifert, eventually an eminently successful 49ers' head coach, planned on a football career in 1962? "Not at all," he said. "I loved football, but I was a zoology major at Utah. Then when I went to graduate school, I became a graduate assistant in football, and found that I enjoyed teaching the technique aspect of the game."

As for Ed Pine, he signed with the 49ers, but their No. 1 draft pick that year, Arkansas wide receiver Lance Alworth, chose the AFL's San Diego Chargers. Pine played only three years with the 49ers, while Alworth would be inducted in the Canton, Ohio, pro hall.

As an aside, the author was working his way through college as a waiter at Big Al's Gashouse, a beer-drinking, banjo-playing, pizza-making establishment in Palo Alto, California. One night, Pine walked in with his 49ers' bonus check. He removed his sport coat and slung it over a chair, then sat closer to the bandstand. Another waiter spotted the coat and the bonus check sticking out of an inside pocket. It was a five-figure check; the waiter returned the coat to Pine. The author can't recall if Pine left a tip on his way out.

Pine joined the 49ers during the franchise's first dark age—a 57–74–7 record in the 1960s, with no postseason appearances and three head coaches. The second dark age era occurred with ruinous Joe Thomas in charge in the mid-1970s, just before Bill Walsh rescued the franchise from oblivion.

Dan Fouts lived through the first dark age as a youngster. "It bothered me then that we weren't winning," he said. "The fans who were there were on the team pretty good; the stadium was rarely full. It was a time of struggling, but you wanted your team to do well. I thought Abe Woodson was awesome. You're a kid, and these players are bigger than life," regardless of their win-loss record.

Young Dan was proud of his father, Bob Fouts, the 49ers' broadcaster, every season. "We used to turn down the television and listen to Dad on the radio," he said. "When he started doing television, it was even better. His 'Red Dog' call came from studying, and from going to training camp, and from being in on the meetings. [Red] Hickey let Dad sit in the back of the room, where he'd pick up on the terms and then incorporate them into his broadcasts."

Hickey had high hopes in 1962, praising the 49ers as "our best squad since 1959." He traded Lou Cordileone to the Rams for defensive back Elbert Kimbrough. Cordileone-for–Y. A. Tittle still rankles older 49er fans, although Cordileone enjoyed success later on while playing for the Pittsburgh Steelers.

Trade-giddy Hickey dealt a future 49er head coach, tackle Monte Clark, to Dallas. Hickey waived C. R. Roberts, leaving J. D. Smith as the team's only initialed running back. Hickey sent wide receiver Aaron Thomas to the Giants for halfback Bobby Gaiters, a much better deal, as it turned out, for the Giants.

The 49ers' "best club since 1959" opened the 1962 season at home by getting smacked around by the Chicago Bears, 30–14. "A ridiculous exhibition of football, wasn't it?" Hickey said. If only it were an exhibition.

Everything about 1962 would be streaky for the 49ers, who lost their first two games, won their next three, lost the next four, won three straight, then lost the last two to finish 6–8.

There were some individual highlights. Woodson, a stellar cornerback and return specialist, was voted All-NFL for the third time after scoring on an 87-yard punt return. Smith had a workhorse season—258 carries, a team record, for 905 yards (3.5 average). Tommy Davis punted for a 45.6 average. And John Brodie completed 57.6 percent of his passes, including 18 touchdowns compared to 16 interceptions. But the offense scored 281 points, while the defense gave up a club-record 331 points, hardly a winning recipe.

Two victories, both against Minnesota, were enjoyed immensely by the 49ers' defensive line—because Norm Van Brocklin, the Vikings' acid-tongued coach, called the Niners' front four a bunch of "donkeys." Charlie Krueger said, "Van Brocklin must have bad eyesight, because if you say something like that, you better have good peripheral vision. He would treat his players awful. He called Tommy Mason, who was a fine halfback and a fine competitor, a horse's-something-or-other. Van Brocklin's problem was that he would open his mouth and there was nothing in it. He was a cold-hearted motherfucker."

So who was "braying" after that 49ers' mule-kicking of the Vikings in '62—21–7 and 35–12 San Francisco victories? "Van Brocklin forgot he was a player when he went into coaching," said Dan Colchico, Krueger's defensive line mate. "That's all I'm going to say."

The biggest downer of that 49er season, however, occurred clear across the country—alas, more of Hickey's doing. In New York City, Tittle had a career year with 33 touchdown passes, opposed to 20 interceptions. And the Giants won the Eastern Conference with a 12–2 record before losing to Green Bay, 16–7, for the NFL title. Brodie had a solid year, but Tittle had more talent around him on both sides of the ball, and that was evident in the final standings.

There were more good-byes said in San Francisco. Assistant coaches Billy Wilson and Mark Duncan quit after the season, reportedly because they disliked Hickey.

Imagine that.

18 1963
Playing Hurt

Dan Colchico was a hardscrabble kid from Port Chicago, a tough waterfront municipality northeast of San Francisco Bay. It was a no-frills, lunch-pail town that put the bluest dye in "blue collar."

The Port Chicago of Colchico's two-fisted youth didn't know the first thing about ambiance. A strong back was more important than social pedigree. Colchico's father, an Italian immigrant, was killed on the job when Dan was six. A hard life inside the Colchico home grew even harder.

"My dad was maybe five foot nine, but he never backed down from anything," Colchico recalled. "When he died, my mom was handed a check for $19.50. I still have that check. My mom worked all her life. She never learned how to drive, and she never missed a day of work. She did the best she could."

Colchico grew up as tough as his father and as determined as his mother. She took the bus, or rode in car pools, and even hitchhiked to get to her various jobs in order to keep food on the table for herself and a son who was growing fast into manhood.

Colchico discovered at an early age that sports could provide a ticket to a better life. So he took to the playing fields of Port Chicago with kids named Lefty, Burly, Benny, Sammy, and Kilroy to develop his skills, including a strong right cross. He was good at most athletic things but best at football, which got him to San Jose State and then to the San Francisco 49ers in 1960. He believed he had arrived at last.

There are more famous 49ers than Colchico, but none more committed. There are 49ers with longer careers, but none who sacrificed as much physically as Colchico. "Crack-back blocking was wide open in those days, and they used to get us pretty good," he said. "One season, I had 140 cortisone shots in

Dan Colchico, pictured here in 1963, was the toughest of the tough, playing through 140 injections one season as a 49ers defensive end and continuing his career even after twice tearing both Achilles' heels. (Dan Colchico collection)

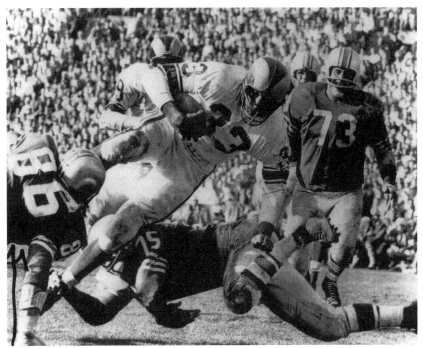

Dan Colchico (86) and Ed Henke (75) double up on Los Angeles Rams' Hall of Famer Ollie Matson in 1962. Colchico received the 49ers' highest team honor, the Len Eshmont Award, that year for his "inspirational and courageous play." (Dan Colchico collection)

my knees and shoulders—two, three shots a day sometimes. I had one operation in January, another one in March. But I played every game that year."

Colchico gave everything he had, physically, to the 49ers and to their training room. There wasn't enough sympathy for how he was living years later. What's left of him wasn't pretty. "There was nothing there in both knees after I was done playing, because it was bone on bone. I've had both knees replaced since," he said, in 2013, over lunch at Mr. Lucky's in Walnut Creek, a half-hour's drive from what used to be Port Chicago.

"I completely severed both Achilles', and partially severed them, too. So I've had four major Achilles' operations," he noted. "I think I'm the only one in professional sports to come back and play after severing both Achilles' twice. I snapped it, and I came back that same season."

Though Colchico wasn't Mr. Lucky in terms of personal health, he soldiered forth, body and soul, at defensive end. "Concussions? They didn't make an issue out of it back then," he said. "They'd give you smelling salts and you went back in. It was part of the game. I played games not even knowing that I had played. The average NFL player lasts four years; I lasted seven years. I even got shot up in my toes and fingers.

"You couldn't put me down. Hey, I grew up on the streets. Nobody messed with me and my Port Chicago friends. No guns, no knives, but we could fight." Port Chicago kids fought out of personal pride, and for what they needed in life. Colchico never stopped fighting. That's how he made it through football. "One game," he recalled, "Charlie Krueger had to tell me which way to move on every play, because I had a concussion."

"Danny was the greatest competitor I ever knew in football," said Krueger.

"Colchico knew only one pace and that was full speed ahead," said Bob St. Clair. They first tangled in practice—St. Clair, the raw-meat–eating tackle from San Francisco, and Colchico, the determined, fearless rookie from Port Chicago. Colchico gave no quarter that day, and that's how he made his mark.

"I picked out the biggest, toughest guy around, Bob St. Clair, and figured if I did good against him, my chances were good," Colchico said of his maiden 49ers' summer camp in 1960. "We had a pretty good battle. I never went to the back of the line to wait my turn. I'd sneak back in to face the tougher guys on the team. I became a starter by the second game."

Filled with cortisone, and physically a time bomb, Colchico refused to take a down off, and he never conceded an inch. "I made a lot of tackles on the other side of the field, because they weren't running my way," he said. "I could never relax. There were some good offensive tackles, like Forrest Gregg of Green Bay, but I held my own. If you tackled Jim Brown, you had to wrap your arms around him, because he had such a relaxation about him, he'd slip away. He didn't run over you. The hardest guy to tackle was John David Crow. He hit harder than anyone. He was tough."

Weeks of losing made Colchico's recovery time seem longer. He suffered the most in 1963, when the 49ers endured their worst season on record. After John Brodie and Billy Kilmer were injured in separate off-season automobile accidents, the 49ers knew that '63 would be an especially long year. Brodie had a broken arm, and Kilmer damaged a leg. Kilmer's season was over before it started. Brodie made it back late in the season, after everything had come undone.

Because of the seriousness of his leg injury, Kilmer no longer was an effective runner. A natural athlete, he converted into a drop-back quarterback, a position he played with remarkable poise in New Orleans and Washington. "He played for 18 years," marveled Krueger, his former teammate, "even with a limp."

Though Brodie was unavailable most of '63, he was instrumental in padding Colchico's contract. When Brodie learned how little money the gritty defensive end was making, he barged into general manager Lou Spadia's office and got him another $1,000.

Jack "Moose" Myers and Dick Voris were hired as coaching assistants, replacing Wilson and Duncan. Locker-room discord continued. An unnamed 49er was asked how many players Hickey had upset. He replied: "How many players are on the team?"

Pro Bowl guard Ted Connolly wouldn't report to camp, explaining, "I can't play with a depressed attitude brought on by unrest and constant bickering." But when he finally showed up with an agent to negotiate a contract, an unheard-of tactic at that time, he promptly was traded to Cleveland, where his blocking led to Jim Brown's best season, with 1,863 rushing yards.

Niners' defensive back Jerry Mertens was lost for the '63 season after knee surgery. Another defensive back, Eddie Dove, was traded to the Giants as Hickey kept sweeping and losing. The 49ers already looked beaten in September.

St. Clair called a players' meeting for "morale purposes." Meanwhile, he waged a "truth campaign" to deny his association with gambler Joe Cannon, who used St. Clair as "window dressing" to promote an oil deal. St. Clair blocked his way through that allegation.

There was some good news on the 49ers' front, however. Joe Perry returned for his farewell season, his 16th, a pro football record for a running back. Leo Nomellini was back, too, for one more season, his 14th, with an NFL-record 10 Pro Bowls and another NFL record for consecutive games, at 174. Leo truly was a lion.

After the 49ers lost their first three games, to the great relief of his disgruntled players, Red Hickey resigned.

Hallelujah!

"Ever have a boil lanced?" Colchico said years afterward.

Steely Dan paused for added emphasis.

"Doesn't Rolaids bring relief?" he asked.

Jack Christiansen, a fourth-year assistant, was named to replace Hickey. But even a needed coaching change couldn't make this 49ers team look good. In Christiansen's first two games, the Niners scored a combined six points.

There was one indescribable interlude, however, to break up the gloom of that depressing season. The Chicago Bears came to town en route to an 11–1–2 record. The Bears were so formidable that year, they won the NFL title by defeating the Giants, 14–10, stifling Y. A. Tittle, who had his finest season, with 36 touchdown passes, compared to 14 interceptions.

Topping the believe-it-or-not category, the Bears' only 1963 loss occurred October 20, against the woebegone 49ers, 20–14. The win was engineered by a waiver-wire quarterback, Lamar McHan, whom the 49ers had claimed only days before for $100. Sometimes, good things can be found in the bargain basement.

After that shocking win, the 49ers and McHan reverted to form, wobbling to the finish with a 2–12 record—the nadir of the franchise's first 32 years. The offense scored 198 points, the defense yielded 391 points. Ouch! Woodson stood out regardless, returning three kickoffs for touchdowns; Able Abe was voted All-NFL for the fourth time.

Even with all those injections and all that losing, Colchico couldn't think of anywhere he'd rather be than in San Francisco. "I'm playing for the 49ers," he said. "This is the place I wanted to be." But if he thought 1963 was difficult, physically, 1964 would be even worse.

Forty-nine years later—his favorite number, 49—Colchico wasn't off the hook medically. Not even close. He had open-heart surgery in 2013, yet one more obstacle for him to deal with. "I still feel weak," he said two months after the operation. "I have trouble opening a cap on a bottle."

He showed two visitors, including former San Jose State running back and teammate Oneal Cuterry, his Concord home while he lugged around his oxygen tank. "What hurts in my body?" he said. "You name it. There's not a bone in my body that doesn't hurt. One day, I was leaking blood through my legs. Before my heart surgery, I'd go to the gym to keep me going."

He gave it to his visitors straight. "If I wake up in the morning and I don't hurt," he said, "I don't open my eyes."

If it were possible, Port Chicago should erect a statue of Dan Colchico with the following inscription: "Here stands the toughest of the tough, the gamest of the game, Port Chicago's stalwart son." Only, Port Chicago no longer exists. "They took it off the map," Colchico said, resentfully.

Port Chicago, that shoreline burg on Suisun Bay in the estuary of the Sacramento and San Joaquin Rivers, became a national story on July 17, 1944. On that tragic day during World War II, munitions being loaded onto a cargo vessel bound for the Pacific Theater detonated, killing 320 sailors and civilians and injuring 390 others.

The majority of sailors killed were African Americans who weren't trained for a naval rating but were put to work as stevedores, with no instruction in ammunitions loading. After that disaster, a half-hundred group of blacks, known as the "Port Chicago 50," refused to load munitions. They were convicted of mutiny and imprisoned until their release in 1946, after the war. But that explosion, and accusations of racial inequality, led to something positive—the desegregation of the Navy in February 1946.

In 1968, Colchico and other Port Chicago residents were evicted from their homes after the federal government bought up the town's property, then demolished the town to form a zone around the Concord Naval Weapons Station's loading docks.

"It was a big sham," Colchico said. But being Dan Colchico, he didn't succumb without a fight. He united Port Chicago's citizens and sued the government. "There were 5,200 acres, and 3,000 people, and we showed where [the government] was wrong," he said. "We both presented our sides, and I beat them in court."

He's proud of that legal victory, but, in 1969, the federal government succeeded in forcing everybody remaining in Port Chicago to leave, thus shutting down the town. "I still get very upset talking about it," said Colchico.

But even though Port Chicago is gone, Colchico, in his heart, hasn't ever left Port Chicago. They were so much alike in character, tough to keep down, gritty to the core.

How else could Dan Colchico have had a football career?

19 1964

The Rainbow Runner

Little was known about Dave Kopay when he joined the San Francisco 49ers in 1964, other than he was a rookie halfback from the University of Washington. Kopay didn't even know himself, the person he was then, and the person he was becoming.

What the 49ers did notice about him right away was that he was ultra-competitive, a macho man, yet quite sensitive. "No matter how hard you hit him, he always got up with a smile," said Dan Colchico. "We nicknamed him 'Psych.' The next year, he said, 'Please don't call me that.'" Knock Kopay backward, pile-drive him into the turf, but don't call him "Psych," the name John Brodie pinned on him because he was always "psyched-up" in practice.

"[Kopay] was a good-looking guy, tough as hell, well-built, a good running back and blocker," said Bob St. Clair. Charlie Krueger said, "People picked on him because he had a reactive personality. I was in the training room one day, getting treatment on my knee. Kopay came in, saying, 'Oh, there's Charlie fake-a-knee.' That meant his time was up. From then on, don't come around me, boy."

Kopay led 49er rushers as a free-agent rookie, though he wasn't the featured back entering the season. But injuries led to more playing time, and he carried 75 times for 271 yards (3.5 average). No 49er rushing leader ever had fewer yards.

Kopay would spend four years with the 49ers and five more years with four other NFL teams. Then, in 1975, three years after retiring, he announced he was gay—the first professional athlete in any American sport to come out.

In his 1977 book, *The David Kopay Story: An Extraordinary Self-Revelation,* he revealed his having an affair with a Washington Redskins teammate, later identified as All-Pro tight end Jerry Smith, who died of AIDS in 1987 without ever admitting he was gay. Kopay's book mentioned his having a "sexual experience" with a male student at Washington and later marrying and then divorcing a stewardess to whom Brodie had introduced him.

"In San Francisco," Kopay wrote, "I poured all my energies into football and lived pretty much without any kind of social life. I did have sex a few times with a woman who was a regular sex partner of some of the other players. I got along all right with my roommates. But these were not the kind of close relationships that last. . . . For four years, I lived within minutes of the great gay capital of San Francisco and never had a real homosexual experience. . . . But in those days, I felt absolutely alone in my private sexual desires."

Without realizing it then, the 49ers had become professional football's first Rainbow Coalition. "I asked Kopay, 'You don't mess with kids, do you?'" said Colchico, after Kopay had announced that he was gay. "He said, 'No.' And I said, 'OK, you're a friend of mine.'"

"There was no way of knowing that he would come out of the closet after football," said St. Clair. "Y. A. Tittle was worried when he heard that Kopay was coming out. He asked me, 'What's he going to say?' I told Y.A., 'What are you worrying about? We all took showers together.'" Tittle had played three seasons in New York before Kopay joined San Francisco. Following knee surgery as a 49er, Kopay was traded to Detroit for third- and fourth-round draft choices. He later played for Washington, New Orleans, and Green Bay.

"Dave wrote that I was one of the most sensitive guys on the team," said St. Clair. "What happened was that if any of our players got hurt during a game, I'd go by the hospital afterward. I went by to see Kopay. He thought I was being sensitive. Some of my teammates said, 'Gee, how sensitive were you?'"

Krueger grew up in a small Texas town, yet he's anything but a Lone Star conservative. "I'm a liberal Democratic-type person," he said, "and I believe in individual rights. Later on, after Kopay had revealed he was gay, he shook my hand and thanked me for the 'decency' I had shown him. I told him that everybody is entitled to their own rights."

Those same individual rights belonged to 49er ticket holders, who had become disenchanted after watching losing football for two years. Thus they bought only 21,000 season tickets for 1964, a drop of 4,000, in spite of a promising draft. The 49ers loaded up for the future by drafting wide receiver Dave Parks in the first round and another quarterback, George Mira, in the second. Then came future Hall of Fame linebacker Dave Wilcox in the third round; a big, fast fullback, Gary Lewis, in the sixth; future All-NFL guard Howard Mudd in the ninth; and dependable linebacker Ed Beard in the 14th.

Then 49er history repeated itself on the obituary page. Vic Morabito, 45, died of a heart attack at his home on May 10, 1964. Like his older brother, the warning signs were there. Vic was hospitalized in 1962 and 1963 because of chest pains. A year later, he was dead.

"I knew Vic," Krueger said. "There were different rules in having a relationship with an owner. We didn't work at the same steel mill. But I didn't have any negative feelings about Vic. I think the Morabitos did a good job bringing this team into the league and surviving until the massive league merger happened.

"I took a class in economics in college [Texas A&M] that gave me insight into the spirit of wealth and distribution. The owners get the benefit from it, then come the lawyers, and then comes the money they give the players—who either do well with it, or they don't. I've been lucky the last few years [with investments]. It's what you do with what you've got. But I didn't have much interaction with the Morabito ladies either."

The 49ers' organizational chart was revised again after Vic Morabito died. The Niners became the only big-league professional franchise, regardless of the sport, to be owned by two women: Tony's widow, Josephine, and Vic's widow, Jane. Lou Spadia was promoted to chief executive officer. This meant that he would be in charge of the team's operations, with tacit approval of the two sisters-in-law. They preferred to stay in the shadows and therefore weren't quoted on football matters.

The author was unable to have Spadia elaborate on his close relationship with the Morabito ladies; he suffered a stroke after a first interview for this book and thus wasn't available for a second interview until three months later. So the author reached out to others.

"More than anything," said Dorothy "Doss" Spadia, "my dad always wanted to honor Tony and Vic Morabito. And then he wanted to run the team for Jane and Josie. Dad never wanted to take any credit for the 49ers. He always wanted to be in the background. He didn't want to be anyone famous. If anything, he wanted to be known as a great dad."

Former 49er Ted Connolly, who became a prosperous real estate investor after football, attempted to buy the team following Vic Morabito's passing. But Spadia stressed, like Tony and Vic had before him, that the team wasn't for sale.

Jack Christiansen brought in his head-hunting Detroit secondary mate, Jim David, as a coaching assistant. Then the Lions mistreated the 49ers in the season opener, 26–17, before 33,204 at Kezar. The 49ers won two of their next three games, then lost seven of the next eight, stumbling to a 4–10 record and another cellar-dwelling season—definitely no confidence-booster.

The season's hallmark moment for the 49ers occurred, negatively all the way around, on October 25. Here is Lon Simmons's radio call of that historic play: "[George] Mira, straight back to pass, looking, now stops, throws, completes it to [Billy] Kilmer up at the 30-yard line. Kilmer, driving for a first down, loses the ball. It is picked up by [Jim] Marshall, who is running the wrong way. Marshall is running the wrong way! And he's running it into the end zone the wrong way, thinks he has scored a touchdown. He has scored a safety. His teammates were running down the far side of the field, trying to tell him, 'Go back.' . . . Marshall has pulled a Wrong Way Riegels here today."

Minnesota defensive end Marshall had, indeed, picked up a fumble and rambled 60 yards in the wrong direction at Kezar for a safety. Edge, 49ers? No, the Vikings still won, 27–22.

"The minute it was picked up, I knew he was going to go the wrong way," Simmons recalled 50 years later. "No doubt in my mind. [Forty-Niner] Bruce Bosley trailed him all the way. Marshall thought the Minnesota bench was cheering for him."

Forty-Niners, other than Bosley, weren't quite sure what had taken place.

"I didn't know what was going on," recalled Krueger after seeing the misguided Marshall get twisted around. St. Clair said, "I was on the field, I turned around, and there he went. It was confusing; I wasn't sure if he was going the wrong way. But I followed Bosley, and if Marshall tried to come back out of the end zone, I would have had a shot at him. But he threw the ball in the stands, so it was a safety."

Marshall's miscue was the second wrong-way run in football history. The originator, Roy Riegels, made his errant turnaround for California in the 1929 Rose Bowl, leading to a deciding safety in an 8–7 Georgia Tech victory. For the rest of his life, he was branded as Wrong Way Riegels. Showing compassion, Riegels sent Marshall a letter. "Don't let this bother you," he wrote. "You'll receive a lot of kidding for the rest of your life. You'll just have to learn to take it and laugh with the crowd."

Marshall, at least, eluded the private hell of being known as Wrong Way Marshall. He remained just plain Jim Marshall. Riegels had relieved him of that enormous burden.

When a team is heading toward a 4–10 season, the home fans aren't hospitable. "At Kezar Stadium, you came through a tunnel with fans all around you," said St. Clair. "One game, a fan poured a beer on me. I had my helmet off at the time, and I jumped up and whacked the guy with the helmet, bloodying his nose. After that, they put a screen over the tunnel.

But we were having a terrible year in '64, and Brodie was worried about being booed before a game. So he asked me if I'd agree to be introduced first as the team captain. So I agreed, but then I tripped over the cement lip of the running track and went tumbling through the end zone. The fans were laughing at me, so when Brodie was introduced immediately after that, no one booed him."

While Parks, Krueger, and Matt Hazeltine made the Pro Bowl, Colchico played his last full season as a 49er, hobbling toward the end of a noble career. Norman Rockwell should have drawn him in the training room, a most compelling sight. Colchico wasn't ever voted All-Pro, and he didn't play in a single Pro Bowl. But he was the ultimate warrior in the eyes of those men he played with and against.

Tributes are like trophies, when coming from such Pro Football Hall of Famers as Forrest Gregg, Paul Hornung, and Jim Otto. "I have great respect for Danny as a football player, one of the best," said Gregg, former Green Bay tackle. "He gave me fits every time I played him." "Dan was in the top level of defensive players," said Hornung, Gregg's Packer teammate. "Dan Colchico was one of the most respected 49ers of that time," said Otto, the Oakland Raiders' ironman center.

"Danny would have played at 50 if transplants and artificial limbs would have allowed it," said 49ers' teammate Howard Mudd.

The 1964 season also marked the end of St. Clair's magnificent career, all of it spent in one place. The NFL had become more civilized over his 12 seasons. "Players, in general, weren't protected at all when I came into the league," St. Clair said. "We could leg whip, body block constantly, leave our feet. I played my first three years without a face mask, then they made us wear them. We were going to strike over that; that's how stupid we were. We thought only sissies wore face masks, and that they'd have us wearing skirts pretty soon. I broke my nose my first year. I pushed it back in place myself. That's why I have a deviated septum today."

After retiring from football, St. Clair worked for Clover-Stonetta Farms, which displays billboards in the Santa Rosa area, north of San Francisco, advertising Clover dairy products. The billboards depict a cartoon cow doing a variety of chores, each chore scripted with a clever play on words.

St. Clair writes some of these scripts. Does he have a personal favorite? "It Isn't Clover until the Fat Lady Sings," he said.

Moo.

20 1965

Parks and Wreck

Dave Parks wasn't a 49er nearly as long as Jerry Rice, but in the brief time he played in San Francisco, Parks was a bolt of lightning compared to Rice's ongoing light show.

Both players were electric, with striking similarities. They each had speed and got faster after a catch. They blocked and played physically. Parks was a mauler, while Rice also flattened larger men, as he did Denver safety Steve Atwater while scoring during the 49ers' 55–10 rout of the Broncos in Super Bowl XXIV.

"David Parks?" marveled John Brodie. "A really beautiful player." Brodie and Parks were as lethal together in 1965 as Joe Montana and Rice, or Steve Young and Rice much later, albeit connecting eras makes for a challenging comparison. "Dave Parks was just awesome," Dan Fouts said, regardless.

The 49ers of the 1960s, additionally, played 14-game schedules, while Montana, Young, and Rice benefited from 16-game seasons in the '80s and '90s. And Brodie and Parks were together only four years, without once reaching the postseason. Thus how do you compare 49ers who never played in a Super Bowl—Brodie and Parks—with those who did—Montana, Young, and Rice—especially when greatness often is identified, unfairly, by Super Bowl appearances?

Brodie had his greatest season, statistically, with Parks in 1965, throwing for a personal-best 30 touchdowns and setting an NFL record with 242 completions. With a club-record 80 catches plus 12 touchdowns, Parks achieved career highs that fall, topping NFL receivers in both categories.

Up to then, the 49ers hadn't a wide receiver with Parks's physicality. He played with the blunt force of a wrecking ball. "He was big, strong, and fast," said Lou Spadia. "When he'd get out front, no one could catch him because he'd run as fast as he had to."

"He was a gazelle, tough, a terrific end," added Charlie Krueger. "I had a lot of respect for David Parks. He could run over a back or juke him, like some of the running backs you see today."

Parks, a six-foot-two, 210-pound first-round draft pick from Texas Tech, was a productive rookie in 1964, with 36 receptions and eight touchdowns. Mathematically, that broke down to one touchdown for every four and a half catches.

And he was merely warming up.

"Offensively, I think there was something that John and I had," Parks said. "We just made things happen. They would try to take me away, and they were never able to because John wouldn't let them. It got to the point where John knew exactly where I'd be. He put so many balls in the air on faith, where he was just counting on me to be there, and for the offensive line to hold up. That took a ton of guts. We made it work."

The 49ers had jacked up their offense in '65. Their first draft pick that year, fullback Ken Willard, would lead the team in rushing with 778 yards (4.1 average), fourth-best in the NFL. The valuable Abe Woodson was traded to St. Louis for running back John David Crow, who gave the 49ers a powerful two-back set in the mold of Green Bay's Jim Taylor and Paul Hornung. Crow, the 1957 Heisman Trophy winner from Texas A&M, also was a weapon coming out of the backfield, with seven touchdown catches.

Making room for Crow, J. D. Smith was traded to Dallas, packaged with tackle-guard Leon Donohue. The 49ers already had another solid wideout, Bernie Casey, to pair with Parks. Casey had led the 49ers the previous three seasons with 53, 47, and 58 catches.

The final piece of the offense: Y. A. Tittle was hired as quarterback coach, although not the happiest of alliances. "I've had three fights in my life, and two have been with Tittle," said Brodie. "They weren't long, and nobody was hurt. One was in the meeting room, the other out on the practice field. But Y. A. and I became good friends."

Over time, Brodie meant. A competitive relationship takes time to develop.

Not since the 1948 team, which totaled 495 points, and the Million Dollar Backfield of the mid-1950s, had a 49ers' offense looked as explosive as in 1965. The Niners erupted in that season's opener with a 52–24 victory over the Bears. Brodie threw for four scores, and Gary Lewis ran 60 yards for another touchdown before a skimpy crowd of 31,211 at Kezar.

Alas, Dan Colchico ruptured his Achilles' again and was lost for the season. The 49ers picked up Dan LaRose from Baltimore to replace him, though there was no replacing Colchico's all-out passion on every down. LaRose was plugged in for just that year.

The Niners next played and defeated Pittsburgh, 27–17, before even skimpier attendance, 28,161, at Kezar. The 49er Faithful clearly were frustrated with all the broken promises.

Though the team lost in Baltimore, 27–24, Parks was magnificent with three touchdowns on nine catches and a franchise-record 231 receiving yards. He trampled Colts' defenders who got in his way, and he was waiting in the end zone to catch his fourth touchdown, the game-winner, when tight end Monty Stickles mindlessly tipped the ball away. "I can't tell you the precise distance of my touchdown receptions, and I can't tell you the patterns I ran to get open," Parks said of that October 3, 1965, performance. "I just remember the one that got away. That's because we had a chance to beat Baltimore, and, oh, what a win that would have been, because they were an excellent, excellent team."

The 49ers took it on the chin again in Green Bay, losing 27–10 to Vince Lombardi's dominant Packers. Returning home, they smoked Los Angeles, 45–21, with Brodie throwing three more touchdown strikes, one to Parks, as 34,703 watched.

The Niners then blew a 21-point lead against visiting Minnesota, which rallied for a 42–41 victory, thus wasting Brodie's three scoring passes to Casey. Losing to Norm Van Brocklin made the day even worse for Krueger and his linemates.

Brodie was 20 of 28 for 289 yards and two touchdowns as the 49ers came up short, 34–28, against Baltimore. The 49ers had the league's best offense, statistically, but hardly the best fan support, as just 40,673 showed up at Kezar, not counting the seagulls.

The 49ers lost their third straight, 39–31, in Dallas, caving in once more on defense. Brodie left the game with a separated shoulder. Backup George Mira threw for two touchdowns, one to Parks, but was picked off twice.

San Francisco's maligned defense was the difference-maker in Detroit. Defensive end Clark Miller picked up a fumble and trucked 75 yards into the end zone for a 27–21 win.

Kicking specialist Tommy Davis, who lasted 11 years with the 49ers in spite of 50 percent field goal accuracy—128 of 256—booted a 22-yarder to beat the visiting Rams, 30–27.

With Brodie's shoulder feeling sounder, he threw a career-high five touchdown passes, while Willard pounded for 113 yards, as the 49ers won their latest shootout, 45–41, at Minnesota. Krueger and friends felt a whole lot better.

The 49ers were on a roll again, making Detroit their fourth straight victim, 17–14, before 34,483 at Kezar. At 7–5, the Niners had a shot at the Playoff Bowl, a onetime NFL novelty that matched the conference runners up.

That opportunity blew up in Chicago as Gale Sayers scored six times to tie Ernie Nevers (Chicago Cardinals) and Dub Jones (Cleveland Browns) for the NFL's single-game touchdown record. The Bears buried the 49ers, 61–20, in the mud at Soldier Field. Sayers scored on runs of 21, 7, 1, and 50 yards; an 85-yard punt return; and an 80-yard pass reception. "He was the most humiliating back I played against," said Krueger. "He had the moves, and he had the speed. The field was sloppy that day, just what we wanted. That will slow him down. Hah!"

The 49ers met Green Bay in the season finale and held the Packers to a 24–24 tie before a season-high Kezar turnout of 45,710, infuriating Lombardi in the process. A Green Bay win would have wrapped up the Western Conference title. Now deadlocked with Baltimore at 10–3–1, the Packers needed to edge the Colts, 13–10, in a tie-breaker before beating Cleveland (11–3), 23–12, for the NFL championship, the last year before the first Super Bowl was played.

After the 49ers' 7–6–1 season, Parks was the team's lone All-NFL pick. The Niners led the league in scoring with 421 points, or 30 points a game. But they had the league's second-sorriest defense, yielding 402 points, one fewer than Minnesota. The Niners hadn't ever scored as many points, or yielded as many—it's hard to outplay your own defense.

Brodie was slighted as an all-league pick in 1965. In the following century, he was asked if the 49ers' chief problem during the dark age of the '60s, and throughout his 17 years with the franchise, was its inattention to defense.

"Duh," he replied.

21 1966

Money Talks

Piracy was the game, and Al Davis was impersonating Captain Kidd. After Davis left the Oakland Raiders to become AFL commissioner, he had one devious goal in mind: raid the NFL's elite quarterbacks. That's what Raiders do; they raid.

Davis's objective, which put him at odds with merger-hungry AFL owners, wasn't to combine the two leagues, but to loot the NFL. He wanted to make the AFL the dominant league. And so he targeted such marquee quarterbacks as Roman Gabriel of the Los Angeles Rams and John Brodie of the 49ers.

Brodie was making $50,000 with the 49ers. The AFL's Houston Oilers offered him a $750,000 package to jump ship. Brodie flew to Texas and, with his attorney brother Bill acting as his legal representative, signed a written memorandum of agreement on, of all things, a cocktail napkin. The quarterback then phoned Lou Spadia, who was in Oregon to watch Lou Jr. graduate from the University of Portland. Right before the ceremony, Spadia received a call in his hotel room. The following conversation took place:

"Hi, Lou, this is John."

"John, what the hell are you doing in Portland?"

"I'm not in Portland, I'm in Houston."

"Houston? What are you doing there?"

"Well, I'm down here with the local football people. They asked me to come down, and they've offered me a contract. I haven't signed it, and you know I want to play for the 49ers. But I've got to think of myself and my family."

Spadia thought quickly: That damned Al Davis!

"Look, John, don't sign anything," he said. "Let me get back to you. I've got to go to my son's graduation, but I'll get back to you. You'll hear from me before the day is out."

Spadia immediately called Jack White, the 49ers' director of scouting, and ordered him to hustle down to Houston. Spadia then phoned Marshall Leahy, the 49ers' lawyer, to check on their legal status. Then he hurried off to his son's graduation, worried whether he still would have a quarterback afterward.

An agreement with Brodie subsequently was reached, and he remained a 49er, receiving the $750,000 over three years. "But the 49ers didn't have to pay it," noted Lou Spadia Jr. "The merger happened right afterward, and the NFL had to pay Brodie. My dad was happy; he had beaten Al Davis."

Unbeknownst to the 49ers, the Oilers, and the NFL, the written memorandum with Brodie's signature disappeared overnight. He accidentally blew his nose into the cocktail napkin, then flushed it down the toilet. But nobody asked him to produce it. "A really good deal," Brodie said, laughing, 47 years later.

Al Davis was forced to return to the Oakland Raiders, because after the merger there would be only one pro football commissioner, Pete Rozelle. Davis fumed at being snubbed. Those two would be mortal enemies from that point forward.

Because his contract negotiations had dragged on, Brodie was late reporting to the 49ers' summer camp; thus he didn't hear head coach Jack Christiansen predict that George Mira would become "a great quarterback." Not just a good quarterback, but great.

Christiansen and other 49er coaches had treated Brodie too often as a No. 2 quarterback for him to forget it. "Crummy deal," he said, in 2013, with still-simmering resentment. "Go away."

Despite the 49ers' continuing failure to produce a playoff team, they raised ticket prices to $5.50. On top of that, they received a $6 million indemnity fee from the Raiders for having invaded 49er territory in the merger. Davis fumed even more, feeling fleeced, convinced by then that Oakland had the strongest team in the Bay Area. And he was correct.

Dan Colchico hadn't recovered from his Achilles' issues, so the 49ers drafted Stan Hindman from Ole Miss as their No. 1 pick. He moved into Colchico's defensive end spot as a rookie.

The 49ers, encountering fan indifference once again, would play only one home game in 1966 where attendance figures reached 40,000, or two-thirds of capacity, and that was the final game of the season.

If 49ers' fans struggled with the team's inconsistencies, imagine the frustration of their broadcasters, club legends Gordy Soltau and Hugh McElhenny, who worked as analysts with Bob Fouts and Lon Simmons. Trying to put a historical spin on all that bumbling and fumbling, Soltau, during one telecast, said, "You'd have to reach back into the argyles to find . . ."

Archives, argyles . . . those 49ers were full of holes.

San Francisco's offense didn't click nearly as well that autumn, dropping 101 points from the previous season. Meanwhile, its oft-criticized defense improved by 77 points, lengthening the franchise's frustration in getting the two on the same page.

The 49ers came out of the gate sluggishly, a 20–20 tie with Minnesota at Kezar. Then they were trampled twice on the road—36–14 in Baltimore and 34–3 in Los Angeles. "We stunk out the joint from start to finish," Christiansen said after the reeking Rams rout.

Christiansen blamed moneybags Brodie, in effect, by benching him and starting Mira. The pint-sized scrambler acquitted himself surprisingly well against Green Bay, passing for two scores and leading the 49ers in rushing in a 21–20 upset win. Brodie, after a week's punishment, started and passed for three touchdowns, with Mira adding a fourth, in a 44–7 throttling of the Falcons in Atlanta. A quarterback controversy, coach?

"Brodie is my No. 1 quarterback," Christiansen insisted. Brodie, who couldn't be sure, strengthened his situation by hitting tight end Monty Stickles with a clutch 21-yard touchdown pass with three seconds left to stun visiting Detroit, 27–24. That stirring win wouldn't be Brodie's first—Baltimore in '57—or last time extracting victory from defeat as a 49er.

"I think it's a real shame that Brodie has not been voted into the Pro Football Hall of Fame," said Simmons. "His statistics were as good as anybody's in those days. He certainly was one of the top quarterbacks of that era. Brodie never had the offensive team around him to go all the way. And the 49ers didn't have a great defense."

The confusing 49ers neither had the offense nor defense in Minnesota, losing 28–3, but they bounced back to beat the Rams, 21–13, at Kezar. San Francisco next tied Chicago, 30–30, the Niners' third tie in 10 games. The Eagles came west and, without a single punch being thrown, eked out a 35–34 win at rainy Kezar as the Niners' defense reverted to form.

The 49ers, after 20 years of trying, continued to run in place, churning hard, but getting nowhere. "It works inside out," Charlie Krueger analyzed. "You want to do well for yourself. If I do all right, then I'll be OK. I didn't walk around with a lot of braggadocio, assurance, hubris. Did I say hubris? But they'll get rid of you in a minute if you're not playing well."

Concluding another season without any sign of future promise, the pogo-stick 49ers whipped Detroit, 41–14, fell to Green Bay, 20–7, stomped on Chicago also by 41–14—holding Gale Sayers to one score—and then were buried by Baltimore, 30–14.

The 49ers ended up 6–6–2. Christiansen, hardly a motivator or tactician, now looked like a .500 coach. "Jack was a very nice guy," said Len Rohde, "and probably too close to the players. He never got to be a hard-nosed guy. He let things slide. He probably would have liked to party with the players rather than come up with a game plan for next week."

Ken Willard finished fourth among NFL rushers, with 763 yards (4.0 average), while Parks was third in catches, with 66, but with only five touchdowns. Parks still was a force, regardless, and joined 49er guard John Thomas, a former college basketball player, as the team's All-NFL picks.

Brodie slipped precipitously from his 1965 position, with 14 fewer touchdowns and six more interceptions. He heard rumors that he would be traded; he first heard such rumors in 1961, when he supposedly was going to the Rams. But in 1966, the New York Giants, who had rescued Y. A. Tittle, were mentioned. "The 49ers do not contemplate trading John Brodie to the New York Giants," said general manager Spadia. "In fact, the 49ers do not plan to trade Brodie to any other team either."

But the 49ers weren't entirely happy with Brodie. For in the next NFL draft, they selected another quarterback, Heisman Trophy winner Steve Spurrier from Florida, as their No. 1 pick. Defense, anyone? Spurrier became the fifth quarterback drafted No. 1 by the 49ers in 17 NFL seasons, compared to just five defensive players taken No. 1 by them over that same period.

That wasn't the smartest game plan for long-term success, and it would show up time and time again.

22 1967

Executive Suite

Lou Spadia, the Horatio Alger hero of the National Football League, completed his improbable rise from handing out jockstraps to handling corporate decisions when he became president of the San Francisco 49ers in May 1967.

He advanced to that position honorably, without trampling a single person to get ahead, and without once violating his code of decency in cheating anyone on his slow progression up the corporate ladder. "Lou was such an honest straight shooter," said Ken Flower. "There was never a hidden agenda. He had a great deal of integrity. He was up-front with you the whole time. And it was not important for him to be recognized as a front man."

The Morabito widows presented Spadia a money clip to commemorate this latest promotion and to acknowledge his loyalty to them and the 49ers' organization. It was inscribed: "For the man who went from office boy to president/owner, thank you for your many years of service. From Jane and Josie."

The 49ers' most devoted employee now was running the show and with a piece of the action, too. Spadia was prepared for this heightened responsibility, despite lacking a college education. He had educated himself in other ways. "He is one of the most intelligent people I've ever met," said daughter Louise "Lulu" Spadia-Beckham. "Absolutely brilliant. He can talk to you about any subject. He was a voracious reader, even into his 80s, constantly trying to improve himself."

Spadia wasn't just a walking textbook, but a well-rounded individual. "He is a man with an amazing sense of humor," Spadia-Beckham said in December 2012. "He is devout in his faith; he goes to Mass every day. He and my mother adored each other, to the point where it was almost embarrassing. They were always holding hands, and he'd pinch her fanny. But you don't want to disappoint Dad, because you know how good a guy he is. He has a lot of friends who like him, not because he was Lou Spadia, president of the 49ers, but because he is a good guy."

Spadia-Beckham is the only one of the four Spadia children who is married. Doss Spadia is twice divorced, Lou Spadia Jr. is once divorced, and Kathleen "Kate" Spadia hasn't ever married. "I tell Doss that I never married the wrong man," said Kate, smiling at her sister during an April 13, 2013, interview in Menlo Park. "Maybe it's an Italian thing, that one of the children never gets married, because she gets to do everything for Dad. After my mom died [in 1976], Dad put his arm around me and said, 'Well, it's you and me.'"

Lou and Dorothy "Maggie" Spadia had the strongest of marriages, so was it hard on Doss to have two marriages fail in the eyes of of her father? "Dad was always happy with whatever I did," she said. "He would tell me how proud he was of me, no matter how I was going to live my life. Being married, not being married, he didn't love me any less. And both my husbands adored my dad."

"He always cared that you were taken care of, protected," said Kate. "Later in life, he really tried to listen to us, to hear our side. And he was a gentleman, the kind you don't see anymore. He opened the door for my mom, and for all of us."

Doss has a staging business, decorating homes for sale, having first borrowed $100,000 from her father to get the business off the ground. She paid him back in full a year later. Kate is an administrative assistant to the president of Schwab Charities.

Spadia's children protected him, too.

"My first year of college, we went to the Rose Bowl parade," said Doss. "Mom was alive, but she was diagnosed with cancer and wasn't feeling well. So it was Lulu, Dad, and I. Dad had reserved bleacher seats, and he was cutting through when someone said, 'If you take one more step, mister, my fist is going into your face.' I pushed my dad out of the way and said, 'You lay one hand on my dad, and you are a dead man.' You don't mess with our family or my dad. Afterward, Dad told someone he was going to change his will—for me."

Doss laughed over her fried zucchini at the Oasis, a legendary Menlo Park beer and burger hangout that's located in the same town where the 49ers once trained. "There was a lot of humor in our family," she said. "My mom was hysterical. I asked her how she trusted Dad on these long [49er] trips. She said, 'You either trust him or you drive yourself nuts.' He'd be on the road and feel something crinkly in his Brooks Brothers pajamas, which Mom always ironed. He'd pull out a note from Mom that said, 'There better not be a broad sitting there.' Dad told me later, 'One thing I'm proud of, I never cheated on your mom.' I told him, 'You know, Dad, that's not really something you should be proud of.'"

Lou and Maggie Spadia formed a strong partnership. "My mom and dad were like soul mates," said Lou Jr. "She was someone who was protective of him, and she gave him a lot of space when he was home. He was devoted to all of us, a real good dad. But he was intense; my mother was laid-back. She stayed home, and our house was immaculate. She monitored our homework, but she included Dad in that. He didn't demand 'A's, but he wouldn't stand for a 'D' or 'F' either."

Lou Sr. was mirthful in a sly way. Good friend and former Pittsburgh Steelers administrator Ed Kiely got a good dose of that mirthfulness when they vacationed together as widowers. "We'd go down to Florida and stay at [New York Giants owner] Wellington Mara's home," Kiely said. "Spadia was very funny. He called up Wellington's wife to thank her for letting us use the place. But he told her that I didn't like the way my room was painted. Then he'd get these paint samples and mail them to the Maras, making it look like I sent them."

Future 49ers president Carmen Policy learned about Spadia's devilish humor from Dan Rooney, the Steelers' owner. "Dan Rooney had developed a very close, strong relationship with Lou Spadia," said Policy. "I would get a lot of stories about Lou from Dan. One story, which had me rolling on the floor, involved their taking a trip to Ireland and Italy, to celebrate their ethnic heritages. Lou told Dan that he would plan the whole trip for them. So now it's time for the trip, and the itinerary shows up. And Dan says, 'Lou, we're in Ireland three days, and Italy eleven.' And Lou says, 'Three days too much?'"

Kiely, who worked for the Rooneys in Pittsburgh, should have warned them about Spadia's sly humor. "He was that kind of guy," said Kiely, "but friendly and warm. He was a wonderful fellow, very honest and curious. He came up as a poor kid, starting with the 49ers the same way I started with the Steelers. He was a good Italian boy, and he visited Italy from time to time. He was very proud of going as far as he did without an education."

Perhaps Spadia needed these humorous diversions to deal with the pressure of the 49ers' losing ways. And he added horticulture as additional therapy.

"There was a lot of losing," said Spadia-Beckham. "Dad had a beautiful vegetable garden with heirloom tomatoes, spinach, and zucchini. He'd come up the driveway at 6:00 P.M., always honking his horn. He'd walk in the door, kiss my mother, get in his gardening clothes, pour himself a drink, and go out to the garden by himself to water and rake. He'd have excruciatingly long days, and I'd see a stressed-out guy. The garden was his solace."

Unfortunately, Spadia couldn't take the garden with him on the road when the team wasn't winning, which was all too often. He might, instead, need some whet-your-whistle solace. "While I was in school in the East," said Kate, "the 49ers had a game in Baltimore. Dad and I went to Mass with Father Hurley and some of my roommates. Then we went to brunch. I had never seen my dad loaded, but he had one too many Bloody Marys. He expected the worse, telling me, 'This isn't going to be pretty.' But Alley Oop [Owens] won the game."

Flower's life was linked to Spadia's from that 1949 training camp introduction to Flower's later involvement with NFL Films, then Flower's sports marketing company, and finally their working together on the Bay Area Sports Hall of Fame. "He affected my life like a father," said Flower. "There was some resentment on Lou's part that he missed out on a college education because of the war. So he took classes in English literature. And in order to write well, he took some special writing classes at San Jose State."

Marking Spadia's first year as president, 1967, the 49ers strung together a six-game losing streak, their longest of the decade. But that team's problems started even before the season. Fullback Ken Willard demanded to be traded to Washington, near his home in Virginia. John Brodie, Clark Miller, and tackle Walter Rock visited with Willard and changed his mind.

Plus drafting Steve Spurrier came with a price: Bernie Casey. A trade had been worked out with Atlanta to get its first-round pick. This meant Casey, one of Brodie's primary receivers, was sent to the Falcons. Casey later retired to become an actor and, as the NFL's Rembrandt, to pursue his passion for painting. But the 49ers, without him, weren't a pretty picture.

George Mira, after the 49ers took Spurrier, sought a trade, but was obligated to report to camp. Dave Parks held out, demanding a new contract at $60,000 per year after his three-year, $100,000 rookie package had expired. Spadia refused, and Brodie feared he might be losing both Casey and Parks. "Yes, cut it out," he said, disgusted, in 2013. "Really good players."

There were more coaching changes. Jim David returned to Detroit and was replaced by Jim Shofner, a subsequent Brodie favorite. Dan Colchico was added to Jack Christiansen's staff, but it would be for one year only. Amazingly, Colchico, even with his Achilles' problems, suited up for New Orleans in 1969, and as a starter, before retiring at 32. "I was playing well at the end," he said, "but it wasn't fun. Doug Atkins, my teammate, thought I was crazy to leave. I just didn't enjoy it anymore."

A Bay Area event of incredible interest happened in 1967—the first 49ers–Raiders game, held at the year-old Oakland Coliseum, the game's site determined by a coin flip won by Raiders captain Jim Otto at Treasure Island, halfway between San Francisco and Oakland. The old school, traditional 49ers were facing, in terms of longevity, the grammar school age, rebellious Raiders for bragging rights. Though a preseason game, it felt like a local Super Bowl. Who would win? It was the 49ers, 13–10, but the Raiders actually were Super Bowl–bound that same season, while the 49ers wouldn't even sniff the playoffs. Again.

The 49ers flew to Minnesota for the season opener. Rookie Doug "Goober" Cunningham broke loose on a 64-yard scoring run, then added a 57-yard punt return to set up another touchdown during the Niners' thrilling victory, 27–21.

The 49ers then blew out visiting Atlanta, 38–7, rushing for 190 yards. After getting stomped in Baltimore, 41–7, they reeled off three wins—27–24 over Los Angeles, 28–27 over Philadelphia, and 27–13 over New Orleans. But in the process, All-NFL guard John Thomas damaged both knees, ending his career.

Christiansen, with a 4–1 jump start, was in decent shape to save his job. Then the wheels came off with a six-game losing streak, the 49ers scoring no more than nine points in five of the six games. Once again, Christiansen benched Brodie. Mira started the last two contests. Spurrier watched it all unravel, wondering if he was inching closer to playing.

Dan Fouts recalled how mistreated Brodie felt. "I was a ball boy at the time," Fouts said. "The 49ers had Mira, and then they drafted Spurrier. They were looking to run John out of town. In pregame warm-ups, my job was to catch the ball for John, hand it to him, and he'd throw it down the field. One day, he was so down in the dumps, he said, 'Screw it, you throw it.' I'm a 16-year-old high school junior, throwing the ball down the field to all these 49ers. . . . It was awesome!"

Fouts had learned as a teenager, because of the access he gained to the 49ers through his broadcasting father, about the inner workings of pro football. "Just watching the players interact, and seeing that they're human beings—they bleed, they cry, they get mad, they get happy; the emotions you can imagine," he said. "And watching them deal with the press, Brodie in particular, it was such a great experience. Then when I started playing football, Chico Norton, the 49ers' equipment manager, asked me what size shoe I wore. 'If you need cleats,' he said, 'let me know.' Then he gave me a pair of shoes. 'They're George Mira's,' he said. I even wore No. 10 in high school because of George Mira."

That 1967 season, Mira stated publicly that he would go to court to prevent the 49ers from stopping his jumping to the AFL's Miami Dolphins (the leagues' merger wouldn't take effect until 1970). Mira, a more mobile quarterback than Brodie, played well in beating Atlanta, 34–28, and Dallas, 24–16, passing for a combined 580 yards and five touchdowns as the season ended.

Guard Howard Mudd and linebacker Dave Wilcox were selected All-NFL. Center Bruce Bosley joined Mudd in the Pro Bowl.

Christiansen judged Brodie's 11 touchdown passes and 22 interceptions before switching to Mira, who had two interceptions along with his five touchdown throws that season. "Had Mira been healthy and available all season," said Christiansen, "it might have made a difference."

Toward the end of the '67 season, the players saw a change in Christiansen. "There was something going on with him," said Frank Nunley, then a rookie linebacker. "He'd come out to practice, start at one end of the field where the offense was, then move to the middle of the field where some of the defensive guys were. Then a half-hour later, he'd move to the other end of the field, then he'd come back to the other side of the 50-yard line, and send us in. Practice was over. It was like he was going through a routine, letting his assistant coaches do all the work."

Perhaps Christiansen saw the end coming. For he was fired on December 20, his 39th birthday, not exactly the best timing, after a 7–7 season. "I'm not going to kick a guy when he's down," Mira said of Christiansen, just before the quarterback started kicking. "But I've said all along that I never felt he gave me a fair shot."

Right afterward, another Brodie trade rumor surfaced, this time involving Minnesota. There was no immediate reaction from Spadia, who had a more urgent matter: he needed a new head coach, and he had to find the right man this time.

For the 49ers had been losers far too long.

23 1968

Turning the Corner

The 49ers couldn't afford another coaching mistake. Since Buck Shaw was booted out in 1954, four different coaches—Red Strader, Frankie Albert, Red Hickey, and Jack Christiansen—had failed to bring an outright conference title to San Francisco, let alone a league championship.

Somewhere, there had to be a coach who could make the 49ers into a consistent winner, perhaps even a Super Bowl champion. And if he was out there, who was he?

Candidates lined up to be interviewed, including Bill "Tiger" Johnson, onetime 49er center and current assistant coach. Three head coaches—Florida State's Bill "Master of the Malaprop" Peterson, Tennessee's Doug Dickey, and Wyoming's Lloyd Eaton—threw their hats in the ring. George Mira, trying his hardest to leave, lobbied for 49er assistant Dick Voris.

So which man was the front-runner?

None of the five, as it turned out.

On Jan. 20, 1968, Lou Spadia lassoed a cowboy from Texas by hiring someone who hadn't been visible on the radar screen: Dallas assistant coach and defensive specialist Dick Nolan. The hiring made sense in one way, because Spadia and Nolan were mirror images of each other: Devout men, family oriented, loyal to the core, driven to succeed. Nolan was more insular and soft-spoken, however, if he spoke at all. *San Francisco Examiner* sportswriter Al Corona, who covered those 49ers, nicknamed him "Mute Rockne."

"I was afraid of Dick Nolan," recalled Charlie Krueger, "because he had come from Dallas. And I was afraid of Tom Landry because he had more player problems than most coaches. It was him and the Bible and Job, and

Job was on welfare. I made some comments about Landry to the press, so I didn't know what to expect from Nolan."

Nolan brought along Landry's complicated Flex defense: a 4–3 front where two players lined up nose-to-nose on the line of scrimmage, while the other two linemen were positioned a few feet back. As he entered his 10th year in the NFL, Krueger had to adapt to a new defensive scheme as well as a new coach. "It worked out fine," he said. "I made the club with Nolan, and I was with him for six years. He was unbiased. He didn't make decisions before they needed to be made. He was a fair man. He was religious; I'm not. But he was a good person."

Other 49er veterans also took a liking to Nolan. "Very professional," said Len Rohde. "He followed the Tom Landry book—business-like, not a lot of fooling around. Not a hard-nosed guy, but let's get it done. A smart coach, trying to understand the players by putting them in the right spots."

"Dick was a straight shooter," added Frank Nunley. "You knew where you were with him all the time."

Well, not every 49er felt the same way about Nolan as did Rohde and Nunley. John Brodie's relationship with Nolan started off poorly and didn't improve. Nolan summoned Brodie to his office for a get-to-know-each-other meeting, but he made Brodie sit for a spell as he shuffled through papers on his desk. Brodie thought he was being treated rudely. "Look, you asked me to come see you," he said. "If you're too busy, do you want me to come back later?"

Nolan realized he was dealing with a no-nonsense individual. As the team's senior member, Brodie had endured more than his share of disappointment. So one more coaching change wasn't about to make him do cartwheels out of sheer joy. Their coach-quarterback relationship began adversely and never really changed.

"Nolan . . . crummy guy," Brodie scoffed in 2013.

However, except for Brodie and a few others, Nolan had a positive relationship with the majority of 49er players. Broadcaster Lon Simmons analyzed the difficult Nolan-Brodie union.

"Brodie was a sharp guy," said Simmons. "One game, Nolan told his offensive coordinator, Jim Shofner, to tell Brodie that he wanted him to come out of the huddle with his head up, and to hurry to the line of scrimmage. So this one time, they're playing the Jets, and Brodie throws a pass that goes through the receiver's hands, and New York intercepts it. So Brodie goes over to Shofner and said, 'Well, at least I came out of the huddle with my head up.'

"John played in some miraculous games, but in one game the 49ers were losing, something like 30–0, and Nolan told Brodie he was going in. And John said, 'Do you want me to go for the win or the tie?'"

That Brodie and Nolan could coexist and achieve together for six years, despite their differences, spoke volumes about the human dynamic.

The 49ers' first draft under Nolan was a launching point for a franchise desperately in need of a liftoff. Nolan, though, had limited input on which players were drafted. Jack White was a part-time 49er scout before becoming the team's director of scouting in 1965. His primary responsibility was the draft, and after a crisp takeoff in the late 1960s, his drafts crash-landed in the 1970s. "He was a big bullshitter," said Louise Spadia-Beckham.

Center Forrest Blue was chosen No. 1 in 1968, followed by linebacker Skip Vanderbundt, safety Johnny Fuller, and defensive linemen Bill Belk and Tommy Hart. Blue and Hart became All-Pros, Vanderbundt and Belk were starters, and Fuller was a reliable fifth defensive back.

Nolan assembled a solid coaching staff in Paul Wiggin, Mike Giddings, Jim Shofner, Y. A. Tittle, Ken Meyer, Ernie Zwahlen, Ed Hughes (Nolan's brother-in-law), and Joe Perry as both an assistant coach and scout. J. D. Smith also was hired to scout. Wiggin, Hughes, and Meyer would become NFL head coaches and Wiggin and Shofner college head coaches.

Monty Stickles was traded to New Orleans for defensive back George Rose, who failed to make the club. But Nolan was eager to dispose of the difficult, though effective, Stickles. In a more important development, New Orleans also landed free-agent Parks after he played out his option. NFL czar Pete Rozelle awarded the 49ers defensive lineman Kevin Hardy, a Saints No. 1 pick, as compensation for New Orleans having signed Parks.

Both the 49ers and Parks were at fault over his leaving. "John Brodie told me, 'Don't go where you don't have a thrower, because you'll be wasted,'" he said. "I didn't really understand the throwing end of it, but I learned what it meant the hard way. John finally told me that I kept him out of a Super Bowl."

Walter Rock, a disgruntled starting offensive tackle, walked out of camp—a Rock in a hard place—and was traded to Washington for a future No. 1 pick in 1970. The 49ers' new training camp in '68 was located on the University of California, Santa Barbara campus, where an important new addition showed up in reed-thin wide receiver Clifton McNeil.

Brodie had a strong camp, and Nolan picked him to start over Mira and Steve Spurrier, who continued as the 49ers' punter. Spurrier and Mira had waited for Brodie to get old, retire, or join the pro golf tour, as he was a superb golfer. But, once again, they couldn't wrest his job.

After Nolan's official debut, a 27–10 setback in Baltimore, he said, "The kicking game has to improve; we're giving the opposition good field position." He toyed with replacing Spurrier with the newly acquired Hardy, a 285-pound punter at Notre Dame. But Nolan stayed with Spurrier.

Nolan's first victory, 35–17 over St. Louis, was witnessed by 27,557 at Kezar. But it wasn't only the kicking game that was bothering Nolan. In Chicago, after the Bears' 27–19 win, he said, "We missed tackles, and we dropped passes. This game will change some things, and it could be personnel."

The 49ers played their fourth tie in four years, 20–20 against the Rams, whose Bruce Gossett kicked two field goals, the tying three-pointer coming with 17 seconds left. If only the 49ers had a reliable kicker like Gossett, wished Nolan.

The Niners finally got it together, winning three of their last four games to finish 7–6–1. Ken Willard said, "We are a much more stable team than we were a year ago." He credited Nolan for the improvement. Willard, after scoring both touchdowns in a 14–12 season-ending win in Atlanta, finished second among NFL rushers with 967 yards (4.3). Brodie wound up third in passing, with 22 touchdowns, opposite 21 interceptions, and 3,020 yards.

The biggest difference offensively was McNeil, who came out of nowhere to catch 71 passes, tops in the NFL, thus filling the void of losing Parks. McNeil's career year brought him All-NFL honors with guard Howard Mudd. Like Parks, McNeil hadn't ever had a quarterback like Brodie to get him the ball. Oddly, McNeil's time in the spotlight lasted all of one season.

By the slimmest of margins, Spadia had two non-losing seasons in his first two years as 49er president. "I don't think he saw a full game until he became president," said Lou Jr. "Before then, he was all over the place during the game, making sure everybody was doing their job."

But a good kind of busy: anything was better than picking up jocks after games.

Eyes of Texas

Charlie Krueger rose from humble Texas beginnings to become a formidable football player and an intellect with a country-like perspective about the diverse world around him.

"I was born upstairs above a fire station," he said. "That's where we lived, in a flat above the fire station. My dad worked for a municipality in Caldwell, a town of about 2,000. Cotton was king, and there was corn, soybeans . . . commodities.

"I was short corn."

Corn that's edible, the kind that grows as high as an elephant's eye, is tall corn. Corn that grows as low as a hound dog's thigh and isn't so edible is known as short corn. The key difference between tall and short corn, according to Krueger's law of economics, is the difference between the haves and have nots.

Though Krueger started out in life as short corn, he wasn't destined for welfare. Quite the contrary, he was bound for glory, so determined was he to make something of himself. He outlasted every other 49er defensive lineman in longevity—15 seasons, or one more than Leo Nomellini, who played offense his first three years in the NFL. And Krueger, over time, would become a very wealthy man. Tall corn, indeed.

Known as the "Textbook Tackle" for his intelligent play, Krueger had his 49er number (70) retired, just like Nomellini (73). "I was very much so honored," he said with textbook diplomacy.

The only difference between these two men: Nomellini is in the Pro Football Hall of Fame; Krueger is in the Texas Sports Hall of Fame. "The numbers don't add up," he said of his chances of making the NFL's hall. "You have to accept that what is is, and what ain't ain't."

Homespun Texas philosophy still shows up in Krueger's vernacular. But don't be misled: this is one fascinating individual. How many other big-hoss football linemen birdwatch; tour silver-mining towns in Nevada; are married to an opera director's daughter; and can discuss a range of eclectic topics, such as the planet's atmosphere, nonstop?

"I've always wondered what's up there, what's down here," Krueger said. "I had some professors who showed me. One professor said that if you go from sea level up a thousand feet, the temperature reduces 2.92 degrees. I thought that was cool. So if you go up 30,000 feet, it's 80 degrees cooler. I read a lot about the universe, like the continental drift. If you take the continents and push

Charlie Krueger received the "Textbook Tackle" designation by playing the position the way it was designed. A 49er fixture over three decades, Krueger later became the first player to win an injury suit against the NFL. 1965 drawing by Dave Beronio. (Dave Beronio collection)

them together, they sort of fit, like South America and Africa. At one time, they were all one land mass."

He reels off such tidbits with the drop of a ten-gallon hat. He combines common sense with curiosity. He isn't a regular opera attendee despite a long marriage to Kristin Adler Krueger, daughter of former San Francisco Opera director Kurt Adler. "He was a complex man," Krueger said of his late father-in-law. "I don't know if he took to me or not. Looking back, I don't know that he should. I did go to the opera after meeting Kris. But where I come from, Caldwell, Texas, it wasn't in my program. I loved Webb Pierce, Flatt and Scruggs, bluegrass."

Krueger is a deep thinker and a sometimes loner, which explained his "Lone Wolf" image among 49er teammates. He was comfortable in a locker-room setting, but equally comfortable in being off by himself, exploring some new aspect of the universe.

He was the 49ers' second of two first-round picks in the 1958 NFL draft behind Michigan halfback Jim Pace. Krueger "hated" college at Texas A&M, where he had a "love-hate" relationship with legendary coach Paul "Bear" Bryant. "He was a very complex, very driven person," said Krueger. "A personality

Charlie Krueger (70) avoids an Atlanta blocker to penetrate the Falcons backfield in 1971. Krueger, whose number the 49ers retired, especially enjoyed beating the Falcons because he deeply disliked their head coach, Norm Van Brocklin. (Charlie Krueger collection)

like his only comes along . . . there is no right word to describe him. He could have had a little megalomania in him. He was a country boy who was driven to Bible things he could quote. And he was driven to drama. He had a helluva influence on my life."

Albeit a complicated influence.

"There wasn't a day in my four years at A&M where I didn't dread going to practice," said Krueger. "You never knew when Coach Bryant would twist off and beat you to death. Scholarships didn't mean anything to him; they only lasted until dark."

Krueger hasn't forgotten Bryant, who was bigger in size than his Texas A&M players, running halfway across the field and slamming into an unsuspecting Aggie's back after that player had done something wrong in practice.

"All of us feared him," Krueger said of Bryant. "But as long as he lived, I never crossed him. Kenny Stabler crossed the Bear [at Alabama], knocked him publicly, and the Bear wouldn't even pronounce Stabler's name after that. You didn't cross [Vince] Lombardi either when he was alive, because he'd cut your ass to pieces."

Because Bryant "worked on fundamentals and basics every day," noted Krueger, he became a first-team All-American and a solid NFL player over three decades. His first 49er season, 1958, though, coincided with Frankie Albert's final year of coaching the team. Krueger, who sat out that entire season with an injury, thought he had left the Bear behind in Texas.

"I broke my arm in the fourth exhibition game," he said. "That was it. Frankie Albert was all I had to look out for after that. Then it was stay away from him as much as you can. He would jerk your chain to deal with [his] boredom. I heard he had depressive situations. His great thing was to crack you by inferences and comparisons. But I never cracked. It was 'yes sir, no sir,' the only four words I used at A&M. On top of that, the cast I wore was crooked, and I now have a crooked arm."

After playing for Bryant, Albert, Red Hickey, and Jack Christiansen—who later was ineffective as head coach at Stanford—Krueger found a sense of relief in playing for Dick Nolan, who brought purpose and direction from Dallas.

Jack White assembled another solid draft class in 1969, taking talented receivers Ted Kwalick and Gene Washington in the first round. UCLA coach Tommy Prothro said, "Kwalick is further ahead at his position than any other [1968] All-American." That included Heisman Trophy winner O. J. Simpson. White also chose linebacker Jim Sniadecki, defensive linemen Earl Edwards and Bob Hoskins, and running back Jimmy Thomas, future 49er contributors.

Meanwhile, the San Francisco Board of Supervisors approved a measure to expand Candlestick Park into a multisport facility for the baseball Giants and the football 49ers. "We do not want to leave San Francisco," Lou Spadia said at the time. "The 49ers originated here, and we feel we are responsible for bringing major-league sports to the coast. We are very much in favor of the Candlestick proposal."

Very much in favor? With the infamous winds at Candlestick Point, situated alongside San Francisco Bay?

For historic purposes, the 49ers actually were tied with the Rams (NFL) and Dons (AAFC) of Los Angeles in bringing big-league sports to the West Coast in 1946.

Nolan was determined to revise the 49ers. After linebacker Matt Hazeltine retired, Bruce Bosley and John Thomas were waived, and Clark Miller was traded to the New York Giants. Then Mira was dealt to Philadelphia for guard Randy Beisler. Mira got his wish, though not his preferred location (Miami), and the 49er quarterback situation was down to John Brodie and Steve Spurrier. Well, it was really down to Brodie.

He started the 1969 opener, inauspiciously, throwing three interceptions as the 49ers lost in Atlanta, 24–12. The downslide continued in Green Bay as Tommy Davis not only missed three field goals, he gave the Packers excellent field position with his short kickoffs, all of which contributed to a 14–7 defeat.

The 49ers' fifth tie in five years, 17–17, occurred against the Washington Redskins, coached by Lombardi, who had ended a brief retirement. The 49ers fell to 1–6–1 after a 41–30 loss to the Rams in Los Angeles. Brodie had a sore arm, which cortisone shots couldn't cure. "Nothing seems to work," he said. So Spurrier started the ninth game and delivered a 24–21 victory in Baltimore, completing 18 of 30 passes for 205 yards, one touchdown, and no picks.

Nolan kept looking for answers. He traded standout guard Howard Mudd to Chicago for Roosevelt Taylor to fill a huge hole at free safety. Davis was let go, and Momcilo "Gabbo" Gavric, a soccer star from Yugoslavia, was signed to placekick. Jon Kilgore was brought in to punt. Both new specialists, unfortunately, wouldn't be so special.

Spadia denied new franchise sale rumors—this time the supposed buyers were a group that included comedian Bob Hope. The 49ers continued their laughable ways with their sixth tie in five years, 24–24, at Dallas. Krueger blocked Mike Clark's 37-yard field goal try with 12 seconds left to, at least, avoid another defeat.

Rookie Jimmy Thomas resembled Superman with two 75-yard touchdowns—on a scrimmage run and a Spurrier pass—as the 49ers beat Chicago, 42–31. Spurrier then went the distance in a snowfall as the Niners lost, 10–7, in Minnesota, where Gavric's low field goal kick hit Vikings' star lineman Alan Page squarely in the helmet.

The futile 49ers ended a 4–8–2 season with Brodie relieving Spurrier and tossing a 22-yard touchdown to wide receiver Dick Witcher with three minutes remaining to beat visiting Philadelphia—and Mira—14–12. Jimmy Johnson intercepted Mira to secure the win.

Gabbo Gavric made only 3 of 11 field goal attempts on the season, though it shouldn't have come as a surprise. He was a defenseman, not a scorer, in professional soccer. "As far as field goal kicking is concerned, a good man can sure win a lot of games," Nolan said, summarizing the season. "Some field goals here and there could have made a difference. I'm counting on trades for experienced men to strengthen the club for next season."

Goodbye, Gabbo.

Brodie finished the season with 16 touchdown passes, 15 interceptions, and a 55.9 completion percentage. Spurrier had 5 scoring passes, 11 pass thefts, and a 55.5 percentage. He hadn't yet demonstrated that he was about to supplant Brodie.

Cornerback Johnson was voted All-NFL and joined linebacker Dave Wilcox, guard Elmer Collett, fullback Ken Willard, and wide receiver Gene Washington in the Pro Bowl.

"Dave Wilcox set himself apart from the rest of us," said fellow linebacker Frank Nunley. "He was not talkative; he did his talking by (pulverizing) people. He had the fame. Jimmy Johnson set himself apart from us, too. Not because he hated anyone; he just was the best pass defender in the world. He'd be 30 yards behind a receiver, and he'd catch up and knock the ball away."

Even with a losing season, a change was taking place with the 49ers that wasn't yet evident to their fan base, the 49er Faithful, or to the world of professional football.

"We could tell, despite our record, that we were there," Nunley said of the team's potential as a contender. "The offense had helped itself quite a bit, our defense had a lot of veterans on it, and guys were in the middle of great careers. I could see us jelling going into the 1970 season. You could see it coming."

For the 49ers, the best years were just ahead.

25 1970

Deliverance

Steve Spurrier positioned John Brodie just where he wanted him—at a distinct disadvantage—in their ongoing competition to determine the better player. Only this time it wasn't throwing a football, but a noontime table-tennis match at the 49ers' summertime dormitory on the UC–Santa Barbara campus.

Spurrier sought any form of gamesmanship superiority over Brodie, even with a ping-pong paddle. And he jumped out to a commanding 19–12 lead. Teammates circled the table, shouting encouragement to both men, yet wondering if Spurrier finally had Brodie's number—at something.

Two more points, and it would be Spurrier's match. Then Brodie mounted a furious comeback. He sliced wicked shots past Spurrier, getting stronger with each point. With tension at its peak and teammates moving in closer, Brodie evened things at 20–20. Then he smacked the ball past Spurrier twice to win.

Brodie promptly laid down his paddle and walked off without saying a word. Spurrier stood there stunned, holding his paddle forlornly. The message was clear: As long as Brodie was on the premises, and healthy, he had the edge.

Competition was Brodie's strong suit. Name the sport, any sport, and he competed well. He had stood out in football, basketball, and baseball at Oakland Technical High School. He held future Boston Celtics legend Bill Russell to a few points in a high school basketball game. "He couldn't hit the broad side of a barn back then," Brodie recalled. Brodie was a boys' city tennis champion in Oakland the very first time he picked up a racket. And he was a scratch golfer. He was, like Roy Hobbs, a natural.

The NFL got a full dose of Brodie's competitiveness in 1970. This was his first season as a 49er when it all came together—talent level, team attitude, coaching, scouting, drafting, trades—following 13 frustrating years of his waiting and hoping.

Brodie, despite the 49ers' miseries of the 1960s, was brimming with confidence before the 1970 season. "I'm looking at our talent against everybody else's," he said, "and I think we have as good a chance as any team of playing in the Super Bowl. I think, potentially, we have a great club. We've filled all our weaknesses."

Forty-Niners in the Super Bowl? Had Brodie lost all his marbles? He wasn't blowing smoke, for he always meant what he said. One reason for his optimism was the positive change at placekicker. The 49ers traded defensive back Kermit Alexander, their all-time interception leader, with 36, to the Rams for Bruce Gossett. Dick Nolan had gotten his man, finally.

Brodie also had a stronger, deeper offense with four capable running backs in Ken Willard, Doug Cunningham, Jimmy Thomas, and Bill Tucker. Bob Windsor and Ted Kwalick brought depth at tight end. Gene Washington and Dick Witcher gave Brodie his best outside receiving targets since Dave Parks and Bernie Casey. And the offensive line of tackles Len Rohde and Cas Banaszek, guards Woody Peoples and Randy Beisler, and center Forrest Blue offered Brodie leakproof protection.

Jack White had a third consecutive strong draft, taking defensive end Cedrick Hardman and cornerback Bruce Taylor in the first round, then selecting running backs John Isenbarger, Vic Washington, and Larry Schreiber, and wide receiver Preston Riley. Vic Washington and Schreiber wouldn't join the team until 1971, while Riley would become an unforgettable name in 49er lore one year later, in 1972.

Hardman provided the 49ers a fierce pass rusher, which they needed almost as much as a reliable field-goal kicker. "He's a great one," defensive line coach Paul Wiggin said after watching Hardman in the Senior Bowl. "He has tremendous speed off the ball."

Making room for the newcomers, the oft-injured Kevin Hardy was traded to Green Bay, and one-year wonder Clifton McNeil was packed off to the New York Giants.

Doug Scovil replaced Joe Perry as kicking game coach, freeing Perry to just scout. Y. A. Tittle and Mike Holovak quit as assistant coaches, with Burnie Miller also joining the staff.

The 49ers hiked ticket prices, with a new ceiling of $6.50—a dollar increase. The fans were about to get a solid return on their investment.

The team launched its silver anniversary season with a 26–17 win over visiting Washington, coached by Bill Austin following Vince Lombardi's death. Brodie was 17 for 20 with a touchdown and no picks. Tommy Hart had three sacks and Charlie Krueger a pair as the 49ers dropped Sonny Jurgensen six times while swatting four passes at the line of scrimmage.

Gossett's impact was immediate; he made four field goals against the Redskins, then two more in a 34–31 win over Cleveland at Kezar. Brodie was accurate once again: 20 of 31 for 227 yards and three touchdowns. The rookie Thomas, a speed back, caught two of them, including a 61-yarder that iced the win. Willard pounded out 105 yards to balance the offense.

Gossett made the difference again in Atlanta, only negatively, as he missed a 19-yard field goal out of Brodie's hold on the game's final play to give the Falcons a gift win, 21–20.

Nonetheless, Willard looked on the bright side: "Our leadership is far superior now to past days. The guys have finally realized that we have talent, and we have power."

Willard wore three hats for the 49ers: leading rusher, team spokesman, and club comedian. He nicknamed middle linebacker Frank Nunley as "Fudgehammer," because "he's built like fudge and hits like a hammer." Willard gave Hardman, a Texan with an outlandish sense of fashion, the sobriquet "Fontana Wagonwheel, the next cowboy star." Willard built a wooden horse, "Sugar," and tethered it to Hardman's locker. Willard kept the locker room loose.

The 49ers recovered from Atlanta by beating the Rams, 20–16, in Los Angeles. Gene Washington caught seven passes for 145 yards, including a 59-yard scoring strike from Brodie, who hadn't yet been intercepted. Brodie also shocked the Rams by scoring on a quarterback draw. And Gossett rebounded: his two field goals settled the outcome against his former team.

Then came another downer. New Orleans intercepted Brodie three times in a stunning 20–20 tie. Two former 49ers, Billy Kilmer and Dave Parks, combined on a 13-yard game-tying touchdown pass with 42 seconds left. A heavier Parks now lined up at tight end, but he still was able to get open. "Everybody's awfully upset," said Willard, "but the more you win, the more they shoot for you. Maybe it's a good lesson."

A good lesson, indeed, as the 49ers reeled off four straight wins. Gossett kicked four field goals, and Brodie hit first-year halfback Isenbarger on a 61-yard touchdown pass in a 19–14 win over Denver. Outside linebacker Skip Vanderbundt preserved the victory with an end-zone interception as time ran out.

The 4–1–1 Niners were in first place, which hadn't happened this far into the season in 11 years. The biggest Kezar turnout in 13 years, 59,335, watched the 49ers dump Green Bay, 26–10. Another 8,500 fans were turned away.

"There's probably no one stronger in football than we are," said Willard.

"We now *expected* to win," Nunley recalled of the team's positive attitude.

The 49ers flew into Chicago and pummeled the Bears, 37–16. Brodie threw for three touchdowns, and Spurrier passed for a fourth.

Then it was on to Houston, where the Niners improved to 7–1–1 with a 30–20 win over the Oilers, featuring three more touchdown strikes from Brodie. Doug Cunningham had 92 yards rushing plus five catches to lead the team in both categories. "My dad, Frank Hardman, was a fan of John Brodie before I ever got to the 49ers," said Cedrick Hardman. "After we played in Houston, I got my dad to come meet John in the locker room. My dad didn't smile much, but he had the biggest grin I'd seen in a while after John talked to him."

Krueger, who spent that afternoon in the Houston backfield, took an instant liking to Cunningham, nicknaming him "Goober" after an *Andy Griffith Show* character. The 49ers stitched "Goober" on the back of Cunningham's jersey—a joke that lasted one game before the NFL's uniform police got wise. Cunningham, a good ol' boy from Mississippi, was fine with it either way. He was easy-going, head to toe.

"One day during a lunch break at practice," said Krueger, "Goober and I went for a ride in my truck. We're up in the hills, where we can see the smog and the traffic down below. And Goober says, 'Charlie, the reason why the world is so screwed up, there are just too many people on the planet, and they've knocked the Earth off its axis.' He was dead serious. I looked at him and said, 'You must be right, Goob.'"

The 49ers' balloon burst after Houston. They were clobbered twice: 28–7 in Detroit and 30–13 by Los Angeles. But with three games left, the 49ers didn't question themselves. They recovered to beat visiting Atlanta, 24–20, notching their first win over the Falcons in four tries.

Two games left. The playoffs loomed.

"This is where you have to take it," Nolan said.

Brodie hit fellow Stanford alum Gene Washington with three touchdown passes as the 49ers won, 38–27, in New Orleans, building their record to 9–3–1. The NFL Niners hadn't ever won 10 games.

One game to go. The playoffs loomed even closer.

That last game, however, matched the two Bay Area teams, and in Oakland. The Raiders already had clinched their division, while the 49ers needed a win to secure their first outright division/conference title in franchise history, still remembering Detroit in '57. "They're not going to give us anything," said 49er defensive end Bill Belk, not expecting playoff-bound Oakland to lay down and play dead, given the tension between the two teams and cities.

Detroit cleared the way this time by beating Los Angeles, 28–23, on Monday night, leaving the Rams one game behind the 49ers. So it all rested squarely on the Niners' shoulders. Brodie returned home to Oakland to seize the moment. "You prepare the best you can and take your best shot. That's all you can do," he said. "I've always been like this."

Brodie gave it his best shot, indeed, passing to Gene Washington and Kwalick for touchdowns as the 49ers shot into a 24–7 halftime lead—the exact halftime margin by which they led the Lions in '57. Only this time, there would be no collapse. The 49ers pulled further ahead to win, 38–7. The NFC Western Division title was theirs, and Brodie's, at last.

"Let me savor this one," he said when queried about the postseason. "It took 13 years to get it. This is my first title since my high school days at Oakland Tech. Now I've got to find a place tonight to celebrate. The team has left that up to me."

The 12–2 Vikings, and their Purple People Eaters defense, were the 10–3–1 Niners' first-round foe in Minnesota. Game day weather dipped below zero with the wind-chill factor. Brodie defied the Yukon-like temperature and set his team's mood by, shockingly, jogging onto the field in a short-sleeved jersey, showing bare skin from his chilly biceps to his frosty fingers.

Wasn't this California kid freezing in the frozen tundra? "No," he said, smiling, 43 years later as he searched for the right words. "Really good throwing."

"When I saw John that day," Hardman recalled, "I thought that was some crazy-looking shit. It was cold, man, but the effect he had on the team was positive. Anyone who had a problem with it, go back in the locker room and don't come out. That's probably my favorite game watching John. The game wasn't that close."

The 49ers won in the chill, 17–14, on Brodie's touchdown passes to wideouts Washington and Witcher, plus a Gossett field goal. The Vikings scored in the waning seconds but clearly were beaten on their turf in their kind of weather by a defense that had no nickname. "Our defense outplayed theirs—that was the key to the game," a selfless Brodie said afterwards.

Frostbite football, interestingly, favored San Francisco. "Minnesota's coach [Bud Grant] felt you had to be tough to play, so the Vikings had no heaters behind their bench," said Lon Simmons. "The teams' benches were

Len Rohde, looking for an Oakland Raider to block in 1974, helped set an NFL record in 1970 when he and line-mates Randy Beisler, Forrest Blue, Woody People, and Cas Banaszek yielded only eight quarterback sacks. (Len Rohde collection)

on the same side of the field, and some of the Vikings were coming over to use the 49ers' heaters. Well, the Vikings were dropping passes, while the 49ers really handled the game, operating beautifully."

The 49ers also benefitted from Brodie's protective front. He was sacked only eight times during the 1970 regular season, an NFL record; then he was dropped just once by the vaunted Vikings defense.

Rohde, having slimmed down from 260 to 205 pounds by 2013, assessed the individual strengths of that offensive line. "It wasn't one thing," said Rohde, beginning with himself. "I tried to be in shape and to use my hands the best I could. I tried to figure out, and be prepared for, what I was up against. It was keep the feet moving, keep your balance.

"Randy was just a good athlete, a natural athlete. Forrest was the most natural of all of us—strong, quick, and could run well. Woody wasn't too tall, but he had a low center of gravity. He had strong legs. He'd get down real low, and you couldn't get him off his feet. He was like a tree stump, and he could run, too. Cas was a very good athlete—a high school all-star basketball player in the Chicago area and a tight end at Northwestern. When the 49ers wanted to make him a tackle, he said, 'My hands are going to get all messed up.' Before you know it, he was there with the rest of us grunts."

Rohde also credited Brodie for the line's success. "John would let us know when he needed some time," said Rohde. "He'd say, 'Just give me another second or two, and I can get the ball to that guy in the corner of the end zone.'"

The 49ers were one game from the Super Bowl—and from fulfilling Brodie's preseason prophecy. Plus, the NFC championship game was in San Francisco. What could be sweeter? Dallas was the opponent. The Cowboys finished 10–4 then beat Detroit by a weird 5–0 playoff score. The 49ers would be playing their final game at Kezar Stadium, their home since 1946, before they moved to Candlestick Park in 1971.

A farewell party? Not quite. Dallas rushed for 229 yards, 143 by the enigmatic Duane Thomas, in a 17–10 victory. Brodie threw for 262 yards, including a 26-yard touchdown pass to Witcher, but that game marked the beginning of the 49ers' futile relationship with the Cowboys in the 1970s.

Simmons recalled how close the 49ers came in their Kezar farewell. "Brodie had Willard free at the goal line, but Brodie was being rushed and couldn't get the ball to him," said the broadcaster. "Then on another play, Brodie tried to throw the ball away, and Dallas made a spectacular interception."

Brodie was cheered as he left Kezar for the final time, a 180-degree change from the "Brodie, you stink" catcalls he had heard for years. He was most deserving of the cheers, having, with 24 touchdowns and 2,941 passing yards, led all NFL quarterbacks. He also had a 59.0 completion percentage and only 10 interceptions. "I've had some other years that weren't bad," he said after the '70 season, "but I felt I threw as well this year as any."

At 35, Brodie was named the NFL's Most Valuable Player for the first time, edging out Oakland's 43-year-old miracle worker, George Blanda.

Brodie, Jimmy Johnson, Dave Wilcox, and Gene Washington, with 12 touchdowns and 1,100 yards in receptions, were voted All-Pro. Rohde joined them in the Pro Bowl. Somehow, Gossett, a difference-maker who converted 21 of 31 field goals, was overlooked.

And after the most satisfactory season in their rocky 25-year football journey, the 49ers hungered for more success.

Nasty Man

Driving with the top down on his 1973 fire-red Cadillac, or "Big Red," Cedrick Hardman felt the ocean breeze on his face as he cruised down the Pacific Coast Highway on a sun-kissed southern California morning.

Hardman's own motor was running, too.

"Concussions?" he said, repeating the question. "The problem with the NFL is they don't hit any more in practice. That way, you find out who can take it. Everybody can't take it. The game isn't for everybody."

Hardman had Big Red rolling at 70 in the fast lane. He then accelerated his personal sermon on NFL head injuries. "It's a vicious game played by vicious people, and they're trying to soften it up," he said. "I never had a concussion, John Brodie never had a concussion, and we hit a lot more back then than they're doing today. That was back when the NFL was the NFL."

If Hardman's speech cut to the bone, well, he was known as "Nasty" when he terrorized NFL quarterbacks in the 1970s. "Somebody did a compilation of defensive ends with sacks on the same team," he said. "There was Carl Eller and Jim Marshall at Minnesota, John Zook and Claude Humphrey at Atlanta, Deacon Jones and Lamar Lundy with the Rams. Tommy Hart and I would have been in the top five. Tommy had 101 sacks, and I had 120."

Big Red, which had nearly 200,000 miles on the odometer in May 2013, no longer sports "NASTY" license plates; Hardman had "sacked" his own celebrity. He proudly noted that the Cadillac still had its original motor, but with a new paint job to catch the sun's rays.

"Bought this car brand-new in '73, bought it for my wife, but she never got to drive it," he said. "She's now living in Houston with my five grandchildren. We had two kids, but my daughter was shot and killed by her boyfriend when she was 19. She was breaking up with him. It's hard for me to talk about that,

Cedrick Hardman in 1976, bearing down on Los Angeles Rams quarterback James Harris, was a "Nasty" sack-master for the 49ers during three straight playoff runs, from 1970 to 1972. Hardman set a team record of 18 sacks in 1971. (Cedrick Hardman collection)

but I believe God has a plan for all of us." Hardman is a devout man despite his Nasty image. He struggled to understand his daughter's tragic death, but he finally gave it over to a higher power, mainly for peace of mind.

Forty-two years had passed, in 2013, since Hardman set a 49er single-season record with 18 sacks in 1971, still the club record for a 14-game season.

He was a 49er from 1970 to 1979, or 10 seasons, which makes him a member of the franchise's 10-year club.

He steered Big Red onto Highway 5, heading to Solana Beach for a lunchtime engagement with Brodie, who lived a half-hour away from Hardman's Laguna Beach residence. Brodie, who is white, is 13 years older than Hardman, who is black. But their relationship is like family.

"John is my favorite 49er," Hardman said, one hand on the steering wheel and his other arm straddling the front seat. "Dick Nolan was my mentor, but John was like a big brother. He took me under his wing. My transition to pro football was made a lot easier by things John did for me. He got me to take a walk with him in Miami. I see this really nice burgundy suit in a store with a matching sweater that costs $325. I wasn't making much money, but John told the salesman, 'Wrap it up.'"

Hardman gunned Big Red to 75, and he was rolling along himself, verbally. Conversing is his very nature, and his tongue wasn't about to decelerate, as it doesn't often brake easily. "Today, they send plays in," he said. "I remember when we were in a playoff game at Candlestick, and they sent a play in. John calls time out and walks to the sideline. By the way he's walking, I got off the bench because I needed to hear this. So John says to the coaches, 'Who in the fuck asked you all to send me a play? Who sent it in?' Everyone turned away, and John went back to the huddle. That was the greatest shit I had ever seen. I knew he was in charge, always in charge."

Hardman laughed, though his laugh was muffled by a soft wind coming in off the Pacific. He leaned in to the passenger. "I was fortunate to play with John my rookie year, when he was the league MVP," he said. "I'd go to different lockers to get courage, and I'd be nervous when I got to John's. But he would always say the right stuff to get my mind right. Before we beat the Rams in L. A. [in '70], John told me to stick around after the pregame meal. He wanted me to be there when he talked with [Steve] Spurrier, Nolan, and [Jim] Shofner. They came over to *John's* table. I'm sitting there in my white suit. John included me in stuff that was overwhelming for someone of his stature."

In 1971, Brodie listened to more trade talk: New England, Cincinnati, et cetera. It never seemed to end, but he now was 36, and the clock was ticking. The 49ers didn't draft a quarterback that year, but the list of players they did draft, outside of offensive lineman John Watson, didn't bode well for the team's long-term future.

Brodie was re-signed at $100,000, significantly less money than his premerger contract—but this time the 49ers were paying, not the NFL.

Nolan, NFC Coach of the Year in 1970, received a new five-year contract at $70,000 per annum. A disparity? Well, both men faced being sacked.

"The players have got to ask themselves: Are they satisfied with what they've got?" Nolan said prior to training camp. "Last year, we took a step in the right direction. But we haven't hit the ultimate—the Super Bowl."

The 49ers traded another 10-year club member, defensive tackle Roland Lakes, to the New York Giants. Then teenager Mark McFadden, son of 49ers public relations director George McFadden, quit his camp job as "The Turk." Mark's job was to inform players to bring their playbooks to Nolan, which meant they were being released; that assignment bothered him, as he had become friendly with many of those players.

Brodie got off to a terrible start in the new season, throwing four interceptions and missing seven wide-open receivers in a 20–17 loss at Atlanta. "It was a 35–10 game for us," he said, "and I ran it into 20–17 for them."

In a subsequent 38–20 win at New Orleans, Brodie showed that his age wasn't an issue. He had a balanced offense that day as the 49ers rushed for 194 yards, 82 from rookie Vic Washington. Then playing on the road for the third straight week, Brodie threw three touchdown passes, two to Ted Kwalick, in a 31–3 wipeout at Philadelphia.

"A real good tight end," Brodie said of Kwalick, "and fast. Whoom-whoom, slow it down. Boom-boom."

Got it, John.

The Niners' nicknameless defensive line of Hardman, Hart, Charlie Krueger, and Earl Edwards had a league-leading 15 sacks by this point but registered no sacks in a 20–13 loss to the Rams in the 49ers' first official game at renovated, and newly enclosed, Candlestick Park before a turnout of 44,000.

"This was one of those games you wished you never had played," wide receiver Dick Witcher said afterward of the Rams, who weren't done yet in making the 49ers wish for better outcomes. But demonstrating the respect that existed between two seasoned pros, Rams defensive tackle Merlin Olsen sacked Brodie, then reached down and picked him up—the type of sportsmanship that no longer exists in today's showboating NFL.

The 49ers won their next four games—13–0 over the Bears, 26–14 at St. Louis, 27–10 over New England, and 13–9 at Minnesota—before being stunned by New Orleans, 26–20, and Los Angeles again, 17–6, leaving the Rams at 6–3–1 to the 49ers' 6–4. "We're back to the same old stuff," said All-Pro linebacker Dave Wilcox. "We've got to win every last one of them."

The 49ers then barely escaped the theatrics of Joe Namath, who came off the bench with a dazzling performance in the Big Apple. The 49ers edged his Jets, 24–21, but only because safety Johnny Fuller picked off Broadway Joe in the end zone to seal the victory. Then the Niners' Gene Washington ran over and shook Namath's hand.

The 49ers next floundered on a Monday evening at home, losing 27–17 to Kansas City, which left San Francisco feeling discombobulated at 7–5.

"No sir, it's not over," Nolan maintained.

"I think we'll go all the way," predicted Rams defensive end Coy Bacon.

The 49ers pulled together in the nick of time, beating Atlanta, 24–3. With the Rams faltering again down the stretch, a Niners' victory over Detroit in the season finale would make them NFC West champs again. Brodie saved another classic performance for when it mattered most, passing for three touchdowns and running 10 yards on a draw play for a fourth score as the 49ers nudged the Lions, 31–27, at Candlestick.

Brodie had delivered the playoffs, personally, once again. "The only thing I run are the gimmies," he said of his touchdown romp. "But it was the only thing left to do."

Then a reporter had the temerity to ask Brodie, in the middle of a celebration, why a veteran of his stature still held the ball on placements. "Because if I didn't," he said dryly, "the ball would fall over"—the good-hands answer, and Brodie had the best hands on the team.

The 49ers, who finished 9–5 to the Rams' 8–5–1, drew Washington's 9–4–1 "Over the Hill Gang," coached by George Allen, as their first-round playoff opponent. The media's focus was the faceoff between the two former 49er Shotgun quarterbacks, Brodie and Billy Kilmer.

"I think we'll beat the 49ers," said Washington linebacker Jack Pardee. "I know our team."

As it turned out, Brodie knew his team better.

"I remember how John set up [cornerback] Pat Fischer," said Hardman. "A classic play-action pass."

Brodie connected with Gene Washington on a 78-yard touchdown pass over Fischer, one of the last white cornerbacks. But it was defensive lineman Bob Hoskins's end-zone recovery of an errant Redskins' punt snap that decided the Niners' 24–20 victory at Candlestick Park.

Once again, the 49ers drew the Cowboys, a 20–12 playoff winner over Minnesota, in the NFC championship game, this time in Dallas. And the Cowboys came out on top again, 14–3. Brodie had generated 13 points in two playoff games against Dallas's Doomsday Defense. Doomsday, indeed, for the Niners.

"We were that close," Len Rohde reflected years afterward. Close, but the proverbial celebratory cigar was being smoked once more in the Cowboys' locker room.

Lon Simmons thought that cigar was lit on a near-miss play. "The 49ers chased [quarterback] Roger Staubach for 30 yards, all the way back to the goal line, and he got away to complete a first-down pass," he said. "That was the key turning point in that game, and the 49ers never could recover from it."

The elusive Staubach wasn't known as "Roger the Dodger" for nothing. Vic Washington rushed for 86 yards that day. Hardman had 12 tackles, including twice sacking Staubach, who couldn't dodge the Nasty one. Hart and linebacker Frank Nunley each had 11 tackles. But the 49ers were corraled by the Cowboys.

The 49ers produced three All-Pros that season—Wilcox, Jimmy Johnson, and Forrest Blue. Brodie had 18 touchdown passes and 24 interceptions, a huge statistical drop from his MVP season. The Niners were aging fast. Besides Brodie at 36, Krueger was 34, and Johnson and Rohde both 33. Unless the 49ers drafted better, their time was running short.

Hardman approached Krueger after the defeat in Dallas. "I told Charlie not to worry," he said, "that we'll win the Super Bowl for him."

The 49ers would win their first Super Bowl 10 years later, although without Krueger or Hardman. Dame Fortune kept straight-arming the Textbook Tackle and sack-master Nasty.

"Even the worst of times was great," Hardman mused as he steered Big Red into Solana Beach and that lunch date with Brodie. "John was a leader. That's what he was, a leader."

27 1972

The Waiting Line

Steve Spurrier had waited five years to replace John Brodie. But even now, having turned 37, Brodie wasn't ready to cede his No. 1 status. Thus Spurrier kept waiting; in terms of his mortality as an NFL quarterback, it was like *Waiting for Godot*.

This isn't what Spurrier, or the San Francisco 49ers, anticipated. Brodie had outlasted Y. A. Tittle, and then Billy Kilmer, Bobby Waters, George Mira, and every other quarterback the organization thrust at him.

Brodie wasn't about to surrender to Spurrier, even if he did have a Heisman Trophy and Brodie didn't. Spurrier had no choice but to concentrate on his punting, but the 49ers took that away from him, too, by drafting Jim McCann in 1971. Spurrier then worked on his golf game.

"Certainly I could play for several other teams, but I'd rather be a backup on a world champion than a starter on a so-so team," Spurrier said. "People who complain about wanting to be traded never amount to anything. The 49ers have treated me well; I want to play here."

No animosity existed between Brodie and Spurrier. They ate together at camp, played golf together. But Spurrier had accepted himself as a backup, which was evident in practice. He didn't display the seriousness that coaches demand. "That's Steve's problem, sloppy practice," said 49ers' passing-game coach Jim Shofner. "You can't be lackadaisical during the week, because it can affect you on Sunday."

Spurrier agreed with Shofner about his uneven practice habits, which dated back to his college days at Florida. "I've never shown great spirit in practice," he said. "The game excites me more. Since college, I've learned to throw the ball harder and sharper. I'm throwing much better now."

Those same NFL critics who questioned Spurrier's arm strength when the

49ers drafted him No. 1 in 1967 weren't any more impressed in 1972. Shofner offered words of caution: "Steve can throw long or short. He can play and win." Big deal, if Brodie took every snap in a game, which had been the situation, basically, for five years. Thus the waiting continued for Spurrier.

Dick Nolan had this crazy idea in 1972: Brodie as a rollout quarterback. An option passer at his age? The Shotgun, now this? Brodie scowled, and Nolan's idea died. Brodie looked for receiver help, so the 49ers drafted Terry Beasley, a speed-burner from Auburn, with their first pick in '72. But that's all Beasley was, unfortunately, a speedster. He had no moves. "Those are the easiest receivers to cover," cornerback Jimmy Johnson pointed out. Thus, Beasley had no long-term future, along with another, colorfully named, rookie wideout, Allen "Jubilee" Dunbar.

Beasley made no friends in the locker room. A free-agent running back, Jimmy Brice of San Jose State, was fretting openly about surviving the final cut. An unsympathetic Beasley said, "I don't know about you, but *I've* made the team." Forty-Niner players had to pull Brice off of Beasley. Brice was cut, but he left the team a hero.

Further 49er dealings: free safety Roosevelt Taylor was traded to Washington. Trusted tight end Bob Windsor, envisioning little playing time with Ted Kwalick there, was traded to New England for a No. 1 pick. Windsor distinguished himself as a Patriot, and as a warrior, by fracturing his leg on a pass catch, then pushing off that same broken leg across the goal line.

The 49ers put together a second brother act (after the Cathcarts, Sam and Royal, in 1950) by signing defensive lineman Rolf Krueger, a free agent from the St. Louis Cardinals. He is Charlie Krueger's younger brother, by 10 years, though not nearly as talented. "It still seems impossible to me that we're teammates," said Rolf. "I was in the second grade when Charlie went off to college." Charlie reflected years afterwards on their relationship: "He was a nice young fellow. I took him swimming when he was young, but it's best that I don't say anything."

They aren't close, which became evident when Rolf didn't attend Charlie's wedding in November 1973. "Rolf is on another page," defensive line coach Paul Wiggin quipped at the wedding reception.

The Fudgehammer, ever-optimistic Frank Nunley, made a bold prediction before the 1972 season. "We won't lose a game to Los Angeles, and we're going to beat Dallas," he said confidently.

The 49ers thrashed San Diego, 34–3, in the season opener. Brodie found Gene Washington wide open for three first-half touchdowns. Len Rohde played in his 169th consecutive game, approaching Nomellini's iron man record of 174 straight.

Brodie then sprained his passing wrist in Buffalo. The Bills' O. J. Simpson, a San Francisco native, said, "I remember sitting in the kids section at Kezar Stadium, watching John Brodie. I'd jump out of the stands at the end of the game to get close to him and the other 49er players." Simpson rushed through the Niners for 133 yards as the Bills won, 27–20.

The 49ers shredded New Orleans, 37–2, at the Sugar Bowl, one week before Brodie joined Johnny Unitas and Y. A. Tittle as pro football's only 30,000-yard passers, albeit in a 31–7 loss in Los Angeles. The Fudgehammer proved a better linebacker than prognosticator.

"We know Brodie's tendencies," said Rams linebacker Isiah Robertson. "He may be right," Brodie shrugged following the 49ers' fourth straight defeat by the Rams.

Then in a 23–17 home loss to the New York Giants, Brodie suffered a high left-ankle sprain. He would be sidelined indefinitely. Spurrier had his long-awaited opportunity. With the 49ers dragging at 2–3, he also had a huge responsibility.

Spurrier's first start, against New Orleans, resulted into another 20–20 tie, just like 1970. Dave Parks was a factor again, catching two touchdown passes from Archie Manning, the father of Peyton and Eli.

The 49ers traveled to Atlanta, where Vic Washington returned the opening kickoff the distance, 98 yards. Spurrier threw for three touchdowns in a 49–14 blowout. The 49ers had found out, indeed, that Spurrier was a gamer. "We can win with Steve," said cornerback Bruce Taylor. "He's got a good arm, and he's smart."

Spurrier connected with Gene Washington on a pair of scoring strikes during a 315-yard passing day in Milwaukee, though the 49ers lost to Green Bay, 34–24. The 3–4–1 Niners rushed for a measly 21 yards, while the Packers' bruising fullback, John Brockington, ran for 133 yards and two scores.

So where would the faltering 49ers go from there, with Spurrier 1–1–1 as their starter? Nolan reshuffled the lineup, replacing Cedric Hardman with Bill Belk, Johnny Fuller with Mike Simpson, and Bruce Taylor with rookie corner Ralph McGill. Hardman's sacks had fallen off, though his demotion would be temporary.

Kwalick saved the day, and likely the season, with an incredible one-handed touchdown catch, leaping high to spear a 25-yard Spurrier throw that beat visiting Baltimore, 24–21. It was Kwalick's only catch of the game, but the talented tight end followed up with two more scores a week later in Chicago as Spurrier tied a club record with five touchdown passes during a 34–21 win. Given a chance to create a spark, Spurrier now seemed on fire.

Hadn't the Fudgehammer said the 49ers would beat Dallas? Well, the Niners won convincingly, 30–10, on Thanksgiving Day in Texas. Linebacker Skip Vanderbundt had the game of his life, returning a Dave Wilcox–induced fumble 73 yards for one touchdown and then scoring again on a 20-yard interception.

The 49ers were 6–4–1 with three games left, and those dreaded Rams coming to town, Nolan looked as if he had aged 10 years. His wife was, naturally, worried. "The pressure is terrific on a coach," said Ann Nolan. "Dick really looks tired after some games. His eyes are sunken, and you can see the circles there. Dick might sleep an hour, then he's up. He's always like this the night before a game."

How could he sleep? Nolan was dealing with an older 49er team that wasn't getting fortification from the draft. The 49ers were on a downhill slide without emergency brakes. Nolan's enemy within was scouting director Jack White. That season, 1972, might be those 49ers' last stand.

The Rams improved their record against the 49ers to 9–1–1 since 1967 with a 26–16 win at Candlestick. "I guess the Rams are just a better football team than we are," Vanderbundt conceded.

The 49ers' backs were pressed firmly against the wall heading into Atlanta. But the team delivered a 20–0 victory along with another Charlie Krueger tirade directed at Norm Van Brocklin, who now was coaching the Falcons. "He insults us a lot and openly shows his disdain and disregard for us," said Krueger. "Van Brocklin coaches through coercion. Winning today is like giving him an all-expenses-paid trip to the hospital for a proper operation."

Krueger didn't specify what kind of operation that might be, but unbeknownst to him, Van Brocklin hid a kindly, benevolent side. After his biological children had grown up, he and his wife adopted several children who needed homes. It's hard to get to know the real person, sometimes, but Van Brocklin was only crotchety as a coach.

Atlanta was 7–6 to the 49ers' 7–5–1 heading into the final week, while the Rams were 6–6–1. A win against visiting Minnesota would notch the 49ers their third straight NFC Western Division title. Going into that game, Spurrier was 5–2–1 as a starter. But with nine minutes left against the Vikings, the 49ers trailed, 17–7, and were backed up on their one-yard line. Brodie, who hadn't played in two months, replaced Spurrier. He once again gripped the dramatic aspect of football by the throat and strangled it: he threw a touchdown pass to Gene Washington and then hit Dick Witcher in the back of the end zone with 25 seconds left, to win, 20–17.

"That's probably my favorite 49er moment," said play-by-play man Lon Simmons, "Brodie's coming off the bench against Minnesota with two scoring drives, the first one 99½ yards, to get the 49ers into the playoffs."

The 49er Faithful, whom Brodie had occasionally flipped off in the past after hearing pregame introduction booing, carried him off the field on their shoulders.

The high and the mighty.

"Brodie's got to be the coolest guy in the world," said guard Woody Peoples.

As cool as the ice in his veins.

"Brodie has to be the whole key—he won it," added Wilcox.

So 8–5–1 San Francisco would play—who else?—10–4 Dallas, only in a divisional playoff, two games from the Super Bowl. Although Spurrier finished fifth among NFC passers, Nolan chose Brodie to start against the Cowboys. Life returned to the way it had been. "I made my decision on years of experience," Nolan said. "Yes, momentum figured into it, too."

Spurrier, who had beaten Dallas on Thanksgiving Day, was upset by the change, but he accepted it nobly. "I'm disappointed," he said, "but Dick said at the start of the year that he would start one guy, and if he was going bad, he'd put the other guy in and go with him. He's stuck with that."

Dallas's starting quarterback, Craig Morton, who had played across the bay at UC–Berkeley, made no bones about the game's outcome. "I guarantee you the Cowboys will beat the 49ers," he said. He was right, though he wouldn't be on the field when the outcome was decided.

Vic Washington returned the opening kickoff all the way, 97 yards, and the 49ers built a 28–13 third-quarter lead at Candlestick Park as fullback Larry Schreiber plunged for three touchdowns. Then, by growing extra conservative, the 49ers allowed Dallas to rally behind Roger Staubach, who replaced an ineffective Morton and delivered 17 unanswered points in a 30–28 Cowboys victory—a win the 49ers fumbled away in the game's final minutes.

Preston Riley only had to recover Toni Fritsch's onside kick, and the victory was San Francisco's. But Riley misplayed the ball, and Mel Renfro fell on it for Dallas. Staubach's ensuing 10-yard scoring bullet to Ron Sellers against rookie strong safety Windlan Hall, subbing for injured veteran Mel Phillips, broke San Francisco's heart with 52 seconds left.

"Nolan wouldn't let Brodie throw the ball in the fourth quarter," Simmons groused. "I told my producer, Stu Smith, that the game was going to come down to an onside kick. Sure enough, it did, and the 49ers didn't recover it."

Three straight postseason games against Dallas, and three straight failures. And Preston Riley, who had just been named the 49ers' special teams player of the year, would become, with one unforgettable bobble, *the most stigmatized 49er in history.*

"Preston Riley just made the last of a whole bunch of mistakes by the team," Hardman said in Riley's defense. "That's the one everybody remembers the most, but he was a good guy and a good receiver."

Rohde still worries about Riley, and how that kickoff mishap may have affected his long-term well-being. "It's so unfortunate," said Rohde. "That's the way it is in life, I guess, how the ball turns. I kind of feel for Preston. I hope he's forgotten about it, instead of having it sit on his mind all these years. You hear the name Preston Riley, and you say, 'Oh, yeah.'"

But 42 years after his fumble, Riley still can't forget. "I've never gotten over it," he said on October 21, 2014. "It has haunted me every day of my life. I don't talk about it a lot, but just talking about it now, I'm about to break up, to lose it. I've been treated for depression a couple of times. I don't like to take any kind of prescription medicine, and I didn't like the way that [depression] medicine made me feel, but I may have to redo some counseling."

Mentally, Riley still can see that onside kick bouncing toward him. "I thought I had the ball in my hands," he said, "but it took a weird bounce over my hands and hit me on the right shoulder pad, and bounced right in front of me."

Nothing can take his mind off that fumble, or the follow-up play that might have reversed his suffering all these years later. "After that onside kick, we still had a chance to win the game," he said. "I caught a pass from John that put us in field-goal range. But [tackle] Cas Banaszek was holding on the play, and it took us out of field-goal range. Well, you can call holding on an offensive lineman every play. But, then, the clock ran out. God knows, I was praying that we would win, but we didn't."

How often have others reminded Riley of that fumble? "There have been a few people over the years that remember it and would say something," he said. "And I've seen it a couple of times on TV. It's mostly just in my mind. That was a big deal, a *big* deal. I have no doubt in my mind that the fumble is why the 49ers traded me."

The 49ers, in 1973, sent Riley to New Orleans, where he was cut by the Saints. He was with Atlanta in 1974 but was released there, too. After football, he did police work for 10 years while building a construction business; at 66, he still was doing construction near his home in Gatlinburg,

Tennessee, when interviewed for this book. "I feel so bad, a lot of sadness and remorse in letting my teammates down," he said. "Golly, I loved all of them. We were headed for the freakin' Super Bowl." Well, not quite yet; there still was the conference championship game to be played. But, sadly, such is the life of Riley.

After the 1972 season, five 49ers—Gene Washington, Kwalick, Forrest Blue, Wilcox, and Jimmy Johnson—were named All-NFL. In Washington's two All-Pro seasons, '70 and '72, he averaged 20.8 and 20.0 yards a catch, numbers that Jerry Rice would have been proud to own. Tommy Hart, with 17 sacks in '72, wasn't even a Pro Bowl selection.

But, ironically, the 49ers' most significant games from their first 26 years were two postseason *defeats:* the collapse against Detroit in 1957, and the Dallas debacle in 1972.

And that third successive playoff loss to the Cowboys, more shocking than the previous two, would haunt the 49ers the rest of that decade.

28 1973
Stroke of Bad Luck

John Brodie and Cedrick Hardman had just finished having lunch in 2013 when a stranger passed by their restaurant table and instantly recognized the former All-Pro quarterback, who had been retired 40 years and was living 400 miles south of San Francisco.

"How you doing, John?" the person asked.

"Beautiful," Brodie replied with a smile.

Beautiful, indeed. Brodie felt good to be talking, and walking. Because in 2000, doctors had predicted that he would have difficulty doing either function again. He suffered a severe stroke that year, which paralyzed his right side and limited his sentences to one word, usually an expletive— as he felt hostility toward the cruel fate that had beset him like a Deacon Jones sack.

Then he stopped being angry and went to work. His competiveness took control. He improved his conversation and his gait. He lectured himself daily, because there was no way he would concede defeat. When Brodie decides to fight back, regardless of the steep odds, he won't give up until he either wins or, at last resort, settles for a tie. If an Arctic afternoon in Minnesota in 1970 didn't stop him from producing the 49ers' first postseason victory, why should a stroke hold him back?

So he moved from his California desert home in LaQuinta to Solana Beach in southern California to receive regular therapy treatments. He also traveled eight times to Russia for stem cell treatments. Gradually, he saw improvement.

Today, he communicates with greater ease, though his speech remains limited. Never the reticent one, he still can make his point with one word, or

No 49er player lasted longer than quarterback John Brodie, photographed here in 1973, who spent 17 seasons with the franchise. Brodie, the NFL's Most Valuable Player in 1970, is deserving of Pro Football Hall of Fame recognition. (John Brodie collection)

one fragmented sentence, better than some people can with a whole paragraph. His new game plan: Win back his life through sheer determination.

Brodie's right arm is disabled, so he isn't playing golf, though he hasn't given up on the idea entirely. Friends say he can still crush a golf ball with one arm. Playing 18 holes might be his next challenge, and he reacts best when challenged.

"When I'm with him, I feel stronger," said daughter Cammie Brodie, one of John and Sue Brodie's four children.

Brodie's notable competitiveness reached new heights when he became the only pro athlete from another sport to win a professional tour golf championship. While a 49er, Brodie won the Northern California amateur golf championship. He paired with Bob Rosburg to win the Bing Crosby National Pro-Am team title at Pebble Beach. Brodie played in two U.S. Open golf tournaments, in 1959 and 1981, a record for the longest gap in between qualifications. And then he scored his "first and only" by winning a senior golf tournament, the 1991 Security Pacific Senior Classic, defeating Chi Chi Rodriguez and George Archer in a three-way playoff.

Brodie is immersed in his rehabiliation, which explains where he is living presently, Solana Beach. His wife, a real estate agent in LaQuinta, several hours away, joins him whenever she can. Though Brodie has family nearby, he can't drive himself to see them.

Wearing beachlike clothing in May 2013, Brodie spoke about his post-stroke progress, his athletic career, and his life. His responses came quickly, sometimes bluntly, often clipped.

"What was it like when the stroke happened?"

"Black. Boom. Jesus Christ! No good."

"You must have been frightened."

"Duh."

"Are you proud of how hard you've fought back?"

"Oh, shit, yes."

"How much better are you?"

"One hundred percent."

"Is more progress needed?"

"Oh, yes. Speech . . . really special."

"Do you feel a special pride in being the longest-playing 49er, at 17 years?"

"Pride, yeah. Oakland Tech, Stanford, 49ers. . . . a real good deal."

"Your entire sports career, that's true, was spent in the San Francisco Bay Area, despite all those trade rumors. But would playing elsewhere have been agreeable to you?"

"I don't know," he said. "[Dick] Nolan, crummy guy."

Hardman: "Johnnnnnnn."

"Did you have a communication problem with Nolan?"

"Yes, thank you."

"Was it related to Nolan's insistence that he had two No. 1 quarterbacks, you and Steve Spurrier?"

"Yes, cut it out."

"Do you feel Nolan blamed you for defeats?"

"Oh, yes. No-good bastard. Cut it out."

"But was your toughest time as a 49er spent during the 1960s?"

"Oh, yes. We had beautiful passing."

"You had Bernie Casey, Dave Parks, and Clifton McNeil to throw to—all quality receivers."

"No, me, Parks, and John David Crow. Then go away."

"Do you mean the 49ers let those two slip away?"

"Yes, cut it out. David Parks, a really beautiful player. Go away. John David Crow. That, too. Christ!"

"Would holding onto Parks have made a difference?"

"Oh, yes. In 1968, really good players. Goddamn! Gene Washington and Parks [together]? Go away."

"Outside of Nolan, did you enjoy your 49er head coaches?"

"No. No. No. No. A really good coach—Shofner."

"You mean Jim Shofner, a 49er assistant, would have made a good head coach?"

"Oh, God, yes."

"What was Red Hickey like as a coach?"

"No good. Go away."

"Did you like Hickey more than Nolan?"

"Yes, Nolan no good. Go away."

Hardman: "Johnnnnnnn."

"You've called Hugh McElhenny the NFL's greatest breakaway back. What about 49er teammate Joe 'The Jet' Perry?"

"Awesome."

"Do you have a favorite game as a 49er?"

"I don't care. But 1970 . . . Vikings. Really good throwing."

"Before 1970, 49er fans booed you, threw objects at you, poured beer on you. How did you survive such abuse?"

"Smart," he said, pointing at his head.

John Riley Brodie was plenty smart. One doesn't survive 17 years with one franchise on pure athleticism. And one doesn't recover from a debilitating stroke without a sharp mind.

Brodie found ways to win in spite of the 49ers' drafting foibles, a defense that failed to stifle opponents consistently, and his own inconsistencies. He never professed that he was perfect. But 1973 presented two new challenges for Brodie—a team that had lost its momentum, and a celebrated quarterbacking career, college and pro, that was fading into the fog.

"We haven't peaked or come close to peaking," Nolan said before the '73 season. "Our best years should be ahead of us." It always behooves a coach to sound optimistic. Certainly, Nolan wouldn't want 49ers' management, or 49er fans, to think the opposite, especially after a third consecutive weak draft, and another raising of ticket prices, this time to $8.50.

Cornerback Mike Holmes was the 49ers' first draft pick in 1973 but missed his rookie year with an injury. He then spent two seasons with the Niners before disappearing as yet another Jack White mistake.

When Preston Riley, the forever fall guy, was traded to New Orleans in '73, Brodie was incensed. Nothing had changed in 2013. "A crummy deal," he said. "Nolan, fuck you."

Brodie even blamed Nolan for Dallas's comeback win in '72, contending that Nolan grew conservative in the second half by strictly running the ball, and thereby killing momentum. "Yes, what's the deal?" he said.

More Dallas fallout, besides Riley's leaving, ensued. Nolan traded defensive lineman Earl Edwards to Buffalo and got a weak return in running back Randy Jackson. The offensive line was made over as John Watson was promoted over Randy Beisler at guard.

And there couldn't be another 49er season without a Brodie trade rumor, this time to Cincinnati. Brodie said he'd retire first. At 38, that was becoming a viable option.

Spurrier, in the interim, visited an eye doctor who convinced him, "If you mentally picture a ball spiraling as you throw, you'll throw a better pass. I tried it, and he's right." Spiraling or downspiraling? Spurrier still was No. 2.

The 49ers opened the 1973 season in intense tropical heat in Miami against the Super Bowl champion Dolphins, who sweated out a 21–13 victory. Brodie benched himself in the second half, completely drained. "I had nothing left," he said, "like someone had just pulled the plug." Other 49ers received oxygen on the flight home and upon landing were hospitalized with stomach and leg cramps.

The Nolan era looked sapped as well, but Bruce Gossett saved the day in Denver with five field goals, including a 37-yarder with 26 seconds left, for a 36–34 victory.

The 49ers obtained wide receiver Danny Abramowicz from New Orleans for a wasted No. 2 pick. For this onetime 49er nemesis, and Saints' "horse" on offense, was ready for pasture.

"Losing to the Rams would make it a long season," said Nolan. The Rams then won in a rout, 40–20, at Candlestick.

Panic time had arrived. Nolan made wholesale lineup changes before the 49ers edged Atlanta, 13–9. More changes would be required after starting fullback Larry Schreiber was lost to knee surgery, and all-purpose halfback Jimmy Thomas required shoulder surgery.

Nolan decided to bench Brodie, who hadn't been effective. Spurrier put up big passing numbers—31 of 48 for 320 yards—even though the 49ers fell, 17–13, to visiting Minnesota.

Brodie started the following week and directed a 40–0 rout of New Orleans at Candlestick. After he retired for the day, Brodie put on an Oakland A's baseball cap in honor of his hometown team, which beat the New York Mets that day to wrap up its second of three consecutive World Series titles.

Things then got wacky in Ninerville: Nolan announced he was sticking with Spurrier. That was it for Brodie. On October 25, 1973, he announced his retirement, effective the end of the season. The team was Spurrier's, at last, but he passed for 12 yards—12 yards!—in a 17–3 home loss to Atlanta.

Wackier still, Brodie was reinstated as starter. But 25 years of chucking footballs, starting at Oakland Tech, had worn out his passing arm. He tossed a team-record six interceptions in a 30–20 loss in Detroit. He threw like the old quarterback he was.

More wackiness ensued. "Singing" Joe Reed, who had a melodic country music voice but an average passing arm, was given his shot at quarterback. He threw two interceptions without a touchdown during a 33–9 wipeout loss to the Redskins in Washington. Vic Washington threw a postgame locker-room temper tantrum over lack of playing time.

Reed failed again in Los Angeles as the Rams toyed once more with the 49ers, 31–13. An emotional scene occurred after the game. Charlie Krueger and Rams guard Joe Scibelli had pounded on each other for 15 seasons, three times a year, including an exhibition and a home-and-home series. Remarkably, in all that time, they hadn't spoken to each other. But at this last match-up, Krueger chased down Scibelli with something on his mind.

"I went up, shook his hand, and said, 'Joe, you've always been square. I'll see you. I'm going to the house,'" Krueger said. "It lasted 15, 20 seconds, and it was over. Joe would die much later of cancer, but he was a pretty decent human, and neither of us was leaving the field crippled." Not then, anyway.

Wacky is as wacky does. After that latest Rams' shellacking, Nolan went back to Spurrier, who sparked two victories—20–6 over Green Bay and 38–28 over Philadelphia.

Then Spurrier fell apart again, this time in New Orleans. The Saints won, 16–0, with a weird conclusion. On the field, Saints owner John Mecom cussed out Abramowicz, who took off after him but was restrained. The 49ers had difficulty catching anything or anybody that day.

More frustrations loomed. The 49ers lost six of their last eight games, to finish 5–9. Brodie asked for, and Nolan agreed, to let him start his farewell game. But he pulled an arm muscle that week and lasted slightly more than a quarter before removing himself as visiting Pittsburgh coasted, 37–14. All the wattage had fizzled out of a once-electric passing arm.

"John Brodie," saluted Steelers defensive tackle Tom Keating, a former Oakland Raider, "is the master of the screen pass. Nobody could set up the screen like Brodie."

"Brodie deserves to be in the Pro Football Hall of Fame," said Frank Nunley, Brodie's 49er teammate. "He ranks right up there with Johnny Unitas and other (Hall of Famers). Brodie was a great leader, and one of the most competitive people I've ever known. He was the NFL's MVP in 1970, and he got the 49ers to their first postseason—three times in a row."

Approaching 78 in 2013, and assessing his medical situation, Brodie still contemplated what caused his debilitating stroke. He had embraced mind-altering Scientology toward the end of his 49er career, when his passing arm hurt, and doctors couldn't find a cure. He truly believes that Scientology mended the arm.

Scientology preaches a technique called "assists"—based on a belief that the spirit can solve the body's difficulties better than regular physical examinations, by putting the spirit in communication with the body, thereby alleviating injury, trauma, and discomfort. That's what it preaches, anyway. A stroke can happen in various ways, but members of Brodie's own family question Scientology's methods, feeling that his eschewing doctors might have led to the stroke.

Does Brodie believe Scientology factored into his stroke?

"No," he said after a short pause.

Regardless of how he was stricken, Brodie didn't give up after the stroke; instead he attacked it with vigor.

"He had so much fun before he had the stroke," Hardman said, grinning, "God had to strike him down." Seated across the same table, Brodie broke up laughing.

Brodie's final season as a 49er didn't end the way he would have liked, but it was more *costly* for six teammates. Hardman, Stan Hindman, Nunley, Bruce Taylor, Vic Washington, and John Isenbarger claimed that they were swindled out of a combined $233,000 by a local investor, Bob Bartels, who then did jail time for his shady dealings.

Some good did come from the 1973 season, however: Dave Wilcox was voted All-Pro for the fifth time, and Forrest Blue for the third time.

But the team's ultimate winner was Krueger, who retired with Brodie. Nineteen years later, Krueger became the first NFL player to win an injury settlement against the league. "I don't know how I won it," Krueger said, in 2013, of his knee-injury suit, "because it was rigged that you wouldn't win, with three league representatives and three player representatives seated across the same table. So it was always a 3–3 tie. The suit started in 1980, and I won in 1992 in the California State Supreme Court.

"It was a long, hard fight. If I had lost, I would have been a bitter mother-fucker. But I want you to know that I had a great amount of respect for Dr. [Lloyd] Milburn [the 49ers' team physician]. He was a player's friend, but my suit affected our relationship."

Nevertheless, Krueger believed his knee injury was misdiagnosed. Had he known earlier how damaged the knee was, he emphasized, he would have retired sooner. He currently uses a cane every day. Even a significant weight loss—he's down from 300 pounds to 207—hasn't alleviated the damage. He is crippled for the rest of his life.

The money settlement didn't make the leg feel any better.

29 1974

Look, Toto, Kansas

"We're looking for a top-flight running back," Dick Nolan projected in 1974 while attemping to stop the 49ers' free fall. Simultaneously, he was searching for his own parachute.

Then draft-room misguider Jack White, who earned his paycheck this time around, presented Nolan with two top-flight running backs. Wilbur Jackson, a six-foot-one, 210-pound power runner from Alabama, and the first African American to play for Bear Bryant, was taken with the 10th pick of the first round. Then Delvin Williams, a six-foot-one, 197-pound jack-rabbit from Kansas, and the perfect complement to Jackson, was drafted in the second round. Wedged in between the two, just ahead of Williams in round two, was tight end Keith Fahnhorst of Minnesota, who would develop into one of the 49ers' premier offensive tackles.

"I was really excited to be a 49er," Williams said. "My junior year of college, I tore my hamstring. And I thought if I ever get a chance to play professional football, I hope it's in a warm climate. Then I was picked to play in the East-West Shrine Football Game. Flying into San Francisco, I saw the area and the hills, and I thought, 'Wouldn't this be great?'"

Well, in pancake-flat Kansas, a haystack looks hilly. "I was a little ticked off that I wasn't drafted in the first round," added Williams. "But when I got drafted in the second round by San Francisco, I said, 'Thank you.'"

The 49ers would say thank you, too, in two years when Williams emerged as a 1,000-yard rusher. But in 1974, NFL rookies weren't certain that there would be a football season. "There was a players' strike," said Williams. "The striking veterans hadn't reported to camp, and though they didn't hassle the rookies, I broke my wrist at San Diego in the first exhibition game. So I was worried. I had alternated with Wilbur, and I knew he would play more because he was a No. 1 draft choice. Even as a second-rounder, you're trying to figure things out."

Nolan was uncertain about things as well, possibly sensing that he had a football team on its way downhill. And so he approached Williams with what amounted to an ultimatum. "Breaking my wrist was a good experience, because it taught me about the business," said Williams. "I was struggling to stay, and Nolan asked me about the cast. 'When are you going to take it off?' he said. That was an indicator to me that Nolan was pressing. So I took it off and fumbled in the season opener at New Orleans.

Ted Kwalick was a superb pass-catching tight end for the 49ers in the early 1970s before jumping to the fly-by-night World Football League, thereby short-circuiting his pro football career. 1972 drawing by Dave Beronio. (Dave Beronio collection)

Somebody grabbed my arm, and I had no strength in the wrist. Dick said, 'That's no excuse.' He had a permanent bad wrist himself, but some of the 49er veterans said, 'It must be the vodka.' Dick, though, was a good man."

The NFL's labor issue, mercifully, was settled prior to the regular season. Then Jackson led all 49er rushers with 705 yards (4.1 average). He was the *Sporting News*'s Rookie of the Year. Williams, fourth on the team in '74 with 201 yards, would lead the 49ers in rushing the next three years, including a then club-record of 1,203 yards in 1976 (4.9 average).

John Brodie's departure factored into the 49ers' disintegration as a playoff team and winner. Nolan tried to find an adequate replacement for Brodie, but five quarterbacks would start for San Francisco in 1974, a death knell regarding the head coach's future.

Then the fly-by-night World Football League blew into town and signed up four 49ers: Ted Kwalick, John Isenbarger, Jim Sniadecki, and Dick Witcher, beginning with the 1975 season. The incensed 49ers traded Sniadecki to St. Louis, which had acquired Ken Willard earlier. Witcher and Isenbarger were dealt to Chicago for kick returner Cecil Turner. Kwalick was made to stay, cruelly.

More problems arose. Vic Washington's anger developed into open hostility. He shouted at Nolan during a lunch break at training camp. Washington was joined by Larry Schreiber in blaming Nolan for the team's "communication problems."

"It happened during two-a-days, and I couldn't believe it. You don't talk to coaches that way," said Williams. "But I liked Vic. He was the kind of guy who fought for what he believed. He later died while fighting the league for his benefits. He and Larry were very good friends." Added Cedrick Hardman, "Vic and I were tight. "If you're going to fight in an alley, you'd want Vic with you."

The 49ers hurriedly traded Washington to Houston for a No. 1 pick (1976) and a No. 3 (1977). As a parting shot, he called Nolan a "dictator." Schreiber lasted another year with the 49ers, but he wasn't the same fullback following knee surgery.

With volatile Vic gone and Doug "Goober" Cunningham lost for the season with a back injury, Jackson's and Williams's importance as running backs increased. Frank Nunley also asked to be traded, but he was denied. Two players traded for, Randy Jackson and Turner, were both cut. Trying to get somewhere fast, the 49ers were going nowhere faster.

The biggest 49er news was the demotion, and phasing out, of Kwalick. He saw sparse action in '74, as he was feeling mothballed. The 49ers brought in tight end Tom Mitchell from Baltimore; a grizzled veteran of 30 with a single-engine pilot's license, Mitchell stepped in as an instant starter. Nolan denied the move was made to punish Kwalick for jumping leagues in '75. "No, sir," Nolan said. "It happens right there on the field. Tom's played better and more consistently [than Kwalick], and I expect him to continue to do so. He's a tough dude."

Williams agreed with Nolan that the change was merited. "Kwalick was proud of his Polish heritage, and being a tough guy. I could see his potential with the catches he made in practice," said Williams. "But I could turn upfield with Mitch, the best blocking tight end I played with. He smoked, drank, and played a helluva game of golf. Kwalick worked for Hyatt, which sent a limousine for him when we played in Atlanta. He stayed in their suite. He didn't room with the players."

Nonetheless, Kwalick was the superior deep threat. Blocking aside, there wasn't a tight end anywhere in '74 who was more athletic than the Penn State alum. Now, if only a 49er quarterback could be found to throw the deep ball.

The 49ers, a work in progress, also had defensive line issues. Bob Hoskins, who replaced the traded Earl Edwards at tackle, was diagnosed with Hodgkin's disease. He played on, doggedly. "Bob always looked like he was angry," said Williams. "He was an intimidator, the angry guy on the team. He would throw you down in practice, more like rookie hazing. I stood up to Bob. Vic Washington was more committed to his toughness than Bob, who was a radical, but really a teddy bear."

The defensive front was thin in other ways. Stan Hindman, who left the team in 1971 in pursuit of a career in art and architecture, returned in 1973 at the team's behest. But he was shifted from end to tackle, where his 235 pounds, better suited for speed than power, proved a liability. "I think Stan was a better artist than a football player," said Hardman.

One position was settled for the time being. Steve Spurrier was, finally, the No. 1 quarterback. "Knowing that the job is his for the first time will make him a better quarterback," said Nolan. "People forget the year he had in 1972."

What wasn't forgotten: Brodie wrested the job back in '72, and Spurrier wasn't exactly gangbusters in '73. And then his '74 coming-out party was called off when he separated his passing shoulder against the Los Angeles Rams in the preseason finale.

Singing Joe Reed was elevated to starter. Tom Owen, a 13th-round pick in '74, would be his backup. Left-handed Dennis Morrison, a 14th-round choice in '73, was slotted as No. 3 quarterback. Nolan looked around for a rabbit's foot.

The 49ers, remembering the unbearably hot Miami opener the previous year, stayed in Lafayette, Louisiana, the week before they opened in New Orleans, acclimating to the late-summer heat and gulf humidity. Singing Joe then threw three interceptions, but the 49ers survived when Saints punter Donnie Gibbs inexplicably fumbled away a perfect snap deep in his territory. Sammy Johnson's nine-yard run with just under two minutes left gave the Niners a lucky 17–13 victory. The Saints then cut Gibbs.

The 49ers returned to a similar climate a week later, beating host Atlanta, 16–10. Reed struggled again—7 out of 22 for 101 yards, one score, and his fourth interception in two games. Bruce Gossett's three field goals saved the 49ers' bacon.

Reed made it five interceptions in three games as Cincinnati thumped the Niners, 21–3, in San Francisco. All three 49er quarterbacks played the following week; statistically, a combined 7 of 20 for 128 yards and two interceptions (Owen and Morrison) during a 34–9 stomping by the visiting St. Louis Cardinals. Reed hit Gene Washington with a 58-yard touchdown pass.

Forty-Niners president Lou Spadia (from right) chats with general manager Jack White, an unidentified person, and Rick Morabito, son of onetime team owner Vic Morabito, during training camp at Santa Barbara in 1972. (San Francisco 49ers archives)

Nolan, now hunting for a four-leaf clover, started Morrison in Detroit. The overmatched left-hander completed only 17 of 40 passes for 171 yards, plus three interceptions, in a 17–13 loss. But he wasn't entirely to blame as 14th-round quarterbacks, as a rule, don't debut as starters before God and Howard Cosell on Monday night.

Morrison, mercifully, received a second start in Los Angeles, but departed early with bruised ribs during another thrashing by the Rams, 37–14. A month later, the 49ers cut him. He wasn't the only quarterback to leave: Singing Joe Reed would exercise his vocal cords next in Detroit.

The 49ers had reached the crisis stage. They traded for 35-year-old quarterback Norm Snead from the New York Giants. But Snead couldn't stop the hemorrhaging either; the 49ers would lose a franchise-record seven consecutive games.

Snead merely was a Band-Aid. The bottom had dropped out in two years, but team president Lou Spadia gave Nolan a vote of confidence. "Dick's job is very secure," said Spadia. Why not? Jack White was largely responsible for the 49ers' descent with inept drafting over a three-year period. "He fooled my father," said Louise Spadia-Beckham. "Dad said White was his biggest hiring mistake."

White selected UCLA defensive tackle Bill Sandifer as the 49ers' second No. 1 draft pick after Jackson in '74. Sandifer tore up a knee in the College All-Star Game. But during rehabilitation, he mentioned that he had had "loose-jointed, sloppy knees" *prior* to his injury—a medical issue that had escaped White. Sandifer wouldn't ever be a factor for the 49ers.

"We had three great seasons," Frank Nunley, "then guys retired, and I don't think we replaced our great players with great players. And Dick didn't take to the losing very well; it affected his personality somewhat. He was a class guy, but he didn't know how to run a business. He loved coaching, but he liked playing better."

Spadia recognized, eventually, that White, not Nolan, was mainly at fault. A good coach doesn't turn bad overnight, unless he repeatedly fails because of bad draft picks and bad roster moves. But the coach, usually, pays the biggest price.

After the 49ers' seven-game funk, Spurrier returned to the team just as Snead was dealing with a sore knee and a sore shoulder. But Spurrier returned as No. 2; Owen now was No. 1. The 49ers won their next two games by a shocking 61–0 margin. Owen threw a 68-yard touchdown pass to Terry Beasley, of all people, and a 20-yard scoring strike to the resuscitated Kwalick in a 34–0 win at Chicago. Owen then connected with Gene Washington twice for touchdowns, and a plodding Manfred Moore scored on an 88-yard punt return, beating visiting Atlanta, 27–0.

So what was those 49ers' true identity? On a miserably cold Sunday in Cleveland, it became clearer. Owen threw five interceptions as the Browns won, 7–0. Flounderers once more.

A few days later, Spurrier demanded a trade after Nolan said he was sticking with Owen, who then split time with Snead in a 7–6 squeaker over Chicago. Even winning was boring.

Owen went the distance as the 49ers defeated New Orleans, 35–21, in the season-ender. Owen threw 184 passes that year, and Spurrier, the anointed starter, three. But by winning four of their last five, the Niners finished 6–8, a slight improvement from the year before, and enough incentive to save Nolan's job.

Two more 49er veterans bowed out. Left tackle Len Rohde retired after 15 seasons with a team-record 208 consecutive games. And future Hall of Fame outside linebacker Dave Wilcox, his knees screaming, said good-bye after 11 seasons.

"The guys I had the most respect for were the right side of the defense: Tommy Hart, Dave Wilcox, Mel Phillips, and Jimmy Johnson," said Williams. "I got to know Jimmy real well, which I thought was a privilege because nobody got close to him. They thought he was a wired guy—the last guy to get to practice, the first guy out of the locker room.

"Jimmy just had his own way of doing things, but those guys were consummate professionals. Dave Wilcox wouldn't practice all week with his knee problems. He'd sit by his locker in a lawn chair, smoke a cigar, and then play the whole game on Sunday. Tommy hardly ever said a word. Mel played with two broken arms. On offense, the players I admired were Woody [Peoples] and Lenny [Rohde]."

Peoples spent 10 seasons with the 49ers through 1977 before moving on to Philadelphia, where he started on the Eagles' 1980 Super Bowl team. He may have been short and squat, but he made the Pro Bowl multiple times. "There are big pieces of meat in the locker room, but that's all they are, pieces of meat," Brodie once said. "Then there are roly-poly guys like Woody Peoples who can play."

The 49ers of the mid-1970s could have used a few more roly-poly studs like Woody Peoples, not to mention a much younger John Brodie.

30 1975

Ladies in Charge

They were unlike all other NFL owners and unlike each other, really. Josephine Verone Morabito Heintzelman Fox was the stay-at-home type, while her sister-in-law, Elizabeth Jane Eddy Morabito, was the party girl.

They were co-owners of the San Francisco 49ers, a unique distinction: There wasn't another franchise in an American major-league professional sport that had two ladies sitting atop its organizational chart.

Lou Spadia, the 49ers president, ensured that the media didn't have free access to the ladies, who inherited their dual ownership after their husbands—the previous owners and half-brothers—had passed away seven years apart.

But in 1975, Spadia lowered the drawbridge over the moat that surrounded the widows' football castle by permitting the author, at the time a 49ers' beat writer for the *Oakland Tribune,* to cross over the bridge.

"I've never looked at ourselves as something special," said Josephine, or Josie, the wife of Tony Morabito, who succumbed to heart failure in 1957. "It's just something that happened, and we've hung on. It's no ego trip, believe me."

"I'm not a women's libber," added Jane, the wife of Vic Morabito, who died of a similar heart condition in 1964. "I don't want to do a man's job. I want them to do the hard work. It's a man's world, let's face it."

The Morabito ladies were content to stay in the background and let Spadia take care of league matters. "Lou is like the person who started sweeping at the plant and wound up running it," said Josie. "He's a very honest man, a qualified man. He has our best interests at heart. We have an organization that works very well together."

Thus Josie and Jane preferred less active roles. "We don't decide who's playing quarterback," said Josie. "We're called in on major decisions, like when we hire a new coach. On the whole, we go along with Lou's decisions almost all the time. When we hire someone, we give him the responsibility and the authority."

Josie didn't mind being called a homemaker or seamstress, because that's who she was, and she was adept at both. "My mom taught grammar school before she married my dad," said daughter Josephine Ann "Midge" Morabito Tassi. "Then she stayed at home and took good care of us, made sure we got to school and back. She was very supportive, helped us with our schoolwork, and made some of our clothes. My mom and my aunt were very different: My mom was more reserved. Jane said what she wanted to say."

Jane accepted that comparison. "Even though Josie and I are very close, we're exactly opposite," she said. "Josie's a homemaker—what a fabulous cook!—while I'm very outgoing."

Bob St. Clair's time with the 49ers (1953–64) overlapped the ownerships, and the obituaries, of the Morabito men. The giant tackle got to know the ladies, too. "Josephine was like a mother to me," he said. "But Jane was kind of on the wild side. She would dance with us. One time after a game, she was dancing with us on top of the table. She was fun."

Jane wasn't just fun; she was active. "Monday, I help retarded citizens," she said. "Tuesday is golf day; I have a 23 handicap. Wednesday, it's bridge. Thursday, it's either golf or dominoes. Friday, I go to the hairdresser. And my weekends are football. I'm very proud of the fact that I'm in football, and I would never get out. I love every second of it."

Josie married twice after Tony died. Her second husband wasn't faithful, but she found happiness again in a third marriage. Jane never remarried. "Being a widow has made me very independent," said Jane. "How many women in my position can do the things and go to the places I go? If I had gotten out of football, I'd have to get married to do the things I do now."

The widows attended NFL meetings, but didn't sit in on the actual meetings. Spadia took care of all official business, while Jane played golf and Josie attended fashion shows. "I don't think I'd add anything to the meetings," said Jane. "That's Lou's job."

Jane passed away in 1992, and Josie in 1995, but their legacy is secure. However, in 1975, their franchise was hardly secure, for Spadia had an important decision looming. A third straight losing season would endanger Dick Nolan's chances of remaining as head coach. How dire was the situation? The 49ers had no games televised nationally in '75; no Howard Cosell, Frank

Gifford or "Dandy" Don Meredith on Monday night. The 49ers no longer were an attractive product in the minds of TV executives. The mighty had fallen—hard!

Another 49er roster shake-up occurred, though some of it was positive. The team had to make room for two drafted linemen, Jimmy Webb (No. 1) and Cleveland Elam (No. 4B), both of whom joined Cedrick Hardman and Tommy Hart on the new "Gold Rush" defensive front.

This meant two defensive linemen had to go. Rolf Krueger retired at 28 without much choice; he wasn't even a microchip off the old block. Stan Hindman retired again, permanently, saying candidly, "I didn't have a very good season." The failed Terry Beasley also retired with 18 receptions over three years. Danny Abramowicz was traded to Washington; his NFL record of catching passes in 105 consecutive games had ended in San Francisco.

The 49ers waived Bruce Gossett, whose field-goal accuracy dipped below .500 (11 of 24) in 1974. Jack White then drafted kicker Steve Mike-Mayer (No. 3B). The 49ers Faithful would rename the soon-to-be unpopular Mike-Mayer "Steve Miss-A-Mile."

No longer an All-Pro center, Forrest Blue was traded to Baltimore, where he hung on as a backup. Replacing him in San Francisco was an ineffective free agent, Bill Reid, whose NFL career would last all of one season. The 49ers' transition was going poorly.

Jean Barrett, a No. 2B pick in 1972, took over for the retired Len Rohde at tackle, and Dave Washington arrived from Buffalo to replace Dave Wilcox—if either man could be replaced adequately. Former Dallas Cowboy Bob Hayes, the Olympic Games' 100-meter gold medalist in 1964, was brought in to take Beasley's place, but "Bullet Bob's" rocket had lost its explosion.

The 49ers lost two assistants to head-coaching positions in two years— Jim Shofner to Texas Christian University, his alma mater, and Paul Wiggin to Kansas City. Wiggin beat out onetime 49er Monte Clark for the Chiefs job, leaving Clark free to interview for other head-coaching possibilities.

The 1975 season began with the same familiar scenario: the 49ers seeking a permanent answer at quarterback. Then veteran Norm Snead, incredibly, threw not one, but two lateral pass fumbles that the Vikings pounced on as they throttled the 49ers in Minnesota, 27–17.

The visiting Rams dumped the 49ers for the 10th straight time, 23–14. The Niners rallied to beat host Kansas City, and Wiggin, 23–3, then lost to Atlanta at Candlestick, 17–3. Snead, booed by the fans, said, "I agree with them."

Snead held onto his starting job, though, and threw for three touchdowns to beat New Orleans on the road, 35–21. Gene Washington scored on 29- and 20-yard tosses, and Tom Mitchell lugged a 60-yarder into the end zone. Bullet Bob was benched after catching one pass.

After the roller-coaster 49ers lost in New England, 24–16, players complained about the off-season promotion of line coach Dick Stanfel to offensive coordinator. "The offense lacks imagination," grumbled one anonymous player.

On October 29, Spadia tap-danced around giving a vote of confidence to Nolan, whose contract expired that season. "I haven't given next year a thought," said Spadia.

The 49ers dropped to 2–5 following a 28–17 home loss to Detroit. Singing Joe Reed, now the Lions' lyrical quarterback, threw two touchdown passes without an interception, while Snead and Spurrier combined for one score and two pickoffs. Could matters get any worse?

Indeed. Mike-Mayer was 5 for 11 on field goals, and 0 for 5 beyond the 30. And he had been drafted specifically as a long-range kicker. Miss-a-Mile was yet another draft-day mistake. "He had a ball that repelled metal," Hardman recalled. "It wouldn't go through the two metal posts to save his life. He took the automatic out of the extra point, made it an exciting play."

Offering further proof that the 49ers had constructed a quarterbacking carousel after Brodie retired, Snead fell off the painted horse, and Spurrier, resurrected once more, climbed back on. The Niners were an amusement park with no amusement.

"I thought Spurrier had all the credentials," said Williams. "Steve was like a gunslinger; he didn't play by the rules. He had a great mind. He'd change plays on the field, and they would work. I don't know if his arm had lost some strength, but then they tried Joe Reed, then Norm Snead, and then Tom Owen even more in my second season. But the first two years, I thought Spur would be the quarterback."

Spurrier became, briefly, the quarterback he had been in '72 by throwing touchdown passes of 42 and 68 yards to Gene Washington and a 19-yarder to Williams, plus no interceptions, as the 49ers finally beat the Rams, 24–23. And of all the people to decide the game, Mike-Mayer kicked a 54-yard field goal with 38 seconds left at the Los Angeles Coliseum. "Here we are in '75, going nowhere," said Hardman. "The Rams are going to the playoffs, and don't you know it, that damn Mike-Mayer kicks a 54-yarder to win it. One of the most enjoyable victories I ever had."

There was one negative note in the victory: Ralph McGill was kicked in the head by Tom Dempsey while missing a 37-yard field goal. Dempsey was born without toes on his right, kicking, foot, and no fingers on his right hand. He wore a modifed kicking shoe with a flattened and enlarged toe surface. His reinforced leather shoe front hospitalized McGill, though briefly.

Before the season, Nolan informed all three quarterbacks that Snead had won the job. Owen took the news quietly, but Spurrier told Nolan, "You're making a mistake." Spurrier backed up his words with two more victories, 31–3 over Chicago and 16–6 at New Orleans, which gave Gene Washington four touchdowns in three games. Jerry Rice is the 49ers' No. 1 all-time receiver, and Washington—not Dwight Clark, not John Taylor, and not Terrell Owens—is clearly No. 2. Both Rice and Washington were gamebreakers, but Washington's 17.9 yards a catch remains the franchise's record.

The unlucky McGill was hospitalized again with head and neck injuries that shortened the career of this No. 2A 1972 draft pick. "McGill was a receiver, not an initiator, when it came to contact," Charlie Krueger pointed out. "That's how you get hurt."

The 49ers had evened their '75 record at 5–5. To hold onto his job, Nolan needed another closing flourish to match the previous season's. A four-game winning streak would enhance his chances. But the season came apart like a toolshed in a tornado. The 49ers lost all four games—27–17 at Philadelphia, 27–13 to Houston, 31–9 at Atlanta, and 26–23 to the New York Giants.

Three starting quarterbacks, combining overall for 15 touchdown passes and 19 interceptions, couldn't prevent the dam from breaking, though the season's failure wasn't just on them. Defensive back Tim Anderson, the 49ers' top draft pick in 1971 who had returned from Canada in '75, was given the opportunity to start, but he looked like a swayback in a derby.

White, who had drafted Anderson and other plow horses, said, "I hope to be back for another year or so as long as my health holds out." He had resorted to sympathy to save his job.

On the subject of health, Bob Hoskins had "a superb season" despite his Hodgkin's disease, said defensive line coach Bob Hollway. And Hardman sparkled with 15 sacks and was named second-team All-Pro. He was the 49ers' only Pro Bowl pick.

Nolan sought a new contract, a new opportunity. "If I am here next year," he said, "there definitely will be changes made." But the day after Christmas, Nolan, the first coach to give the 49ers a playoff presence, was fired.

Happy Holidays, Nolan family.

"A change was needed," Spadia said. But those close to Spadia said the firing wounded him deeply, because Nolan was such a good man. "It came as a shock," said Nolan. "It's part of this business. I've been in this business for 22 years, but things like this never get easy."

Two days after Christmas, a former 49er was floated as Nolan's successor.

31 1976

Winds of Change

Lou Spadia's depression returned in 1974, shortly after his father's death. It worsened the following year, after his mother passed away. Then after his beloved Maggie, 55, died of cancer on March 30, 1976, he couldn't pull himself out of bed. He was so gripped with depression, his children discovered, he couldn't even cry over losing his wife.

Three straight losing seasons, and then having to fire Dick Nolan, only added to Spadia's depressed state. But there was 49er business to attend to, so on January 13, 1976, Spadia hired Monte Clark as the team's seventh head coach. Thus, Clark became the second 49er player, after Frankie Albert, to lead the team. "I couldn't find a hole in the guy anywhere," Spadia told the media. "He has character, background, experience, and he has been with a winner wherever he has gone. He's a great eyeball-to-eyeball guy. He looks you right in the face and communicates with you."

Clark, San Francisco's fourth draft pick in 1959, was a USC alumnus who spent three years as a 49er lineman. He moved on to Cleveland and eventually to the Miami Dolphins as Don Shula's assistant, molding an excellent offensive line that led the charge for a two-time Super Bowl champion. "A learning attitude is very important with me," Clark said upon taking over the 49ers. "I want my players thinking that way, whether it's the last day of practice or the 15th year they've been playing. I want my team to have a hard-working image. I was that way myself."

Nolan graciously congratulated the 49ers on Clark's hiring. "He's worked hard and certainly deserves the chance," Nolan said. "He'll do a helluva job."

What happened a few months later at Spadia's home popped straight out of a novel, a moment hardly anticipated in reality. Kate Spadia hasn't

Lou Spadia and his wife, Maggie, are joined by longtime friends, Pete and Barbara Gianinni, at a Roaring '20s party in 1971. Lou and Pete were friends while growing up in San Francisco, and that friendship led to Pete's becoming the 49ers ticket manager. (Louise Spadia-Beckham collection)

forgotten that poignant scene. "Dick Nolan came to the house after Mom had passed away," she said. "I greeted him at the door and said, 'Dick, you may not want to come in because Monte's here.' He said, 'It's OK.' Well, he walked in, and he and Dad hugged, and then Dad cried for the first time since Mom died. Dick cried, too, the two of them just bawling. And Monte was bawling, too."

Nolan showed once again that he was a first-class human being. Now Clark had the same responsibility, as Nolan had in 1968, of turning the 49ers into a playoff team. Clark moved the 49ers' summer training camp from overcast Santa Barbara to sunny Santa Clara and then rearranged his roster.

"Wilbur Jackson and I had been stacked at the same position," said Delvin Williams. "When Monte came, he put me at halfback and Wilbur at fullback—a real confidence-builder for Wilbur and me, and for the team. We had a chance."

But the players wondered if Spadia had hired a Marine drill instructor, by mistake, as head coach. "Monte was the best offensive line coach ever," said Cedrick Hardman. "The only problem was that if he didn't kill you, you'd be all right. We'd practice three times a day. One day, we lost a whole offensive line. Everybody got hurt, but Monte could interchange people and get results. We'd hit, hit, hit. We had goal-line hitting before a game. You don't see that today."

Maggie Spadia prepares a Thanksgiving turkey for the family in 1968. Lou and Maggie met as San Francisco teenagers, and Lou gave up playing the accordion on the spot when he saw Maggie dancing with another man during their courtship. (Louise Spadia-Beckham collection)

Clark's master plan began with disassembling the quarterback carousel that had turned the franchise into a carnival. To make the carousel music sweeter, and the carnival less of a sideshow, he pursued Jim Plunkett. On March 27, 1976, the 49ers mortgaged their immediate future by trading Tom Owen, two No. 1 draft picks in '76 and a No. 1 and No. 2 in '77 to New England to bring Plunkett back home. The San Jose native had attended nearby Stanford, became its only Heisman Trophy winner, upset Ohio State in the Rose Bowl, and then was the NFL's No. 1 overall pick in 1971.

"I was really enthused about Jim's coming," said Williams. "You'd hear that he was gun-shy, and not as good as he was, but we had the makings of a really good team in 1976. Our quarterbacking had been like a revolving door. That causes uncertainty. Maybe there's a weakness you have, and that may cause some doubt in your mind when Merlin Olsen and Deacon Jones are waiting for you on the defensive line. And if the quarterback can't pass, the defense knows you're going to run, and they can shut that down."

Gene Washington, who moved from quarterback to wide receiver at Stanford to create room for Plunkett, was excited about their teaming up again. "It certainly means a winning season for the 49ers," said Washington. "He's a great passer; there's nothing he can't do."

But Washington was remembering a Plunkett who wasn't damaged goods. His five seasons in New England had taken its physical toll. The Patriots hired Chuck Fairbanks as head coach in 1973, and he installed the option offense he used at Oklahoma, where the quarterback was a rollout passer. Plunkett was a dropback thrower—strictly. When he began running the option, either pitching out or keeping the football, he now had a bull's-eye on his powerful chest. In 1975, he turned up the field with the ball, and 49er linebacker Dave Washington separated his left shoulder with a clean, but forceful, hit.

Steve Grogan replaced Plunkett that day; the Patriots won, 24–16; and Grogan was Fairbanks's new fair-haired quarterback. Then Nolan was fired, Clark was hired, and in 1976 Plunkett became a 49er, with a chance, he hoped, to resurrect his career.

Though Plunkett wasn't the fluid passer in San Francisco that he had been in college, Clark believed one quarterback still beats five. So he dealt Steve Spurrier to Tampa Bay for wide receiver Willie McGee, linebacker Bruce Elia, and a No. 2 draft pick that year. The sprinterlike McGee was the key component in the deal, giving Plunkett another wideout weapon to pair with Gene Washington.

Spurrier lasted nine seasons in San Francisco despite all the uncertainty and turmoil. Reflecting on his up-and-down time as a 49er much later, he remarked, "I should have worked harder." His one full NFL season as a starter in Tampa Bay resulted in an 0–14 whitewash in 1976. Released by the Buccaneers a year later, he entered coaching. No one ever doubted his football mind, and he became eminently successful coaching at Florida and South Carolina, with a disappointing two-year 12–20 run with the Washington Redskins sandwiched in between.

The Morabito family had owned the 49ers from the mid-1940s through 1975. But that ownership was in jeopardy in 1976. Wayne Valley, who dropped out as coowner of the Oakland Raiders following an ugly court battle with Al Davis, sought to buy the 49ers, based, partly, on his admiration for Monte Clark.

However, before the 49ers could be sold legally, the team had to be first offered to its minority owners, including Franklin Mieuli, who grasped at the opportunity by teaming up with former San Francisco mayor Joseph Alioto to submit an ownership bid. Valley, seeing that he was blocked, bowed out. But the winds of change kept blowing, and they shifted easterly.

Clark, in addition to being the 49ers' head coach, was given front-office power. He named Howard White as director of college personnel, then demoted Jack White to area scout, where he was best suited The 49ers drafted two promising offensive linemen in Randy Cross and John Ayers, a roster-filling quarterback in Scott Bull, and a tough running back in Paul Hofer.

Terry Beasley, who retired after the '75 season, showed up, oddly, at training camp in '76. As soon as he got his reporting check, he left for good. Good riddance to bad news.

Clark wanted less fudge on the Fudgehammer, so Nunley dropped his weight from 240 to 218. "I don't have one pair of pants I can wear," he complained with his perpetual smile.

Plunkett was unimpressive during the preseason, even though the 49ers were 4–2. The one exhibition highlight was 11th-round draft pick Hofer's scintillating 47-yard touchdown run with a minute left that put away Kansas City, 21–13. "We ought to pass the collection plate for that kid. He made some tremendous runs today," said Jimmy Johnson, returning for his 16th, and final, NFL season as a still-agile 38.

The '76 season began with a mistake. Green Bay's Johnnie Gray intercepted Plunkett's first official pass as a 49er and returned it 15 yards for a touchdown. Plunkett recovered nicely and threw twice to McGee for touchdowns of 24 and 29 yards. Williams scored twice more, including a 59-yard run, while rushing for 121 yards. The 49ers made Clark's debut a winner, 26–14, on the road.

Then the dynamic Walter Payton rushed for 148 yards and two scores, and Chicago's defense exposed the 49ers' makeshift offensive line by sacking Plunkett six times during the Bears' 19–12 win before 44,158 at Candlestick.

The 49ers rebounded in Seattle as Plunkett threw for three touchdowns—two to Gene Washington and one to McGee. And Ralph McGill, daring further punishment, scored on a 50-yard punt return to fatten a 37–21 victory.

But the star-crossed McGill was rehospitalized with a third concussion after the 49ers literally sacked the visiting New York Jets, 17–6. The Gold Rush had eight sacks that day, three by Jimmy Webb and two each by Cedrick Hardman and Tommy Hart. Joe Namath went down five times and backup Richard Todd three times. Clark's post-game view: "This win is nothing to write home about."

Then on a Monday night, the 49ers perfectly scripted a 16–0 win over the Rams in Los Angeles. Plunkett found McGee and Tom Mitchell for touchdowns. But the real story, again, was the formidable Gold Rush, which sacked James "Shack" Harris no fewer than 10 times. Hart had a career game, with six sacks and two forced fumbles that led to 10 points.

Hardman and Cleveland Elam had two sacks apiece. "I have never seen a defensive line dominate an offensive line like the 49ers did tonight," said the Rams' Merlin Olsen.

"I had four five-sack games in my career, but the game I enjoyed the most was beating the Rams, 16–0, in 1976," said Hardman. "I'd have to say that 1976 was the most fun year I had playing football. We were really excited. We had Delvin and Wilbur, we had Plunkett, Gene, and Willie McGee, arguably the fastest player in the league. We had the best front four in the game, we had a solid secondary, and we had a great coaching staff. We had a great [defensive line] coach in Floyd Peters, who was an enforcer, and like a second head coach."

The 49ers blasted New Orleans, 33–3, at Candlestick to improve to 5–1. Plunkett threw scoring strikes to Wilbur Jackson and Gene Washington. The Gold Rush added seven more sacks, giving it 24 in three games, and 29 overall, tops in the NFC. "They beat us every way you can beat a team," said Saints coach Hank Stram.

But it was a pyrrhic victory. McGee broke his leg and was lost for the year. Clark, in an emergency, traded running back Sammy Johnson to Minnesota for wide receiver Jim Lash, who proved to be ordinary. McGee's injury popped the 49ers' balloon. "What happened in 1976, and this was the key to the whole thing, was when Willie McGee broke his leg," Williams said. "He was a 9.2-second sprinter, so they couldn't double-team Gene. After Willie broke the femur, we struggled."

The Gold Rush managed to keep the 49ers in the hunt with six more sacks—37 in seven games—in a 15–0 silencing of visiting Atlanta. The 49ers were 6–1, and seemingly on fire. "We're cognizant that it gets tougher from here on," cautioned Clark.

He was so right. The 49ers' promising start was shattered the next week in St. Louis with some football follies. Niners' return men Anthony Leonard and Hofer let the opening kickoff, mindlessly, roll by them. The surprised Cardinals jumped on the ball to set up their first touchdown. "I thought it was *Candid Camera*," Clark said. "I have never seen that happen before."

Cornerback Jimmy Johnson was beaten deep for a touchdown for the only time that season on Jim Hart's 77-yard pass to track sprinter Mel Gray. But Williams rushed for a club-record 194 yards and three scores that afternoon, so the 49ers still could have won the game. However, the unreliable Steve Mike-Mayer missed a 23-yard field goal with 1:57 left and the score tied at 20–20. St. Louis's Jim Bakken then won it in overtime, 23–20, on a 21-yard field goal—which the accident-prone Leonard set up by fumbling away a punt.

Delvin Williams looks for daylight in rushing for 1,203 yards, then a franchise record, in 1976. Williams, a second-round 49ers' draft pick in 1974, teamed up with Wilbur Jackson to form a powerful two-back set. (Delvin Williams collection)

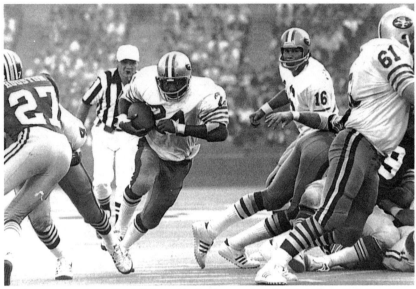

Delvin Williams takes a handoff from Jim Plunkett against the Washington Redskins in 1976. While Williams rushed for 1,203 yards that season, Plunkett played himself out of the 49ers quarterback position and then off the 49ers roster entirely before resurrecting his career with two Super Bowl wins as an Oakland Raider. (Delvin Williams collection)

A crazy day. Then the season got crazier.

Mike-Mayer missed a field goal of 32 yards and had a 39-yard low kick blocked as Washington won, 24–21, at the 'Stick. Williams's 180-yard rushing performance and three touchdowns, including an 85-yard pass from Plunkett, went for naught. Mark Moseley settled the outcome with a 39-yard field goal.

The 49ers' precipitous downslide reached 6–5 after a 21–16 loss in Atlanta, despite Plunkett's two touchdown throws to Washington and a 23–3 defeat by the visiting Rams.

Clark replaced the off-target Plunkett with, first, Scott Bull, and then newcomer Marty Domres. Another quarterbacking carousel? "It's like something mysterious," Clark said of the four-game losing streak. "I can't figure it out."

Quarterback coach Doug Gerhart had it figured out, criticizing Plunkett: "I'm not happy with Jim's results, and I don't think he is either. It looks to me like he has lost some strength in his arm. He's not on target like he should be." Plunkett responded: "It's nothing to do with arm strength. What's disappointing is if a guy is open, I'm not getting the ball to him. Maybe it's a lack of concentration."

An erratic Plunkett bounced his passes occasionally. Later on, he assessed his two below-the-quarterback-curve seasons in San Francisco, while noting that he was sacked 26 times each season. "I became cautious, afraid to make a mistake," he said. "I'm a mentally tough guy, but I was no longer the aggressor. And it showed in my throwing, which became timid, half-certain, and off the mark. After McGee went down, Jim Lash wasn't fast, so defenses began doubling on Washington, who was playing with a broken wrist. The 49ers went to a control passing game."

Plunkett also threw with a pulled right rib muscle in '76. So Bull started in his place in a Monday home game against Minnesota; only this was a night for runners, not passers. Bull threw only eight times as Jackson rushed for 156 yards and Williams for 153—shades of Hugh McElhenny and Joe Perry—as the 49ers won, 20–16. Bull did score on a 1-yard plunge.

"Minnesota was a must game," said Williams. "We had been in a tail-spin, with a new coach and a bunch of young guys. So we didn't have the maturity or much room for error. [ABC's Monday-night announcer] Alex Karras was saying on TV how the Vikings were missing tackles. I have that on tape. I wanted to punch him. That was the most exciting game I played in, to go over 1,000 yards on Monday night on national TV. And only three times in the history of pro football had two backs on one team rushed for 150 yards in the same game."

Newly enthused, the 49ers headed for San Diego, where more gloom awaited. Plunkett started the game but produced zero offense. Bull came in and threw a 13-yard touchdown pass to Hofer to force overtime. Miami Dolphins retread Mercury Morris then scored as the Chargers won, 13–7. But Mike-Mayer missed three more field goals—of 45, 40, and 29 yards. Clark fought to keep a sense of humor. "This game was like the *Gong Show,*" he said. "It should have been gonged."

Bull got the call again in the season finale at New Orleans, though Plunkett was healthy enough to play. "Jim isn't playing as well as we know he can play, and he knows he can play," Clark explained. "Scott has come through when put in tough situations. But don't write Jim off; everything is there. He just needs to get his confidence. I'm certainly counting on Jim to come back strong next year. But it's up to him."

Bull led the 49ers to a 27–7 win over the Saints, throwing a 20-yard touchdown pass to Washington and scoring on a 15-yard run. The fizzling 49ers finished 8–6 after their sizzling start. Mike-Mayer's .500 field-goal accuracy (14 of 28) deep-sixed the team's postseason plans. He missed too many makable field goals. "We could have easily been 10–4 and in the playoffs," Williams lamented. Plunkett's disappointing homecoming—13 touchdown passes, 16 interceptions, two benchings—damaged the 49ers' postseason hopes as well.

Still, the future looked bright. Williams and Jackson were a strong two-back set. The Gold Rush set a team record with 61 sacks—Tommy Hart with 16, Elam with 14—to lead the NFL. Hart was named All-Pro for the first time and joined Elam and Dave Washington in the Pro Bowl. Gene Washington was overlooked, although his six touchdown receptions with a broken paw gave him 15 scores in two years.

The 49ers then said so long to franchise icon Johnson. The oldest starting cornerback in NFL history at 38, Johnson gave up only a 9-yard pass to the Saints' Don Herrmann in his farewell game. "The consummate cornerback," Williams said of Johnson. "At the same time, Willie Brown was with the Raiders. You got to see two guys playing cornerback the way it should be played."

John Brodie played 17 years with the 49ers, Jimmy Johnson and Joe Perry 16 years, Charlie Krueger and Len Rohde 15 years, and Leo Nomellini 14 years. Those old Niners sure had staying power.

The holdover 49ers from 1976 were confident that Monte Clark would find the missing pieces necessary to make the playoffs in 1977.

He was the right coach, in the right place—at the wrong time, however.

For that easterly wind had shifted west.

32 1977

New Boss Man

The Franklin Mieuli–Joseph Alioto bid to buy the 49ers amounted to a smokescreen. The two men didn't have the capital to pull it off, and they knew it all along. They intentionally warded off Wayne Valley as a favor to Al Davis, a game plan that would become evident in time.

Nevertheless, rumors of a 49er ownership change wouldn't die, though Lou Spadia maintained, "We do not have a 'For Sale' sign hanging on our front door." No signs were necessary: on March 31, 1977, the Morabito era ended in San Francisco. Edward J. DeBartolo Sr. of Youngstown, Ohio, purchased the 49ers for a reported $16.5 million, a mere fraction of his total worth, which was, he estimated, "somewhere between $5 and $10 billion."

DeBartolo placed his son, Edward "Eddie" J. DeBartolo Jr., 30, in charge. Then junior named Joe Thomas as general manager, an implosive move, like hiring Red Hickey to run the football operations. Watching that scene from Oakland, Davis laughed. He knew, of course, of Thomas's self-destructive nature. And you don't think Davis had the DeBartolos' ear? Don't forget; he was responsible for selling the 49ers.

The Morabito ladies, it turned out, were in a bind. They couldn't find buyers, so they paid Davis, of all people, a $100,000 finder's fee to locate new owners. Four years later, the very same Joseph Alioto became Davis's attorney in the Raiders' move from Oakland to Los Angeles. From Mieuli and Alioto to Davis and Alioto—these arrangements don't happen by accident.

"Tony and Vic told Josie and me that if anything happened to them, we should get out of football if we had any sense," Jane Morabito said in 1975. Spadia encouraged the ladies, finally, to take that step, while unaware of how such a transaction would affect his tenure with the 49ers.

"My mom told me that she was glad she got out of it when she did," Josie's daughter, Josephine Ann "Midge" Morabito Tassi, said in 2013. "The old-school owners were gone. The new ones, she said, were in it as a tax shelter. She kept a percentage of the 49ers until the team was sold. My aunt Jane kept hers until the end of her life. Then it became her son Ricky's."

Under male ownership again, the 49ers entered into their most chaotic period, orchestrated by the distinctly unlikable, myopic, and clearly-over-his-head Thomas.

At the introductory press conference, DeBartolo Sr.'s countenance was pasty, wrinkly, disturbing. One observer said, "It looks like he just stepped out of a coffin." Son Eddie had a huge pompadour, reminiscent of a 1950s teen idol, along with a innocent boyish smile that suggested Daddy had given him the combination to the vault.

"Cedrick [Hardman] and I went to the press conference," said Delvin Williams. "We're kinda in the back of the room. Eddie had lots of hair. Cedrick said, 'He doesn't look much older than us.' He looked like Michael Corleone, but he was very businesslike." Williams wasn't aware that Youngstown, Ohio, had a Corleone-like aura.

"We're just players; they don't tell you," said Williams. "But the [Morabito] women didn't have football minds; their husbands did. Cedrick and I had gone to see Monte [Clark]. He told us, 'They're going to sell the team, and they want me to stay. But I won't do it because they want me to give up my power to Joe Thomas.' Monte said he didn't trust Joe and couldn't work for him. He had a passionate dislike for Joe."

Spadia's depression returned after the sale. "The depression would only arise when there was a feeling of personal failure. That was the last straw, when he lost his presidency," said Kate Spadia. "He couldn't get out of bed. He had to go to a hospital and work his way out. Then he went to the Donatello [Hotel] to stay. He had depression most of his life."

Thomas offered Spadia a bone; a community relations position. Thomas tried to strip Spadia's masculinity along with his presidency. After shunting him to a small office at the team's Redwood City site, he, spitefully, took away Spadia's executive chair without his knowledge and left him a folding chair in its place.

Thomas wasn't yet done spewing venom. He ordered Spadia, like some office boy, to go fetch him postage stamps and a sandwich. Spadia was loyal, but he wasn't a lackey. He resigned on the spot from the franchise he loved and owed so much to, but which he no longer recognized. "The one thing that hurt my dad the most was when Joe Thomas was hired by the 49ers," said Doss Spadia. "He was so mean to my dad. He wasn't a nice man. I never heard my dad say anything mean about anybody, but he didn't care for that man."

Spadia left the 49ers after 34 years of devoted service. Future 49ers' president Carmen Policy, a onetime attorney, was legally involved with the Morabito-to-DeBartolo ownership transfer, but he couldn't believe how badly Thomas mistreated Spadia.

"Joe Thomas was such a catastrophe," said Policy. "And Lou tried to handle [his demotion] with grace, trying to maintain the history of the 49ers past and their connection to the community. He tried to advise Eddie and the dad, when he could, in an appropriate way, for their own good and the sake of the 49er franchise. Mr. DeBartolo Sr. loved to have dinner with Lou at Fior d'Italia. The DeBartolos liked Lou Spadia a lot; he was a great guy whose soul was part of San Francisco. They found him to be a straightforward, honest businessman."

Spadia was through serving the 49ers, but he wasn't done serving the community. Together with Bill Dauer, president of the San Francisco Chamber of Commerce, he founded the Bay Area Sports Hall of Fame—a hall without a hall. BASHOF plaques float among local airports, where passengers can read about their heroes before boarding.

"What my dad was thinking," Lulu Spadia-Beckham said of BASHOF, "was that, 'I'm a kid who grew up on a hill in the Potrero, played baseball, loved sports. What was the likelihood of me, the son of immigrants, making it to this position in life? There's going to be another kid in the Potrero who, if we give him a football or a baseball, maybe he can make something of himself, too.'"

Spadia ran BASHOF as responsibly as he had the 49ers. The first class of inductees in 1980 was a who's who of local sports legends: Joe DiMaggio, Willie Mays, Bill Russell, Ernie Nevers, and Hank Luisetti. The unpredictable Russell didn't attend the dinner, so Spadia made certain from that point forward that dinner attendance was mandatory for induction. Spadia himself was inducted, against his own objections, in 1999.

Spadia kept up his connection with the 49ers, but from a safe distance. "Lou became more involved with us after Joe Thomas was gone," said Policy. "That's when I got to know Lou, because of the Bay Area Hall of Fame and the San Francisco Chamber of Commerce. Lou would be involved with our annual luncheons with the chamber and on special events. We even took him

Lou Spadia was unceremoniously ousted by the 49ers after rising in the organization from clerk and towel boy to team president and owner. He later cofounded the Bay Area Sports Hall of Fame, which surprised him with his own induction in 1993. (Louise Spadia-Beckham collection)

on road trips when he wanted to go. And the more I got involved with the 49ers at the league level, the more I realized how revered and respected Lou was within NFL circles."

By the time Spadia's employment ended with the 49ers, Thomas already was wreaking havoc. He ripped photographs of 49er greats off the walls and tossed them out with 49er records and other franchise history. "We're creating a new history," he rudely announced. Thankfully, 49er employees, behind his back, retrieved whatever memorabilia they could from the dumpster.

Bob Hoskins, who had played courageously with cancer in his body, was waived by the 49ers prior to the Morabito-to-DeBartolo turnover after failing a physical because of blood clots in his legs. The Hodgkin's had returned, and he would pass away, at 34, in 1980.

"Bobby had the biggest heart of anyone that I know," said Carolyn Hoskins, his widow. "Everyone was saying that he would lose weight as a 49er because of the radiation, and he was defiant not to do that. During treatment [for Hodgkin's], he gained nine pounds. There was talk that Bill Sandifer was going to take his starting job. Bobby just kinda laughed about it. 'It's competition,' he said. 'We'll see what happens at training camp.' And he never lost his job.

"But he started to lose his hair. Everyone back then was wearing an Afro. So he went to the barber shop and had all his hair shaved off. No one knew who he was. When Bobby played, I remember the 49ers were a family, caring about one another as family. When he passed, I got 2,000 sympathy cards, and every card had something positive about what Bobby, as a person, as a man, had done in helping others. People would see him and be uplifted."

Some twenty years ago, Carolyn Hoskins joined the Northern California chapter of the NFL Alumni Association, which actively fund-raises for youth activities. She serves on the chapter's executive board. Older, Morabito-era

Lou Spadia (second from left) and Mario Basso (far right) join Pro Football Hall of Fame inductee and NFL Players Association president Gene Upshaw and other unidentified figures at a 1990 golf event benefitting the Bay Area Sports Hall of Fame. (Mario Basso collection)

49ers such as Gordy Soltau, Jerry Mertens, and Larry Schreiber became chapter members and officers. Younger, DeBartolo-era 49ers are not as involved with the group.

"Young NFL alumni do it their own way today," Soltau said, in 2013, expressing personal disappointment. "They make so much money that they don't have to pool their resources like we older alums do. They're not interested in getting together with the old guys. We've raised about $100,000 a year for the last 33 years for kids."

Bob Hoskins's teammates, Williams and Hardman, personally witnessed the deterioration of the 49ers under Thomas—a 5–9 record in 1977, and a 2–14 mark in 1978, under three different head coaches: Ken Meyer, Pete McCulley, and Fred O'Connor.

"Joe Thomas was intolerant; we were all walking on eggshells," Williams recalled. "Supposedly, he paid well, but he started cutting people, trading veterans, and telling others they were making too much money. It felt like a one-man show. I rushed for 931 yards in '77, and could have gotten 1,000, but I think Joe wanted to keep me healthy so he could trade me. I didn't trust him, and he screwed me on my contract. He said he was going to make it retroactive, and he never did."

In 1978, Thomas did trade Williams, to Miami, where he rushed for 1,258 yards. Hardman had no contract issues with Thomas but clearly didn't understand the man. "I thought Joe Thomas resented the game, and the people who played the game," said Hardman. "I didn't see much love, and he enjoyed pissing people off. He was proud of that. I knew he was an evil person. He'd dress in red, and he looked like the devil. All he needed was some horns."

But the red-clad devil did have an angel tucked away inside. "He treated me real good," Hardman pointed out. "He said he wanted to keep me, but he didn't give signing bonuses. I told him that didn't matter to me. Chicago wanted to give me a $177,000 signing bonus through my agent, Nick Buoniconti, but it wasn't worth it to me. I wanted to play in San Francisco. Joe gave me a great contract, and he made me a captain."

Hardman's head coach in '77 had a ball. "Ken Meyer had more fun than any coach I ever knew," he said. "He knew he was only going to be there one year. Every time we had a team party, he and his wife had more fun than anyone. They'd get on the dance floor and run everybody off. I didn't know a 5–9 season could be so much fun."

Meyer was fired after the 1977 season, Gene Washington's final act as a 49er after a spectacular nine-year run. He went out brilliantly that season, with a 19.9-yards per catch average, plus a team-high 32 receptions and five touchdowns, despite 49er quarterbacking woes.

Finally, in 1978, Eddie DeBartolo realized his mistake and fired Thomas; then DeBartolo hired Bill Walsh off the Stanford campus. And Walsh created an NFL dynasty.

Hardman's last year as a 49er, 1979, was Walsh's first. That year also was the physically diminished O. J. Simpson's second and final season in his native San Francisco. "One day, we were on the ground stretching before practice. Bill came by, shadow-boxing," Hardman said in Big Red on the ride back to Laguna Beach after lunching with John Brodie. "So O. J. said, 'In a fight, coach, I'd put my money on Cedrick.' And I said, 'I'm no boxer, but I am a fighter.' Bill looked at us kind of funny. I heard he was a boxer in college [San Jose State], but I didn't mind talking back to a coach. My nickname was 'Nasty.' O. J. and I were friends. We hung out quite a bit; the rest of the team was children. But I don't want to say anything about what has happened to O. J. since. I have my opinion, but I'll keep it to myself."

Jim Plunkett and Simpson, whom Thomas got from Buffalo for three No. 1 picks, were awful trades for the 49ers, costing the franchise a combined six No. 1s and a No. 2. By then, Simpson was a shell of his former greatness. But Plunkett, after being waived in 1977, regained his health and confidence in Oakland, and his career took off like never before.

Hollywood has missed out on Plunkett's life story: It's a sports saga like no other. Raised by two blind parents in San Jose, he experienced a cancer scare at Stanford, where he was asked to move to defensive end. He resisted and won the school's only Heisman Trophy. Then he quarterbacked a huge Rose Bowl upset over Ohio State. After being the NFL's No. 1 overall draft pick in 1971, he was let go by both New England and San Francisco and then claimed only by the Raiders, who let him heal physically and emotionally. He went from "washed up" to wonderland—two Super Bowl championships and a Super Bowl Most Valuable Player award.

An Oscar, anyone?

Williams believed the Dolphins would remove the stigma of his having played for Thomas and the disappointment of seeing the 49ers descend into the NFL sewer. But Miami teal didn't translate into greener pastures for Williams.

"My first year there, I went to graduate school," he said. "Though I was academically ineligible my first year at Kansas, I graduated from college on time. I signed up for some classes in Miami because I didn't know anybody there. I felt like the odd man out. I was going to play for one of the greatest coaches [Don Shula], and Miami had a great offensive line. But it was a totally different atmosphere with a run-down training facility."

Becoming a 1,000-yard rusher again and a first-time All-Pro didn't mellow Williams out. So he got into cocaine. "I didn't drink a lot, but you'd go to a party and it was social to take some cocaine," he said. "It became a way to relieve the stress of football, playing with a broken wrist or something. I didn't like marijuana; it put me to sleep. And I already had sleep apnea. Cocaine was a matter of survival."

Williams grew up with an alcoholic father and a brother who is a recovering cocaine addict, like Delvin Williams's daughter. He has two cousins hooked on heroin. So his family tree had some shaky branches. Williams started smoking at nine and took his first drink early in life.

"The Dolphins were the only sports organization in Miami when I played there, so they got all the attention," he said. "Shula wanted to know about my cocaine. He had heard about it, probably from league security. Shula had a daughter on drugs. But [cocaine] didn't affect my play."

Williams is clean today, he stressed. Upon retiring from football, he decided to do some public good. So he founded Pros for Kids, recruiting pro athletes to offer guidance to youngsters about sports and life. Word of his project reached the White House, and guess who came to dinner? "Mrs. Reagan got involved, and I started playing politics. She came to three of my dinner functions," said Williams. "We had 1,200 show up one time. Then she invited me to a White House dinner. I wore a tuxedo, sat at her table, and met President Reagan. I love Mrs. Reagan. She was wonderful to me."

Pros for Kids failed to attract enough sponsorships, so Williams's dream died after 10 years. "I didn't take a salary for two years," he said. "It was more selfish than anything; Pros for Kids was my recovery from drugs. But I was getting tired, with just me in charge. I burned out."

Williams is among a small fraternity of 49ers who played for the Morabitos and the DeBartolos. The franchise's amazing story entered a new chapter in 2014 when the 49ers moved into the brand-new Levi's Stadium, home of the 2016 Super Bowl—a brand-new stadium in Santa Clara, not San Francisco.

"A lot of NFL teams do this," Bob St. Clair pointed out. "The New York Giants and Jets play in New Jersey. But for some reason, with me being raised in San Francisco and having played my high school, college, and pro ball there, I have more nostalgia. I wish the move hadn't happened. So it's hard for me to take, big time."

"It just doesn't seem right," said Bob Fouts, who grew up in Sacramento but has lived in San Francisco most of his life.

"I was wondering what name they'd use when they moved down there," said Pete Wismann. "But it doesn't bother me; it's just business."

Len Rohde lives in Los Altos, a 20-minute drive from Santa Clara. He didn't see the 49ers' relocation as a big deal. "I think it will be outstanding," he said in 2013. "The 49ers have a history in Santa Clara. Tony Morabito went to school there, and Buck Shaw coached there. A lot of fans from there drove to Kezar and Candlestick. But I can't imagine their not being called the San Francisco 49ers. Santa Clara will sell the seats and keep the revenue anyway. It would be a shame to lose that name, 'San Francisco 49ers.' It's tradition."

Carmen Policy, the 49ers' president during their dynasty run, worked for the City of San Francisco in trying to prevent the franchise's move to Santa Clara. "The 49ers needed a new stadium, there's no question about it. And if there was no way possible to get a stadium in San Francisco, then I could understand their going elsewhere in the Bay Area, where a stadium could be done. But I think they're missing out on so much by being outside of the heart of the city."

Policy was "bothered" that the baseball Giants and the basketball Warriors were promised new facilities, yet the city's longest tenant, the 49ers, had to leave. "Now, I know the economics, and the dynamics, of a football stadium are different than a ballpark," he noted. "But the truth of the matter is that people kept fumbling the ball when it came to putting a stadium together. The 49ers, in my opinion, would have been so much better off by staying in San Francisco.

"Keep in mind what's happening. The big companies, the Silicon Valley giants (in the Santa Clara area), their young people want to be in San Francisco. So it's not like people were fleeing the city; the young people know there's a heart and soul here, a presence, and they want to be close to it. The farther you get away from it, the more you suffer. Staying in the city would have been better for the 49ers, no question, and better for their fans."

What would the Morabito men, Tony and Vic, say about the 49ers leaving San Francisco? For there wouldn't be a 49ers' franchise without Tony Morabito. "Tony was San Francisco all the way," said Dave Beronio. "He would not have approved of moving the team to Santa Clara. He didn't take a penny out of the 49ers' business the first three years. The 49ers started out badly in San Francisco, and built and built and built. Now I'm surprised by the seat situation [in Santa Clara], and the high prices. Tony's not able to see any of this, but I don't like the team's moving either."

Josephine Ann Morabito Tassi is Tony and Josie Morabito's only living child; their other daughter, Grace Ginella, died in 2007. Tassi was asked how her father would have reacted to the team's relocating. "I'm not quite sure," she said. "Unfortunately, that's progress, although we may not like it."

But she remains curious as to why more public attention wasn't focused on San Francisco's indifference toward the 49ers, and how the city just let them load up and drive away. "It just shows how people are," she said, "and how less they care."

The 49ers couldn't get a new stadium in San Francisco. But the Giants, who arrived there in 1958, 12 years after the 49ers started, got a brand-new ballpark. And the Warriors, who left Philadelphia for San Francisco in 1961 and then moved across the bay to Oakland in 1972, plan to move back to San Francisco and into a new arena by 2017.

So how could politicians in San Francisco, "The City That [supposedly] Knows How," have shown such disrespect to their oldest, and most accomplished, sports franchise?

"I guess they just felt it was something to do on a Sunday," said Tassi.

Epilogue

Lou Spadia died at The Sequoias, a San Francisco care facility, on February 16, 2013, three weeks after his 92nd birthday. His death occurred five months after he told the author, "Oh, I've got a few months left." Was he being truthful, or did an ensuing stroke hasten his passing?

"I think he wanted it so badly," said daughter Doss Spadia. "At one point, in July 2012, he wanted to call in hospice. It was too early." July 2012 was two months before Spadia was first interviewed for this book. His stroke occurred four days after that interview. In Spadia's mind, his time left on Earth was growing shorter.

"Two years before [his death]," said Doss, "he said, 'I'm getting ready to die.' He just didn't enjoy living anymore. Toward the end of his life, there were very few times he would smile. He became more of a recluse. I would just sit there and hold his hand. He had suffered so many losses in his life that he didn't want to see his friends anymore. He'd say, 'I don't want to talk. I'm tired.'"

Spadia remained lucid into his 90s, but his body was failing. He felt useless walking around on a cane. "All he wanted to do was swim again, and his right leg was paralyzed," said daughter Louise Spadia-Beckham. "So he would do stretching exercises for an hour. Walter, his therapist, would say, 'We're done for the day.' And Dad would say, 'Let's do ten more.' Finally, the body said, 'We're done.' Two weeks before he died, he couldn't keep any food down."

Spadia-Beckham and her father spent valuable time together toward the end. "He told me that he had no regrets," she said. "But he said, 'Some guys have all the luck.' He was talking about his depression, and then his having the stroke. And, of course, there was my mother's passing away. Everyone knew know much in love Lou and Maggie were."

Dorothy "Maggie" Spadia died in 1976. The author asked Lou years afterward if he had ever come close to remarrying. He mentioned a lady, though not by name, and said they nearly wed, before discovering that she already had been married four times. Seeing her as an opportunist, he called it off. But there would be another romantic interlude.

"After my mother died, and Dad got older, he dated younger women who were beautiful," said Spadia-Beckham. "Pat Doherty and my dad really loved each other. They worked together at the San Francisco Chamber of Commerce, where the Bay Area Sports Hall of Fame office was located. But he wouldn't marry her because of the age difference."

Pat Doherty was 29 years younger than Lou Spadia when they dated. She is an artist who worked for *San Francisco* magazine after leaving the chamber, and now has an administrative art position in Marin County. A talented oil painter, she specializes in dessert paintings, like cakes and cupcakes.

"Everyone loved working with Lou. He was fun, and he was a perfectionist, down to the very last detail," Doherty said in a 2013 interview, a few months after Spadia's passing. "It was a good transition for him after the 49ers. Lou and I hit it off right away. Was there love? Absolutely."

She dabbed at some tears.

"He called me Patricia; he never called me Pat," she said. "He'd tell us at the office, 'I know I'm a lot older than you, but in my mind, I'm your age.' I think our age difference bothered him, but there was nothing anyone could do about it."

Doherty was asked if they had discussed marriage. She replied that it's too personal a subject to discuss publicly. "We were very close friends, and we enjoyed doing things together," she said. "He had a lot of social activities, and he would say, 'Patricia, I need a date.' But I wouldn't say we were a couple."

She visited him at the care facility as his life was ebbing. "He was a very special man," she said, "really one of a kind."

She dabbed at more tears.

Spadia didn't entertain many friends at The Sequoias, and he shooed away even his closest friends. "When I saw him at the care facility," said Mario Basso, a best friend since their teen years, "he wouldn't talk to me. He was embarrassed looking the way he did. Katie, his daughter, told me to take him for a ride in his wheelchair. But when my wife and I got to the front door, out we went, the bum's rush."

As Doss Spadia explained, her father was physically worn down, and tired of talking, even with his dearest friends. The life he knew, and cherished, already was over in his mind.

Lou Spadia and longtime friend Mario Basso, with his wife, Carolyn Basso, and an unidentified youngster, pose at an 1987 gathering. Lou and Mario grew up together during the
Depression, both from poor families, and then excelled as adults, Mario in the insurance
business and Lou in the football business. (Mario Basso collection)

He did watch the 49ers, his 49ers, lose to Baltimore in the Super Bowl
on February 3, 2013. "The Super Bowl was his last good day," said Spadia-
Beckham. "He was in his bed wearing his 49er cap. He had a little bit of
food and was able to keep it down. He got excited watching the game. He
was lucid. Somebody made a long run, and he said, 'Did you see that?' He
wasn't upset that the 49ers lost. He said, 'It's just nice to be a fan.'"

In the final months of his life, Spadia chose to say goodbye to those who
mattered to him most. Though in failing health, he managed to write six
letters—all in one day, in his own handwriting, and on his own personal
stationery. "He was that way, even in his 90s," said Spadia-Beckham. "If
he had a job to do, get it done. Nothing waited."

Spadia wrote to Doherty, Ken Flower, Basso, and others. Basso read his
letter to the author: "Dear Mario: I may have waited too long to do this,
but I still have the energy to have this sent to you. It expresses the love
that has been in my heart these many years together. My words can never
fully express what you've meant to my life. I would have been an empty
shell without you. A love like ours is eternal. Lou."

Near the end, Spadia received a letter from Ann Nolan, widow of Dick

Close friends and business associates Ken Flower and Lou Spadia appear together at a charity event in 2002. Flower, a native San Franciscan and a basketball star at USC, looked up to Spadia as a father figure. (Ken Flower collection)

Nolan, whom he hired and fired: "Dear Lou: Louise gave [daughter] Nancy pictures of Dick and you, and Nancy e-mailed them to me. They brought back many good memories of you and Maggie, our trips to games and dinners at wonderful restaurants with Josephine and Jane. Those years were Dick's happiest coaching years, and he had no regrets, but was always sorry he didn't make the Super Bowl. Thank you for giving him the opportunity to work for you and the Forty Niner organization. A belated Happy Birthday [January 21], and I hope your health continues to improve. Fondly, your friend, Ann Nolan."

At 4:00 P.M. on February 16, 2013, Spadia sent Louise out of his room to pray for him. When she returned, he had passed on. "He must have known," she said. "And he died on my daughter Maggie's birthday. My Maggie is named after his Maggie."

The commissioner of football, or any professional sport, isn't a privileged position. A common man can become commissioner. The most famous commissioner, Pete Rozelle, rose from average stock.

So is it possible, with a different set of circumstances, that commoner Lou Spadia, the self-educated offspring of Italian immigrants, could have risen to NFL commissioner?

"I'm sure he would have been able to handle the challenge," said Ken Flower. "Family and activity would have been a hardship, moving the family east. But if all the parts fell into place, Lou would have been a fine mediator with his ability to get along with all types of people. And he had a fine business sense. Negotiating and rights fees, he would have been able to handle.

"I think he would have made a fine commissioner."

Notes

Author Dave Newhouse saw his first 49ers game in 1948, started writing about them in the 1960s, was a 49ers beat writer from 1970 through 1976, and has covered the Niners as a columnist for the *Oakland Tribune* since 1979. His longtime involvement with the franchise has led to many conversations, interactions, and other background information included in this book without specific dates.

Introduction

Ken Flower, Lou Spadia, and Louise Spadia-Beckham, conversations with the author, June 29, Sept. 4, 12, 2012; Pete Wismann, Bob Sinclair, interviews with the author, Sept. 25, 2012, Feb. 6, 2013; Paul Zimmerman, "Dr. Z's All-Century Team," *Sports Illustrated,* Aug. 30, 1999; Carmen Policy, interview with the author, Nov. 14, 2014.

1. Pre-1946

Josephine Morabito Fox, Lou Spadia, and Mario Basso, interviews with the author, Nov. 22, 1975, Sept. 21, 2012, Mar. 8, 2013; Allen E. Sorrell quotation from Spadia. Details of the pugilistic careers of James J. Corbett and Abe Attell, from *Boxing Register* (Ithaca, N.Y.: McBooks Press, 2002); Ken Casanega interview, June 4, 2014.

2. 1946–47

Dave Beronio, Paul Salata, Jesse Freitas, interviews with the author, Sept. 27, 2012, Apr. 30, 2013, Mar. 22, 2014; Wismann and St. Clair interviews; Elmer Layden quotation and further information about the 49ers' 1946 and 1947 seasons from National Football League Properties, Inc., *The NFL's Official Encyclopedic History of Professional Football* (New York: Macmillan, 1977); George Preston Marshall, George Halas, Harry Wismer, and Buck Shaw quotations from *Oakland Tribune* files; 49ers' 1946 and 1947 game summaries, honors, and transactions from *Tribune* files and Ron Juanso, *San*

Francisco 49ers 1995 Media Guide (Sacramento, Calif.: Herald Printing Company, 1995); Bruce Lee, San *Francisco Chronicle,* Sept. 2, 1946; Bill Leiser, "As Bill Leiser Sees It," *San Francisco Chronicle,* Sept. 9, 1946.

3. 1948

Len Casanega interview with author, June 4, 2014; Ken Casanega, Spadia, Freitas, and Beronio interviews; Jim Breuil, Tony Morabito, and Jim Cason quotations from *Oakland Tribune* files; Joe Perry quotations from Dave Newhouse, *The Million Dollar Backfield* (Berkeley, Calif.: Frog Books of North Atlantic Publishing, 2000). Other references include National Football League Properties, Inc., *NFL's Official Encyclopedic History of Professional Football* and Herb Michelson and Dave Newhouse, *Rose Bowl Football since 1902* (New York: Stein & Day, 1977); 49ers' 1948 game summaries; and transactions from *Tribune* files and Juanso, *San Francisco 49ers 1995 Media Guide.*

4. 1949

Gordy Soltau, Lou Spadia Jr., Kate Spadia, and Sam Cathcart, interviews with the author, Sept. 28, 2012, Dec. 1, 2012, Apr. 13, 2013, and Oct. 31, 2014; Ken Flower, Dave Beronio, Paul Salata, Pete Wismann, Tony Morabito, Buck Shaw, Ray Flaherty, Glenn S. "Pop" Warner, James Clark, and George Preston Marshall quotations from *Oakland Tribune* files; pro football's league histories and Buddy Young quotation and additional information about the 1949 season from National Football League Properties, Inc., *NFL's Official Encyclopedic History of Professional Football;* 49ers' 1949 game summaries, honors and transactions from *Tribune* files, and Juanso, *San Francisco 49ers 1995 Media Guide.*

5. 1950

Joe Vetrano Jr., interview with the author, May 2, 2013; Spadia and Soltau interviews; Tony Morabito quotation and 49ers' 1950 game summaries and transactions from *Oakland Tribune* files and Juanso, *San Francisco 49ers 1995 Media Guide* and Katie Lewis, *San Francisco 49ers 2006 Media Guide* (New Washington, Ohio: Herald Printing Company, 2006); Joe Vetrano Sr.–Buck Shaw conversation from Dwight Chapin, "Mining for Gold (and Red)," *San Francisco Chronicle,* July 18, 1999; anonymous coach quotation from National Football League Properties, Inc., *NFL's Official Encyclopedic History of Professional Football.*

6. 1951

Salata, Soltau, Wismann, and Lou Spadia interviews; Buck Shaw, Tony Morabito, and Joe Kuharich quotations from *Oakland Tribune* files; Y. A. Tittle quotations from Newhouse, *Million Dollar Backfield;* 49ers' 1951 game summaries and transactions from *Tribune* files and Juanso, *San Francisco 49ers 1995 Media Guide* and Lewis, *San Francisco 49ers 2006 Media Guide.*

7. 1952

Bob Fouts and John Brodie, interviews with the author, Mar. 7, 2013, May 1, 2013; Lou Spadia, St. Clair, Wismann, and Beronio interviews; Buck Shaw, Dr. Bill O'Grady, Tony Morabito, and Johnny Lujack quotations from *Oakland Tribune* files; Hugh McElhenny quotations from Newhouse, *Million Dollar Backfield;* 49ers' 1952 game summaries and transactions from *Tribune* files, Juanso, *San Francisco 49ers 1995 Media Guide* and Lewis, *San Francisco 49ers 2006 Media Guide.*

8. 1953

George Seifert, interview with author, Apr. 5, 2013; Spadia, St. Clair, and Gordy Soltau interviews; Y. A. Tittle, Johnny Unitas, Chuck Bednarik, and Paul Wiggin quotations from Newhouse, *Million Dollar Backfield;* Leo Nomellini and Bruno Banducci quotations from *Oakland Tribune* files; 49ers' 1953 game summaries and transactions from *Tribune* files and Juanso, *San Francisco 49ers 1995 Media Guide* and Lewis, *San Francisco 49ers 2006 Media Guide.*

9. 1954

Wismann, Soltau, St. Clair, and Bob Fouts interviews; Buck Shaw, Tony Morabito, and Hampton Pool quotations from *Oakland Tribune* files; 49ers' 1954 game summaries and transactions from *Tribune* files and Juanso, *San Francisco 49ers 1995 Media Guide* and Lewis, *San Francisco 49ers 2006 Media Guide.*

10. 1955

St. Clair, Bob Fouts, and Soltau interviews; Y. A. Tittle, John Henry Johnson, and Pat Summerall quotations from Newhouse, *Million Dollar Backfield;* Hugh McElhenny, Red Strader, Tony Morabito, and anonymous player quotations from *Oakland Tribune* files; 49ers' 1955 game summaries and transactions from *Tribune* files and Juanso, *San Francisco 49ers 1995 Media Guide* and Lewis, *San Francisco 49ers 2006 Media Guide.*

11. 1056

Bob Fouts, Soltau, and St. Clair interviews; 49ers' 1956 game summaries and trans-actions from *Oakland Tribune* files and Juanso, *San Francisco 49ers 1995 Media Guide* and Lewis, *San Francisco 49ers 2006 Media Guide.*

12. 1957

Josephine Ann Morabito Tassi, Dennis Anderson, interviews with author, May 2, 2013, Aug. 27, 2014; Seifert, Brodie, Beronio, St. Clair, and Soltau interviews; R. C. Owens, Red Hickey, Tony Morabito, Y. A. Tittle, and Wally Willis quotations from *Oakland Tribune* files; 49ers' 1957 game summaries and transactions from *Tribune* files, Juanso, *San Francisco 49ers 1995 Media Guide,* and Lewis, *San Francisco 49ers 2006 Media Guide.*

13. 1958 •

Lon Simmons interview with author, Sept. 14, 2014; Kate Spadia and St. Clair inter-views; Charlie Powell's boxing record from *Oakland Tribune* files and *Boxing Register;* Y. A. Tittle quotation from Newhouse, *Million Dollar Backfield;* Vic Morabito, Red Hickey, and Tony Zale quotations from *Tribune* files; 49ers' 1958 game sum-maries and transactions from *Tribune* files and Juanso, *San Francisco 49ers 1995 Media Guide* and Lewis, *San Francisco 49ers 2006 Media Guide.*

14. 1959

Charlie Krueger interview with author, Apr. 16, 2013; Brodie, St. Clair, and Soltau interviews; Red Hickey quotation from *Oakland Tribune* files; 49ers' 1958 game summaries and transactions from *Tribune* files and Juanso, *San Francisco 49ers 1995 Media Guide* and Lewis, *San Francisco 49ers 2006 Media Guide.*

15. 1960

Dan Colchico, Len Rohde, and Dan Fouts, interviews with author, Feb. 13, 2013, May 29, 2013, Mar. 29, 2014; Simmons interview; Charlie Krueger, John Brodie, and Red Hickey quotations from *Oakland Tribune* files; 49ers' 1959 game summaries and transactions from *Tribune* files and Juanso, *San Francisco 49ers 1995 Media Guide* and Lewis, *San Francisco 49ers 2006 Media Guide.*

16. 1961

St. Clair and Krueger interviews; John Brodie, Ed Henke, Bruce Bosley, Abe Wood-son, Vic Morabito, Red Hickey, and Norm Van Brocklin quotations from *Oakland*

Tribune files; 49ers' 1960 game summaries and transactions from *Tribune* files and Juanso, *San Francisco 49ers 1995 Media Guide* and Lewis, *San Francisco 49ers 2006 Media Guide.*

17. 1962

Dan Fouts, Seifert, Colchico, and Krueger interviews; Red Hickey and Norm Van Brocklin quotations from *Oakland Tribune* files; Forty-Niners' 1961 game summaries and transactions from *Tribune* files and Juanso, *San Francisco 49ers 1995 Media Guide* and Lewis, *San Francisco 49ers 2006 Media Guide.*

18. 1963

Colchico, Krueger, and St. Clair interviews; Ted Connolly, Bob St. Clair, and anonymous player quotations from *Oakland Tribune* files; Port Chicago, California, 1944 naval explosion and 49ers' 1962 game summaries and transactions from *Tribune* files and Juanso, *San Francisco 49ers 1995 Media Guide* and Lewis, *San Francisco 49ers 2006 Media Guide.*

19. 1964

Doss Spadia interview with author, Apr. 13, 2013; Charlie Krueger, Colchico, St. Clair, and Simmons interviews; Howard Mudd, Forrest Gregg, Paul Hornung, and Jim Otto quotations from *Oakland Tribune* files; Dave Kopay quotations from *The David Kopay Story: An Extraordinary Self-Revelation* (New York: Arbor House, 1977); Roy Riegels quotation from Michelson and Newhouse, *Rose Bowl Football since 1902;* Forty-Niners' 1963 game summaries and transactions from *Tribune* files and Juanso, *San Francisco 49ers 1995 Media Guide* and Lewis, *San Francisco 49ers 2006 Media Guide;* Lon Simmons play-by-play radio broadcast, KSFO, San Francisco, Oct. 25, 1964.

20. 1965

Brodie, Dan Fouts, Krueger, and Lou Spadia interviews; John Brodie quotation on Tittle from Newhouse, *Million Dollar Backfield;* Dave Parks quotations from *Oakland Tribune* files; 49ers' 1964 game summaries and transactions from *Tribune* files and Juanso, *San Francisco 49ers 1995 Media Guide* and Lewis, *San Francisco 49ers 2006 Media Guide.*

21. 1966

Lou Spadia Jr., Brodie, Rohde, Krueger, and Simmons interviews; Lou Spadia, John Brodie, and Jack Christiansen quotations from *Oakland Tribune* files; 49ers' 1966 game summaries and transactions from *Tribune* files and Juanso, *San Francisco 49ers 1995 Media Guide* and Lewis, *San Francisco 49ers 2006 Media Guide*.

22. 1967

Ed Kiely and Frank Nunley, interviews with author, Apr. 17, 2013, Nov. 5, 2014; Lou Spadia Jr., Louise Spadia-Beckham, Kate Spadia, Doss Spadia, Flower, Colchico, Brodie, Dan Fouts, and Policy interviews; Jack Christiansen and George Mira quotations from *Oakland Tribune* files; 49ers' 1967 game summaries and transactions from *Tribune* files and Juanso, *San Francisco 49ers 1995 Media Guide* and Lewis, *San Francisco 49ers 2006 Media Guide*.

23. 1968

Krueger, Rohde, Brodie, Louise Spadia-Beckham, Lou Spadia Jr., Nunley, and Simmons interviews; Al Corona quotation from *San Francisco Examiner* files; Dick Nolan, Ken Willard, and John Brodie quotations from *Oakland Tribune* files; 49ers' 1968 game summaries and transactions from *Tribune* files and Juanso, *San Francisco 49ers 1995 Media Guide* and Lewis, *San Francisco 49ers 2006 Media Guide*.

24. 1969

Krueger and Nunley interviews; Tommy Prothro, Lou Spadia, John Brodie, and Dick Nolan quotations from *Oakland Tribune* files; 49ers' 1969 game summaries and transactions from *Tribune* files and Juanso, *San Francisco 49ers 1995 Media Guide* and Lewis, *San Francisco 49ers 2006 Media Guide*.

25. 1970

Cedrick Hardman interview with the author, May 1, 2013; Brodie, Rohde, Krueger, and Simmons interviews; Paul Wiggin, Ken Willard, Dick Nolan, Bill Belk, and John Brodie quotations from *Oakland Tribune* files; Forty-Niners' 1970 game summaries and transactions from *Tribune* files and Juanso, *San Francisco 49ers 1995 Media Guide* and Lewis, *San Francisco 49ers 2006 Media Guide*.

26. 1971

Hardman, Brodie, Rohde, and Simmons interviews; Dick Nolan, Dick Witcher, Dave Wilcox, John Brodie, and Jack Pardee quotations from *Oakland Tribune* files; Forty-Niners' 1971 game summaries and transactions from *Tribune* files and Juanso, *San Francisco 49ers 1995 Media Guide* and Lewis, *San Francisco 49ers 2006 Media Guide*.

27. 1972

Preston Riley, interview with author, Oct. 21, 2014; Rohde, Krueger, Hardman, and Simmons interviews; Dick Nolan, Ann Nolan, Steve Spurrier, Jim Shofner, Jimmy Johnson, Rolf Krueger, Paul Wiggin, Frank Nunley, O. J. Simpson, Isiah Robertson, John Brodie, Bruce Taylor, Skip Vanderbundt, Woody Peoples, Dave Wilcox, and Craig Morton quotations from *Oakland Tribune* files; 49ers' 1972 game summaries and transactions from *Tribune* files and Juanso, *San Francisco 49ers 1995 Media Guide* and Lewis, *San Francisco 49ers 2006 Media Guide*.

28. 1973

Brodie, Hardman, Krueger, and Nunley interviews; John Brodie, Dick Nolan, Steve Spurrier, and Tom Keating quotations from *Oakland Tribune* files; 49ers' 1973 game summaries and transactions from *Tribune* files and Juanso, *San Francisco 49ers 1995 Media Guide* and Lewis, *San Francisco 49ers 2006 Media Guide*.

29. 1974

Delvin Williams interview with author, Apr. 24, 2013; Louise Spadia-Beckham, Hardman, and Nunley interviews; Dick Nolan, Vic Washington, Larry Schreiber, Bill Sandifer, John Brodie, and Lou Spadia quotations from *Oakland Tribune* files; 49ers' 1974 game summaries and transactions from *Tribune* files and Juanso, *San Francisco 49ers 1995 Media Guide* and Lewis, *San Francisco 49ers 2006 Media Guide*.

30. 1975

Jane Eddy Morabito interview with author, Nov. 22, 1975; Josephine Morabito Fox, Josephine Ann Morabito Tassi, St. Clair, Hardman, and Williams interviews; Stan Hindman, Lou Spadia, Dick Nolan, Jack White, Bob Hollway, Steve Spurrier, Charlie Krueger, and anonymous player quotations from *Oakland Tribune* files; 49ers' 1975 game summaries and transactions from *Tribune* files and Juanso, *San Francisco 49ers 1995 Media Guide* and Lewis, *San Francisco 49ers 2006 Media Guide*.

31. 1976

Kate Spadia, Williams, Hardman interviews; Lou Spadia, Monte Clark, Dick Nolan, Gene Washington, Frank Nunley, Jimmy Johnson, Merlin Olsen, Hank Stram, Doug Gerhart, and Jim Plunkett quotations from *Oakland Tribune* files; 49ers' 1976 game summaries and transactions from *Tribune* files and from Juanso, *San Francisco 49ers 1995 Media Guide* and Lewis, *San Francisco 49ers 2006 Media Guide.*

32. 1977

Carolyn Hoskins, interview with author, Nov. 4, 2014; Beronio, Wismann, Bob Fouts, St. Clair, Rohde, Hardman, Williams, Kate Spadia, Doss Spadia, Louise Spadia-Beckham, Josephine Ann Morabito Tassi, and Policy interviews; Edward J. DeBartolo Sr., Jane Eddy Morabito, Lou Spadia, Joe Thomas, and Gordy Soltau quotations from *Oakland Tribune* files.

Epilogue

Lou Spadia and Pat Doherty interviews with the author, Sept. 4, 2012, May 28, 2013; Doss Spadia, Louise Spadia-Beckham, Basso, and Flower interviews; Ann Nolan letter provided by Louise Spadia-Beckham; Lou Spadia letter provided by Mario Basso.

References

The Boxing Register. Ithaca, New York: McBooks Press, 2002.

Clark, Christine Setting. *St. Clair: I'll Take It Raw*. Charleston, South Carolina: Book Surge Publishing, 2005.

Estes, John. *The Pride of Port Chicago: Dan Colchico and the Golden Age of Football*. Kearney, Nebraska: Morris Publishing, 2012.

Georgatos, Dennis. *Game of My Life San Francisco 49ers: Memorable Stories of 49ers Football*. Champaign, Illinois: Sports Publishing LLC, 2007.

Jacobs, Martin. *San Francisco 49ers*. Mount Pleasant, South Carolina: Arcadia Publishing, 2005.

Juanso, Ron. *San Francisco 49ers 1995 Media Guide*. Sacramento, California: Herald Printing Company, 1995.

Lewis, Katie. *San Francisco 49ers 2006 Media Guide*. New Washington, Ohio: Herald Printing Company, 2006.

McGuire, Dan. *San Francisco 49ers*. New York: Coward-McCann Sports Library, 1960.

Michelson, Herb and Dave Newhouse. *Rose Bowl Football since 1902*. New York: Stein & Day, 1977.

National Football League Properties, Inc. *The NFL's Official Encyclopedic History of Professional Football*. New York: Macmillan, 1977.

Newhouse, Dave. *The Jim Plunkett Story: The Saga of a Man Who Came Back*. New York: Arbor House, 1981.

———. *The Million Dollar Backfield*. Berkeley, California: Frog Books of North Atlantic Publishing, 2000.

Smith, Robert. *The Illustrated History of Pro Football*. New York: Madison Square Press, 1970.

Tuckman, Michael W. and Jeff Schultz. *The San Francisco 49ers: Team of the Decade*. Rocklin, California: Prima Publishing & Communications, 1989.

Index